ALSO BY NAT HENTOFF

SPEAKING FREELY

SPEAKING

FREELY

A Memoir

by NAT HENTOFF

 ALFRED A. KNOPF · NEW YORK · 1997

THIS IS A BORZOI BOOK
PUBLISHED BY ALFRED A. KNOPF, INC.

http://www.randomhouse.com/

Library of Congress Cataloging-in-Publication Data
Hentoff, Nat.
Speaking freely: a memoir / by Nat Hentoff.—1st ed.
p.   cm.
ISBN 0-679-43647-2 (alk. paper)
1. Hentoff, Nat—Biography. 2. Authors, American—20th century—
Biography. 3. New York (N.Y.)—Intellectual life—20th century.
4. Journalists—United States—Biography. 5. Jazz—Historiography.
I. Title.
PS3558.E575Z476   1997
818'.5409—dc21
[B]   97-6353   CIP

Manufactured in the United States of America
First Edition

For Margot, who is my life

if the rhythm section ain't making it, go for yourself.

—BEN WEBSTER

Gary Fisketjon, who edited this memoir, made a vital difference. What Jo Jones was to drumming, Gary is to the rhythms of a book.

Contents

CONTENTS

SPEAKING FREELY

INTRODUCTION

A few years ago, I gave a lecture on free speech at Trinity College in Hartford. On my arrival, I learned from a student that two weeks before, an official of Minister Louis Farrakhan's Nation of Islam had been there to bring hard truths to Trinity.

"He mentioned you," the student said. "He called you the Antichrist."

That had been it, I was told. No further explanation. And, alas, no job description.

I had been less than reverential to Minister Farrakhan in my columns in the *Washington Post* and the *Village Voice*, so I was not surprised to be on his enemies list, but I had not expected to be quite so highly elevated.

There was a subsequent phone message from someone purporting to speak for the Nation of Islam. It had to do with my imminent destruction. But I didn't take it seriously; Minister Farrakhan was trying to move into the mainstream then, and it would have been poor public relations for one of his white critics to be obliterated.

Words do wound, and they're intended to—as are many of mine. Readers are entitled to strike back, verbally. The only death threat I've taken to the police came from a Jewish group which objected strenuously to my insistence that Israel could survive as a Jewish state only if there were an independent Palestinian state in what was then known as the Occupied Territories.

The letters from the Jewish group were not fevered, but they seemed quite firm of intent. I called the New York Police Department's Intelligence Division (somewhat of an oxymoron, as I should have remembered from the 1960s, when some members of the department's Red Squad used to pretend to be radio reporters on the street but held their microphones upside down).

Two detectives came to the *Village Voice*. They told me to separate the mail I received, and not to open letters from people I didn't know. They would come and inspect those letters from time to time. I told the detectives that practically all the mail I got was from people I didn't know, and much of it contained leads for my column. So I couldn't wait for them to go through that mail. Well, then, they said, just be very careful on the street for a few weeks. Very careful. Watch people coming and going very closely. Especially anyone who comes close to you.

For two weeks, the smile of a stranger on the street was like an assassin's tip of the hat. And in every baby carriage that came toward me, there was surely—under the blanket—an Uzi machine gun.

Finally, I couldn't stand it anymore, and decided that if the threats were real, there was nothing I could do anyway to protect myself. I stopped peering into baby carriages, and pretended I was no longer afraid.

I remembered what Duke Ellington had told me years before. The musicians he liked to hear, he said, were "beyond category"—belonging to no school. Sometimes, he went on, they angered listeners who liked their music with labels attached. And sometimes they were put down—hard. But those musicians, he added, also had the most fun because they never stopped surprising themselves. Duke's airy advice to me as a writer was to go for myself.

Duke Ellington was dead by then, but I think he would have been amused when I became a pariah to some at the *Voice*—my home base—and many other places in the early 1980s and beyond. This Jewish atheist civil-libertarian, imperfect pacifist, committer of civil disobedience against the Vietnam War, had declared himself to be pro-life. I was the only declared pro-lifer at the paper since its founding in 1956. Three women editors stopped speaking to me, and the other staff members pretended in pity not to notice—as if I were dying of some horrible but thankfully non-infectious disease.

How I came to be, to my own surprise, a pro-lifer will be a later part of this narrative. The consequences continue to be beguiling.

I was invited, for instance, to lecture at an upstate New York college on my apostasy as a person on the Left. Two weeks before the engagement, the professor who had asked me to come called in embarrassment. The women on the lecture committee had decided that the students could only bear so much free speech on the question of abortion. My lecture was aborted. However, the professor said, I would be welcome to come the next year and talk on a subject I'd written a book about: the evils of censorship. There was no trace of irony in his voice.

The next year I did come, and talked about free speech *and* abortion, greatly annoying a chief benefactor of the college—a determined liberal—who told me I was a self-hating Jew. She knew, she said, because she was Jewish. I missed the connection, until she assured me that all authentic modern Jews were pro-abortion.

I would have liked to tell of some of my adventures as a heretic to a friend, Malcolm X, who had a quick, sardonic sense of humor and was decidedly beyond category. Among them:

My lives as a radical (according to the FBI); an "enslaver of women" (according to pro-choicers); a suspiciously unpredictable civil-libertarian (according to the ACLU); a dangerous defender of alleged pornography (according to my friend Catherine MacKinnon); an irrelevant, anachronistic integrationist (according to assorted black nationalists); and, as an editor at the *Washington Post* once said, not unkindly—"a general pain in the ass."

As for Malcolm, I first met him before I knew what he looked like. Soon after I came to New York in 1953 to be an editor of *Down Beat*, a jazz magazine, I began hearing from some black musicians about the Nation of Islam; its leader, Elijah Muhammad; and a young organizer for the Nation, Malcolm X. As a reporter, I sought him out, and we became friends.

REMEMBERING MALCOLM

In the 1950s, such influential intellectuals as Daniel Bell and Norman Podhoretz had discovered that the ideological wars were over in the United States. President Eisenhower was a symbol of the calming of the nation, except for certain troublesome minorities who, after all, had no other place to go.

But soon the black labor leader A. Philip Randolph began speaking of the "unfinished revolution" of blacks claiming their constitutional—and economic—rights. Embodying his words were Freedom Riders, black and white, in the South; black students sitting at white lunch counters; and biracial civil rights demonstrations in the North.

It was before Malcolm X's picture had been in the white press. Indeed, when I first went to see him in the mid-1950s, very little about the Honorable Elijah Muhammad's Lost-Found Nation of Islam in North America had appeared in the white media. I knew something of the Black Muslims because I read the black press and because many jazz musicians had been telling me about the growing, disciplined numbers of Elijah Muhammad's straightbacked legions. And they had talked about this tall, lean prince of the Nation of Islam, this Malcolm X, who was one hell of a soloist.

I was freelancing at the time, and often wrote for *The Reporter*, which, in addition to the usual back-of-the-book arts section, focused on covering what had not previously been reported in national and international politics. My editor there had never heard of Malcolm or Elijah Muhammad, so he told me to go ahead.

Having called Temple Number 7, of which Malcolm was minister, I was told to meet him at a luncheonette on Lenox Avenue. It was owned and operated by the Nation of Islam, which had been increasingly involved in trying to establish a self-supporting black economy.

The appointment was for late afternoon, and when I got there, I wasn't there. Not to the blacks behind the counter, or the customers. I was the only white on the premises. I finally asked for a cup of coffee. There was no response. A few minutes later, when I looked up from the *Times*, there was a cup of coffee before me on the counter. Nobody had served me. The cup had just decided to fill itself.

There was a jukebox in the luncheonette, and throughout the hour or so I was waiting for Malcolm, only one song was played. Continually. "A White Man's Heaven Is a Black Man's Hell." The rhythms were sinuously West Indian, and the male singer was a high tenor—supple in phrasing and pleasing in texture. It was somewhat less pleasing if you were white and listened to the words. I walked over to the jukebox to read the name of the singer. Louis Farrakhan. It didn't mean anything to me then.

I kept on reading the *Times* and looking up expectantly whenever the door opened. Not knowing what Malcolm looked like, I was willing, indeed eager, to believe that he was everyone who came in. He never was.

After an hour, it began to occur to me that either Malcolm X wasn't going to show up at all or I was being tested in some way. In any case, I'd had enough. I jammed the newspaper into my coat, and walked toward the door. A tall, lean man with glasses and an amused look, who had been sitting at a corner table reading and making notes, looked up and said to me, "You looking for somebody?"

"Malcolm X."

He smiled. Not in any friendly way. "You've found him," he said. Malcolm motioned to a chair across the table from him.

We talked for a couple of hours. That is, he talked. His voice never rose, but his intensity was such that the words kept coming at me like the quick, hard left jabs of a well-tuned boxer. He spoke of the necessity of black separation, from which would come self-respect and self-sufficiency. And he talked of the North being "up South." Walking down Lenox Avenue, I still felt the cool, sharp breeze of his wit. And his merriment. Malcolm had been having a good time.

The Reporter printed my piece and, later, a long letter from an NAACP official protesting that so much space had been given to a minor cult. The official prophesied that long after the Nation of Islam and Malcolm had gone, the NAACP would still be responsibly here. (Actually, I had also greatly underestimated Malcolm and, for that matter, the Nation of Islam. At the end of my article I had written: "Malcolm X may yet be an executive in the Urban League, but Elijah Muhammad is more likely to end as Marcus Garvey did—with little left but pictures of himself addressing huge crowds years before.")

After our first meeting, I would occasionally call Malcolm in connection with various civil rights pieces I was doing for the *Voice, Commonweal,* and other places. If he wasn't in, he would invariably call back. Malcolm was well organized. Occasionally he would initiate a call to get my reactions to the way in which the press was playing a story about him, or to read me part of a speech he was going to deliver. He figured I might want to use some of it. My wife, Margot, ordinarily unafraid of anything, never got used to answering a call from a "Mr. X."

I'd see him on occasion at press conferences, and we were on a couple of radio and TV panels together. I enjoyed watching him outmaneuver reporters and academics who either were convinced that he was an irredeemable racist or felt that with sufficient cultivation he might eventually see the light and join the editorial board of the *New York Times*.

On one television show, Malcolm and I had a particularly sharp exchange about violence. Neither of us yielded ground. He seemed to enjoy the jousting. As we became friendlier, we argued more. I was, and am, an imperfect disciple of the radical pacifist A. J. Muste. Malcolm could never have been mistaken for a pacifist in terms of strategic theory—although he himself was among the least violent men I have known and, so far as I know, was never directly involved in any violent actions, despite his rhetoric. Anyway, we argued a lot about force, the effective threat of force, and its therapeutic and political uses.

I didn't realize it during my first meeting with him at the luncheonette, but Malcolm was a man of considerable and piercing wit. If someone used a word imprecisely, or in a way that revealed what he *really* meant, Malcolm would pounce with delight. He was also a stinging analyst of the print and broadcast press, none of which intimidated him in the least.

His broader sense of humor manifested itself when he invited me and my wife to a pantomime put on by the Nation of Islam at Town Hall. We were the only whites there, and were seated in the middle of an orchestra row, surrounded by empty seats. It was as if we were in quarantine.

The pantomime had to do with the indictment, in the Nation of Islam scriptures, of "white devils"—created by an eerie black scientist, Yakub, 6,000 years ago—as the originators of all evil. It ended with a vivid prophecy of the imminent terminal punishment of the white man for all the destruction and pain he had caused. Watching from our place of internal banishment, I felt as if I were back in the luncheonette on Lenox Avenue. I saw Malcolm, in the wings, watching us and laughing heartily. He asked me afterwards, with as straight a face as he could muster, if I had enjoyed the afternoon.

On one occasion I became quite angry at something he had said. It seemed gratuitously mean-spirited at a time of much anticipation. The place was a hotel in Washington on the eve of the 1963 March on Washington. In the lobby, reporters were cornering various civil rights dignitaries. On assignment from Westinghouse Radio, I had just come in, bearing, with pride and discomfort, a god-awfully heavy Nagra tape recorder.

But there was such good feeling in the air that the Nagra almost became weightless. Across the room, I noticed Malcolm surrounded by members of the press, and he saw me. Smiling mischievously, he waved and shouted across the room, "Hey, Nat Hentoff, I bet you think you're here for a real historic event! You've been fooled, like everybody else."

He was wrong, of course, in terms of such results of that day—and the force behind it—as the Civil Rights Acts. On the other hand, I would not now relish a debate with Malcolm on the state of the majority of blacks in the ghetto—with a recording, in the background, of Martin Luther King's "I Have a Dream" speech.

I heard from Malcolm again in 1964, during his pilgrimage to Mecca. He was very proud of having made that journey, writing to Alex Haley: "I think I'm the first *American born*

Negro to make the actual Hajj. . . ." The pilgrimage also effected a profound change in his ideas about race and racial separateness. As he wrote in a letter to an assistant, "I have been utterly speechless and spellbound by the graciousness I see displayed all around me by *people of all colors.*"

Written on his way home, Malcolm's postcard to me said: "In my recent travels into the African countries and others, I was impressed by the importance of having a working unity among all peoples, black as well as white. But the only way this is going to be brought about is that the black ones have to be in unity first."

The last time I saw Malcolm was a few days before he was killed on February 21, 1965. It was by chance. I had come to radio station WBAI in New York to tape a program, and Malcolm had just finished one. At first he seemed in good spirits. Laughing, he told me some gossip about a writer we both knew who was notorious for his ability to talk publishers into sizable advances for books that usually were never heard of again.

Rather suddenly, Malcolm turned somber. His house in Queens had been firebombed on February 14. He told me that soon after, needing a few hours of quiet to finish an article, he had checked into a hotel under an assumed name. He thought he had taken more than sufficient care not to be followed, but as soon as he entered his room, the phone rang, and a voice said, "Hello, Malcolm."

I had never seen Malcolm afraid before. But fear was in him that afternoon at the radio station. He said he did not expect to live much longer. And the last thing he said was, "Whatever happens, it won't be Elijah."

He didn't say any more. What I thought he meant then, and what I still think he meant, was that the CIA had targeted him. Malcolm had been wiretapped and surveilled by the FBI in the interests of "national security" from the time he had become reasonably prominent, and probably before. He had said he was certain the CIA was on his trail when he was in Africa. Malcolm was, after all, becoming more and more of a figure of symbolic significance in the Third World, and he planned to become a familiar presence, pillorying the United States, at the United Nations.

Twelve days before his assassination, Malcolm was scheduled to speak at a meeting in Paris, but the French government refused him entrance to the country as an "undesirable." French authorities explained that Malcolm's speech could have provoked demonstrations undermining "the public order." It did not say whether an American agency had asked that Malcolm be kept out.

There was another theory. In his 1973 book, *The Death and Life of Malcolm X* (Harper & Row), Peter Goldman speculates that Malcolm was barred from France because the French had "acted on the representation of two of their lately liberated colonies, Senegal and the Ivory Coast, that Malcolm—aided and abetted by Nasser and Nkrumah—might try to overthrow moderate pro-Western governments like their own."

Did the CIA also believe that?

I have been a journalist too long to be ensorcelled by conspiracy theories. I cite the CIA possibility here because of what Malcolm said to me and because of what the CIA's record during the 1960s says about that obsessive agency. In those years the CIA was a nation unto itself, accountable to no one. We shall probably never know if there was any CIA involvement in the murder of Malcolm X. This is not the kind of information that comes pouring forth when you make a request under the Freedom of Information Act.

It is true that the shots were fired by emissaries of the Nation of Islam. But the real question is: who sent them?

Despite what Malcolm said about not having long to live, his murder stopped me cold. I heard about it on a portable radio in Washington Square Park, while pushing the carriage of my younger daughter. Looking up, she thought something had happened to me.

All that intelligence, energy, passion, and capacity for evolving leadership—gone. In the years since, I have often thought of what might have been if Malcolm had still been alive—organizing, analyzing, and teaching.

There has been much speculation about why Malcolm was cut down, but I doubt there will ever be a definitive investigation, since so much time has passed. What does stay in my mind—having seen a number of replays on television of the murder at the Audubon Ballroom—was the inertness of nearly all the armed local and federal undercover cops in the audience. (Their presence was confirmed two days later by the *New York Herald Tribune*.) As the fatal shots were fired, the cops just sat there, as if they were watching a show.

There was a widely disseminated photograph in *Life* magazine of Malcolm's bodyguard, Eugene Roberts, leaning over him, earnestly giving his leader artificial respiration. Roberts, as it turned out, was at the time an undercover member of the New York Police Department's Red Squad. Malcolm had even more enemies than he knew.

Over the years, when lecturing at colleges where at times adherents of the Nation of Islam have been in the audience, I have told of a college appearance in upstate New York that Malcolm made a year or so before he died. After he spoke, a student was to field the questions from the audience. A young black man rose. He didn't have a question; instead he unleashed a brutal philippic against Jews—all Jews, from the beginning of time, and then some: They sucked the blood out of blacks, out of black communities. They controlled everything—the White House, the press, the banks, the music business. All whites were oppressors, but Jews were the particularly relentless and remorseless cause of black misery—from the teachers they sent to make black kids think they were dumb to the rotten meat they sold in their stores in the ghettoes.

Malcolm had had enough. He rose, pushed past the student moderator, and said to the young black man, "What you're doing is what has so long been done to us. Bigotry doesn't help anybody, including the bigot. It's a waste of energy, a waste of your mind. Listen, I don't judge a man because of the color of his skin, I don't judge people because they're white. I don't judge you because you're black. I judge you because of what you do and what you practice. I'm not against people because they're Jews. I'm against racists."

Malcolm told me a story one day. Before his trip to Mecca, when he was still a total black separatist, he had been interviewed by Dr. Kenneth Clark, an unyielding integrationist, for a book. Clark's research on the psychological damage done to black children in segregated schools had contributed to the Supreme Court's decision in *Brown v. Board of Education.* In the interview Malcolm had said to Clark, "If you are born in America with a black skin, you're in prison. . . . The Honorable Elijah Muhammad teaches us that integration is only a trick on the part of the white man . . . to lull Negroes to sleep, to lull them into thinking that the white man is changing. . . ."

Dr. Clark's son, Hilton, had been much taken with Malcolm X, whose presence was such that his entrance into a room or onto a platform riveted attention. It was partly because of his reputation—he was a man of such "disciplined power," as Kenneth Clark had said, that he could face down the police, as he had done during a confrontation in Harlem between black Muslims and the cops. Except when I saw fear in him just before he died, Malcolm had developed an air of command, of crisp authority.

The younger Clark was also becoming more and more interested in the separation Malcolm was preaching. His father was quite disturbed.

"Dr. Clark shouldn't worry," Malcolm told me with a smile, a large smile. "I won't take his son away. I wouldn't do that."

Aside from what might have happened nationally if Malcolm had lived, I miss the man—his wit, his swift intelligence, his warmth, when he wasn't in the arena. And, quiet as it was kept, his tenderness. He was indeed a dangerous man.

"ARMIES OF NEGROES MARCHING
AND COUNTERMARCHING IN THE AIR,
SHINING IN ARMOUR"

Six years before Malcolm X was assassinated, I went down South to explore what A. Philip Randolph—who had the sound and cadences of Jehovah—called "the unfinished revolution."

Randolph had organized the first all-black labor union, the Brotherhood of Sleeping Car Porters, as well as the first federal Fair Employment Practices Committee. In the 1940s, Randolph was responsible for integrating the armed services and became best known for the resounding 1963 March on Washington for Jobs and Freedom.

John Adams had been prescient. In an 1821 letter to Thomas Jefferson, Adams had said: "I have seen slavery hanging over this country like a black cloud for half a Century. If I were as drunk with enthusiasm as Swedenborg or Wesley, I might probably say I had seen Armies of Negroes marching and countermarching in the air, shining in Armour."

Starting in the late 1950s, armies of blacks *had* been marching and countermarching in the South. They were Freedom Riders and also students involved in sitting in at lunch counters, public libraries, and jail.

Their determination was infectious. Soaring, integrated

choruses of "We Shall Overcome" were heard throughout the country; and among blacks there was pride that a new world—as Duke Ellington titled a composition—was a-coming.

During a concert in London around this time, Dizzy Gillespie dedicated a number to "Mother Africa." I'd known Dizzy for years. Under the banter and the hip comedy, he was what used to be called "a race man." Not a separatist—most of his bands were integrated—but in no way an "Oreo."

That night in London, he looked at the audience with a characteristically mocking smile, and said, "We're going to take over the world, so you better get used to it." A few nights later, a group of British jazzmen held a private party in Dizzy's honor. Toward dawn, he shared his highly roseate vision of the future with them:

"You've lost Asia and Africa, and now they're cutting out from white power everywhere. You'd better give up or begin to learn how it feels being a minority."

Before his pilgrimage to Mecca, Malcolm often celebrated that vision, but I didn't hear it from many blacks in the South then. Their minds were concentrated on surviving the present.

Before leaving on that Southern trip, I got a safe-conduct pass from Bayard Rustin. A tall, elegant black American with a skillfully manufactured upper-class English accent, Bayard worked closely with A. Philip Randolph and Martin Luther King. Rustin was a remarkable organizer—as in the 1963 March on Washington—and a shrewd political strategist.

When I told Bayard of my itinerary for the Southern journey, he said, "Some of the black activists that you want to see won't talk to you. They don't trust whites asking questions. But they'll talk to you if you show them this."

Rustin wrote on a piece of paper that he knew me, vouched

for me, and would appreciate it if anyone reading this would help me.

The pass worked. Every time. But I had no pass to show to whites.

In Montgomery, I tried to get into a cab driven by a black man, but he said he couldn't take me. Whites had to take white cabs. That was the law. I gave the white cab driver the address—the home of the Reverend Ralph Abernathy, who had succeeded Dr. Martin Luther King as head of the Southern Christian Leadership Conference. The cab driver looked at me as if I were crazy. He said I must be crazy. "That nigger's house was bombed, don't you know that? His church too."

I nodded.

"So what are you, crazy?"

"I'm a reporter," I said. "I have to interview him."

"I won't take you all the way." He looked at me with what I took to be pity and scorn.

From where we stopped, I could see the powerful spotlights that Abernathy now had focused on his home all night long.

"The light's on all the time, day and night," the cab driver said. "But it won't do any good. So go ahead and get yourself shot."

Mrs. Abernathy peered through a crack in the front door, read my Bayard Rustin pass, and let me in. Ralph Abernathy, who had been Martin Luther King's chief lieutenant for a long time, led me into the living room. Stocky, he usually seemed rather impassive, moving and speaking slowly—unless he was preaching or addressing a meeting.

That night he told me he came from Marengo County in Alabama, some hundred miles down into the "black belt." His father owned his one-hundred-acre plantation.

"I never worked a day for a white man," Abernathy told me with evident satisfaction.

It was a down time for "the movement" in Montgomery. Abernathy had taught sociology at Alabama State, but now, he said, "I get very little open support from the black Alabama State faculty. It's a state-supported school, and they're afraid. And my congregation has fallen off in recent weeks. Oddly, it didn't fall off during the bus protest [the protest that began when Rosa Parks wouldn't change her seat on the white section of the bus], but these days, some of the teachers are not coming. And there are others who are afraid to come because the church might be bombed again."

The next day, Sunday, in his office in the church, Abernathy's spirits were up. He had just preached a fiery sermon. It was a surgingly musical call-and-response performance. In the classic tradition of the 1920s recordings of black preachers I had collected, he roared like a trombone, prophesying freedom. The congregation filled his pauses with exultant responses.

Abernathy did not speak in the calm, intellectual, analytical diction of the night before. Watching and listening to him, I had a sense of what black preaching might have been like before either of us was born.

Back in his office, I asked Reverend Abernathy what he thought of Elijah Muhammad and the Nation of Islam. The Nation seemed to be harvesting many souls, I said.

"Well, now"—Abernathy shook his head at my naïveté—"I don't think they'll get much stronger. But I don't think the Negro has time—or needs to—apologize for the crackpots in his community. We have a right to our crackpots as you do to yours."

On another visit to Montgomery, this time for *The New Yorker*, I was picked up at the airport by E. D. Nixon, who, for some fifty years, led the civil rights movement in Alabama. Nixon had also been founder and president of the Alabama branch of the Brotherhood of Sleeping Car Porters and Maids. Through the years he had taken considerable risks in working for black voters' rights and public-school desegregation.

In December 1955, when Rosa Parks was arrested in Montgomery for refusing to move to the rear of a city bus, E. D. Nixon and Virginia Durr, a white supporter of constitutional rights, had put up her bail.

As the black protest against the treatment of Rosa Parks began, it was E. D. Nixon who had persuaded a young preacher, Dr. Martin Luther King, to head the boycott organization—the Montgomery Improvement Association—that Nixon had helped create.

Meeting E. D. Nixon at the airport, I felt somewhat in awe of this historic figure. He had a commanding presence and unequivocal self-confidence. He took me to the home of Clifford and Virginia Durr—who were to be the main subjects of my article for *The New Yorker*.

Clifford Durr, a lawyer, had spent nearly twenty years in Washington in various New Deal agencies, including a term as a member of the Federal Communications Commission. A man of clear principles—rare in Washington then as now—Durr had declined reappointment to the FCC in 1948 because he refused to support Harry Truman's loyalty programs for federal employees. And he had represented some of the victims of that hunt for subversives.

Durr's stand for due process and the First Amendment made him a person of suspicion in Washington. In 1951 he came back to Montgomery to practice law. There he was largely isolated by whites because he worked with E. D. Nixon and young black lawyers on various civil rights litigations, including a case that ended segregated busing. As the *Encyclopedia of African-American Civil Rights* (Greenwood Press, 1992) notes, "His championship of civil rights cost Durr most of his white Montgomery clients."

His wife, Virginia—a sister of Josephine Black, Supreme Court Justice Hugo Black's wife—had a long history of advocacy for civil rights. During the Montgomery bus boycott, she had put together car pools for black workers.

The Durrs had agreed to talk to me on condition that they not be named as sources for the story. The antagonism toward them in white Montgomery was rising, and although they were not withdrawing from their civil rights work, they thought they might become less effective if they were given more press attention—especially from the outside.

We talked for a long time. I learned about the inner dynamics of the powerful local newspaper, the *Montgomery Advertiser*, and the moral topography of the dominant whites in the city. I also found out something about the inner politics of the legislature and the courts. As I left, the Durrs cautioned me again not to use their names and to disguise parts of the article so they could not possibly be identified. When I got back to New York, I spent a lot of time doing just that, and felt proud of my skill at multiple disguises.

The day after the *New Yorker* issue with my article appeared, the *Montgomery Advertiser*, with malicious glee, condemned Clifford and Virginia Durr for speaking to a Northern carpetbagger who had clearly come to Montgomery to defame the city and its citizens and stir up racial unrest. The Durrs, the paper said, were accomplices in this attack on Montgomery.

I read my article again and again, but couldn't figure out how my disguises had unraveled. A long time afterward, a reporter in Montgomery told me that E. D. Nixon had been under police surveillance at that time, and as soon as he met me at the airport, I came under surveillance too. A plain-clothes cop had followed me to the Durrs' home, and later told the *Montgomery Advertiser*.

I tried to tell this to Virginia Durr, but she never forgave me.

By contrast with my feelings that I had, indeed, somehow betrayed Virginia and Clifford Durr, it was in Nashville that I came across the most heartening story of my Southern trip.

Robert Lilliard—one of the black lawyers defending the sit-in students who had been arrested for violating segregation laws—was talking to a mass meeting at a black church. There were many mass meetings of support in those days and nights. Domestics came and laborers, as well as professionals and students.

Lilliard was telling of an exchange in a Nashville courtroom the day before, in which the white judge had asked Lilliard, "Are *all* the Negro lawyers of Nashville representing the defendants?"

"Every one!" Lilliard replied.

"That's the finest spirit of stick-togetherness I've seen in this community," the judge said.

"Me too, Your Honor."

In succeeding years, in the South and in the North, some of that spirit became marginalized as black separatists gained some recruits—and as many whites forgot the tune of "We Shall Overcome."

During those early years of "the movement," moreover, there was a lot of angry prophesying among some radicals in it, who felt strongly that eradicating discrimination was only a minimal beginning; after that, integration into the society as it was then was unacceptable, unthinkable.

Singer Joan Baez, who committed civil disobedience at induction centers in protest against the war in Vietnam—and marched with Martin Luther King—was a friend of mine. She told me one afternoon of her not-so-passive resistance to some of Dr. King's goals:

"I loved Dr. King and wanted to work with that revolution, but he and I agreed on very few things. I kept asking him, 'What is it you're trying to do? Why aren't you trying to change the system?' At that point, for instance, banks run by blacks were growing out of some of his organizations, and this development was considered revolutionary.

"Dr. King would say, 'Well, the black keys and the white keys on the piano are out of tune. We have to get them into tune, and this is one way.' My answer was, 'But the whole fucking orchestra is shot, so what good are black banks going to do?' "

I tried to argue with her. Black banks might help some blacks who had been stiff-armed by white banks—to get mortgages and loans that Joan had no trouble getting. But her radical visionary spirit did not brook such parochial concerns.

Similarly, Charles McDew—chairman of a black Southern group of extraordinarily courageous young black and white civil rights activists, the Student Nonviolent Coordinating Committee—was saying at around the same time:

"I want to be able to make up my own mind as to how much of this society I'm willing to integrate with. Too many of the 'freedom riders' don't think beyond integration. But men ought not to live and die for just washing machines and big television sets."

That struck me as easy rhetoric, and rather elitist for a civil rights warrior. A good many of the people McDew and SNCC were registering to vote—at considerable danger to all concerned—would have liked washing machines and big television sets just fine.

I was surprised, therefore, when I met Chuck McDew. This was before SNCC had become a separatist redoubt under the "Black Power" leadership of Stokely Carmichael, whose enemies list came to include not only Southern sheriffs and other racists but also whites in general and Jews in particular. Later, Carmichael targeted me as one of those "Zionist Jews" who tried to suppress black truth.

In McDew's time, SNCC fought bigotry without harboring bigots. He and a number of his colleagues came up North to get support for SNCC, and some press attention. We met at my office at the *Village Voice*, and I was struck by the absence of reverse racism—which was already building elsewhere among some blacks—in these visitors from SNCC. They considered themselves radical because they were planning deeper changes that had to be made across the board—deeper, they thought, than the NAACP or the Southern Christian Leadership Conference was capable of imagining.

Chuck McDew was particularly impressive. Utterly determined, but remarkably free of racial stereotyping, he reminded me of a jazz musician I greatly admired—Charles Mingus. And like Mingus, there was joy as well as anger in him. He put his considerable energy into organizing for the vote, for schools that worked, for respect. Although the "nonviolent" part of the Student Nonviolent Coordinating Committee's credo was not a commitment deeply held by some of the SNCC organizers, it was by McDew.

By this point I had spent several years writing about some of the leading adherents of nonviolence in the United States— especially A. J. Muste, who was an adviser to Martin Luther King. It had been King who told me that A.J. turned him on to the power of nonviolence when King was in Crozer Theological Seminary in Pennsylvania.

"A.J. had come to lecture," King said to me one afternoon in New York before he was to address a labor union rally. "He looked old, though he wasn't then. And there wasn't much drama [in] how he spoke. But he made you pay attention. I wasn't a pacifist then, but the power of A.J.'s sincerity and his hardheaded ability to defend his position stayed with me through the years. Later I got to know him better, and I would say unequivocally that the emphasis [back then] on nonviolent direct action in the race relations field is due more to A.J. than to anyone else in the country."

Muste's insistent emphasis was on *active* nonviolence, not just on passive resistance. He climbed over fences into nuclear-missile bases to protest preparations for war, and he was involved in direct civil disobedience at the Pentagon and other sites where violence was being nurtured. I got to know A.J. well, and wrote a book about him, *Peace Agitator* (Macmillan).

Admiring A.J. and the nonviolence of Chuck McDew, I tried to be a pacifist—what was then called an absolute pacifist. I studied the theory, and imagined the practice. The hard part would be, what would I do if someone attacked me or my family physically? I was accustomed, though not always pleasurably, to dealing with fierce verbal attacks on me for what I had written. But no one, since I was a boy, had hit me—yet. So I had no idea how I'd react.

One day my wife, Margot—a relentless pragmatist—asked me, "What would you do if I were attacked on the street?"

"Why," I said, remembering a frequent phrase of A.J.'s, "I would interpose my body between him and you." And I got all puffed up with my dedication to nonviolence.

Margot hit me as hard as she could—and she can hit very hard—in the stomach.

I did not hit her back, but my pretensions at being a pacifist were deflated. I knew then that I would not have just interposed my body.

As a bruised pacifist, I was delighted to have met Chuck McDew, who struck me as someone who would interpose his body in times of violence visited upon him—and probably had done so. Of all the civil rights leaders I met in those years, McDew was the most open. He wore no masks.

I lost track of him until 1993, when I was researching an article on blacks and Jews in the South during years of "the movement." It was a fragment of a message from jail written in 1961 by Robert Moses—a much-respected, wholly nonviolent leader of the "Eyes on the Prize" forces.

The fragment is printed in *The Tree of Liberty: A Documentary History of Rebellion and Political Crime in America*, compiled by Nicholas Kittrie and Eldon Wedlock (Johns Hopkins University Press).

In Amite County, Mississippi, in 1961, Robert Moses had been arrested and beaten for "trying to register our niggers." From jail, Moses sent this message:

> We are smuggling this note from the drunk tank of the county jail in Magnolia, Mississippi. Twelve of us are here, sprawled out along the concrete bunker. . . . Charles McDew ("Tell the Story") is curled into the concrete and the wall. . . . Later on, Hollis will lead out with a clear tenor into a freedom song, Talbert and Lewis will supply jokes, and McDew will discourse on the history of the black man and the Jew.
>
> McDew—a black by birth, a Jew by choice, and a revolutionary by necessity—has taken on the deep hates and loves which America and the world reserve for those who dare to stand in a strong sun and cast a sharp shadow.

I had never known Charles McDew was Jewish. (A similar surprise—but one that engendered greatly different feelings on my part—came in 1996, when Louis Farrakhan told Henry Louis Gates in *The New Yorker* that he believed he had Jewish antecedents. That would make Farrakhan, I thought, a classic self-hating Jew.)

I often think of McDew as emblematic of a time when— despite the fierce tensions—the Promised Land, though very distant, seemed, eventually, accessible. It seems so very long ago—longer than the actual forty years—that Chuck McDew, as a student at South Carolina State College, organized four hundred or so students to sit in at dangerous white lunch counters in Orangeburg, South Carolina, and later worked on the Freedom Rides.

I remember, time and again, those forty years ago, holding a black hand somewhere, singing "We Shall Overcome."

We thought we would.

BLUES FOR LIBERALISM:
MY VISIT TO ADLAI STEVENSON

For a time, the exhilaration of the civil rights movement intersected with the indignation of the antiwar demonstrations. Against the strong urging of Roy Wilkins, head of the NAACP, Martin Luther King made resistance against the Vietnam War part of the black freedom movement. The battle for justice, King said, was indivisible. Demonstrations against the government on both counts increased, and I was part of some of them, sort of.

I became skillful at avoiding the eyes of cops ready to pounce and collar defiers of the law, and I never did get arrested, but I felt guilty each time I saw my comrades pushed into a paddy wagon. Not very guilty, though.

There was one experience during the war years that began to change how I defined myself politically—or, more accurately, how I defined myself, period. I had been reading the French novelist Georges Bernanos, who had vigorously opposed the Vichy regime during the time of Hitler and lived in exile in Brazil from 1938 to 1945. One sentence by Bernanos kept reverberating in my mind:

> The horrors which we have seen, the still greater horrors we shall presently see, are not signs that rebels—

insubordinate, untamable men—are increasing in numbers throughout the world, but rather that there is a constant increase, a stupendously rapid increase, in the number of obedient, docile men.

In June 1965 I was a member of an anti–Vietnam War delegation that met at the United Nations with Adlai Stevenson, then the United States ambassador to much of the world. Stevenson, in his campaigns for the presidency in the 1950s against Dwight Eisenhower, had been the resounding spokesman for principled liberalism. Witty and crisply articulate, he retained a large following of idealists, especially among intellectuals. Of all those then in public life, Stevenson, we believed, understood us on both moral and political terms. He spoke for us.

Among us in the delegation were Dwight Macdonald, the acerbically astute intellectual with expertise in many fields; Harvey Swados, a writer with particular knowledge of the labor movement; A. J. Muste, the direct-action pacifist; and David McReynolds, whose military carriage belied his long-term devotion to the War Resisters League, where his income was less than that of a sanitation worker. Also on hand was Paul Goodman, whose intellectual curiosity was boundless, and who often created solutions to various social problems that were so lucid and logical that politicians considered them impractical.

Three weeks before Stevenson's sudden death, we had come to ask him to resign and "become the spokesman for that which is humane in the tradition of America." We wanted him to lead the nation out of Vietnam and other places where America was compounding injustice.

It was also an appeal from our own impotence. We did not know how to stop the war. Bobby Kennedy was not yet in opposition; just before this visit, some of us had gone to see him in his New York apartment overlooking the East River, and he implied that the time had not yet come for him to declare himself—if he was going to declare himself.

Eugene McCarthy had not yet been heard from as the gunslinger who would retire LBJ. So Stevenson seemed to be the one widely respected political figure, among liberals, who might be able to rally all those middle-class parents who were deeply troubled about the war—particularly about the danger to their draft-age sons—but didn't know what to do.

As for me, I was also curious to see for myself why this remarkably elegant political figure, who had meant a great deal to me during part of my twenties, was ending his public life as a liar for his country at the United Nations. He was supporting official American positions on Vietnam, Cuba, and the Dominican Republic that were being exposed in the press as plainly untrue.

As I came into the room, I also remembered how a woman I knew—who was not given to making heroes out of politicians—cried inconsolably the night Stevenson first lost to Dwight Eisenhower.

From the moment Stevenson welcomed us to his United Nations office, I tried to resist his charm. I am wary of charm in government officials because its presence resembles the manners of exceptionally skillful morticians. But Stevenson's charm was immediately enveloping.

As genuinely gracious and as unfeignedly courtly as Stevenson was, it was difficult for me to indict him to his face for complicity in the killing in Vietnam. Some of the radical young at the time, however, would have had no hesitancy in greeting Stevenson with "Up against the wall, motherfucker!"

But what I saw and reacted to was an encapsulated man who, of all things, wanted something of *us*. God knows what it was. Certainly not absolution. That was not part of our job description. Perhaps it was understanding. We were all adults, we must certainly understand the rules of the game. Surely, now that we had talked to him, we would realize that his essential humanity and compassion had not changed. And we would recognize the difficult, pragmatic challenges of his present situation.

This yearning to be understood—and I came to realize it was that—was implicit in much of the conversation. But Stevenson was also clearly trying to make us see that the reason he was at the United Nations was that his post there afforded him access to power. Accordingly, there was the ever-present possibility that he could persuade Lyndon Johnson to listen to him, to really listen to him. But if Stevenson did what we asked of him now, what would he be then? A superfluous footnote to these critical times—a balding, well-spoken loser. Again.

We visitors were far too politically marginal to impress someone who had the connections to change the direction of the country. He, at least, could get the truly powerful on the telephone.

Our talk with the ambassador at first was about American intervention in the Dominican Republic. Briefly, awkwardly, he tried to defend the involvement, but several of us were so primed with facts that, finally, Stevenson tacitly conceded the weakness of his position by not continuing to advance it.

The rest of the time, Vietnam was the subject. For a while my attention wandered. I knew the questions and could predict the answers. At times, instead of following the play of the polemics, I watched Stevenson's eyes, which were a very clear blue. As a politician and diplomat, he'd had much experience in keeping his eyes clear of whatever he was feeling. But there were moments of open vulnerability.

There was hurt when the truthfulness of a past statement by him was being shredded. Alarm showed for an instant at another point. He was being pressed hard, and maybe he was afraid he might succumb to spontaneity and say something that could deeply embarrass him later when he'd have to insist he'd been misquoted. As a gracious man, he would find it painful to imply then that we were liars.

But he was clearly shaken after a lucid, devastating analysis of American policy in Vietnam by David McReynolds. Anguished, Stevenson asked, "But what the hell *can* we do?" Alternatives were suggested, but the implication from his side of the room was that none of them could be "sold" to LBJ.

After about an hour, Adlai Stevenson had regained control of himself and his priorities. He was a thoroughly professional player of the game, according to the rules of the insiders—and, although not all the way inside, he was still an insider.

At the door, he shook our hands and said, "You honor me by coming. I do not often have a chance to have this kind of dialogue with people like you." He really seemed to mean it, but it had been more of a duel than a dialogue. He had withstood our attempts to change the rules by which he lived, but he appeared to have experienced no pleasure or relief in proving his loyalty to LBJ.

When he died soon after of a heart attack on a London street, I was saddened. He had been with his good friend Marietta Tree, and had said to her as he walked away, "Keep your head up high."

Reading the tributes to him, I wondered at how certain writers thought they were honoring him by playing the game whose rules had trapped him. In the *New York Times*, Sam Pope Brewer wrote from the United Nations:

> One conspicuous testimonial to the reputation of Mr. Stevenson is the fact that, though he had been misled by his own government into denying any United States responsibility for the Bay of Pigs invasion of Cuba, not even hostile

delegates accused him of dishonesty when that responsibility was exposed. His personal integrity was always accepted as being above suspicion.

But what does that mean? How immutable is personal integrity if, after its possessor has been betrayed by his superiors, he continues to serve a lying government?

The most disappointing farewell to Stevenson was Murray Kempton's "The Long-Distance Runner" in the *New York World-Telegram*. Along with I. F. Stone and George Seldes, Kempton was my mentor as a journalist for reasons that are evident in the beginning of Kempton's piece: "He died, of course, in a public place. So many times, when the worst thing had happened, he had to endure it in a public place. He seemed always lonely and never given the release of being alone."

But Kempton ended his column:

> For all of us who remembered him from the moment he captured us, he was not a public man but a personal possession, the embodiment of our own honor. He was the only public man of whom we demanded that, when he was ordered to lie, he must refuse. But he did not belong to us; he belonged to his country. He would have stayed the course. "Patriotism is not short, frenzied outbursts of emotion," he told the American Legion in 1952, "but the tranquil and steady dedication of a lifetime." We have lost a long-distance runner.

Patriotism, then, is staying the course: my country right or wrong, truthful or mendacious. And if the war in Vietnam is part of the course, then we must salute and carry on.

A leading liberal of the time, James Wechsler, editor of the *New York Post*, wrote of Adlai Stevenson:

He was a citizen of the world; he was also a patriot in the noblest sense of that vulgarized word. . . . His continued service at the UN, in the light of the rebuffs and even indignities he intermittently suffered in dealing with Washington's military-diplomatic bureaucracy, embodied the highest form of selflessness and responsibility.

To whom was Adlai Stevenson being responsible during those years at the United Nations? Us?

My mourning for Adlai Stevenson began before his death.

But there was some of Adlai Stevenson in me, as I grudgingly recognized the next year, 1966. During that summer on Fire Island—where Margot and I had a house—there was a visitation from members of the new Black Power version of the Student Nonviolent Coordinating Committee led by Stokely Carmichael, who had made it clear that whites were not wanted in "the movement."

Margot wrote about that event in the *Village Voice*, but she left something out because I asked her to. She very much didn't want to, and she was right.

First, Margot sets the scene:

On the last Saturday in August, Seaview held its annual rite of reconciliation between the white left-liberal and the American black man—a fund-raising benefit for SNCC. . . .

Seaview . . . has long been a lode worth mining for fund-raisers of "progressive" organizations. . . . This year, however, when the posters went up announcing the SNCC benefit, the atmosphere was not the same. Black Power was abroad in the land, the bad fairy was coming to the christening. Stokely Carmichael was going to speak. Conversation became animated on the streets of Seaview. . . .

"What's he coming for, anyway? I thought they don't want anything from us anymore."

At the fund-raiser, I was asked to be among those doing the pitch for money. I consented. When it came time for Carmichael to speak, he was, as Margot reported,

> Very mild. Very reasonable. Not much of a firebrand. . . . Nothing insulting. The crowd is disappointed. Tonight was supposed to be different. For once, the lines would be drawn and they could finally withdraw their support.
>
> Black Power and Stokely Carmichael were going to let them go. But Carmichael wasn't letting go. No, he says, SNCC does not reject white support—only white leadership of black men. No, he is not a racist.

Before Carmichael spoke, he and the rest of the SNCC entourage were in an upstairs room that no one else was allowed to enter. Margot and I were exceptions, because I was going to do a money pitch. As the SNCC members were about to go downstairs and socialize with the white liberals, Carmichael said to his colleagues, "We gotta play nice nigger for the white folks sometimes."

Margot originally included that remark in her piece. It was the epiphany of the evening. I talked her into deleting it because, I said, whatever was said in that room upstairs was privileged. We weren't there as journalists, but rather as an ad hoc part of the SNCC team for that evening.

Actually, I was covering up for Carmichael. If that quote had got out, fund-raising for SNCC might well be blighted in other places. And, I discovered, I was still enough of a white liberal to want to protect blacks from themselves.

Margot ended her story in the *Voice*:

> On August 29, two days after the Seaview benefit, SNCC held a fund-raising rally in Harlem. The *New York Post* cov-

ered it and quoted Carmichael as saying, "In Cleveland they're building stores with no windows. All brick. I don't know what they think that'll accomplish. It just means we have to move from Molotov cocktails to dynamite."

A Seaview woman showed the quote to her husband. "That isn't what he was like here," he said.

"Well," her husband answered, "maybe he was misquoted."

THE JAZZ CAPITAL OF

THE WORLD

My continued, nearly obsessive interest in "the movement"—civil rights and antiwar—also intersected with my main line of work during those years.

In 1953 I had left Boston, my exuberantly anti-Semitic hometown, to come to the big leagues, New York, as an associate editor of *Down Beat*. From the time I was eleven, jazz was my vocation, the equivalent of a religion. As a kid, I spent everything I made in after-school jobs on records by Bessie Smith (I once found a treasure trove of her trumpeting blues in the basement of an Irish music store); Billie Holiday (three for a dollar); Duke Ellington; Count Basie; and Peetie Wheatstraw ("The Devil's Son-in-Law").

At nineteen I was hired as a radio announcer at WMEX in Boston, and soon talked the boss into letting me have some of the unsold time for a jazz radio program. Because of the program, I was able to interview most of the legendary—and not so legendary—improvisers who came to town: Charlie Parker, Duke Ellington, Charles Mingus, and Dizzy Gillespie, among others.

I also broadcast regularly from the city's most uncompromising jazz club, the Savoy Café, where the clientele was mostly black. The presence of some whites—especially white women with black men—agitated and angered the police, who often harassed Steve Connolly, the owner and bartender, by discovering such offenses against the public weal as the absence of soap in the rest rooms. Steve, anticipating this charge and the attendant fine, was always careful to have fresh bars of soap there. But somehow, whenever the cops came, the soap had disappeared.

The racial-sexual tension also worked in reverse. A large, grim black police detective used to follow us at a block's distance when I walked a black singer-pianist home from the Savoy. I didn't go into her room, but that didn't diminish his resentment.

Still, the Savoy was the most satisfying place I'd ever been. On my nights—and days—off, I was always there.

In the argot of an earlier time, I was jazz-crazy.

The chance, therefore, to leave Boston to work full-time for a jazz magazine in the jazz capital of the world was a dream come to life. I was told I'd be paid $150 at *Down Beat*. Because salary checks at my job at WMEX were handed out every other week, I figured that I'd have to make do in New York on $75 a week. I didn't dare object, for fear of jeopardizing that ideal job. Besides, I was used to eating out of cans. Still, it was a relief to find out that the $150 came *every* week.

I was in the clubs just about every night. Whitney Balliett of *The New Yorker* had described jazz as "the sound of surprise." I already knew that, but in New York, the surprises could be more stunning because the competition was so much fiercer. A musician originally from the Midwest had told me what Coleman Hawkins had said to him one night back home. "Bean," as the inventor of the jazz tenor saxophone was called, because he had so much going on in his head, gave booming advice to the young player:

"You're pretty good, kid, and you've got a hell of a reputation here, but you'll never know how good you are, or how bad, until you come up against the musicians in New York."

One night I was at Café Bohemia, a club in Greenwich Village, where Oscar Pettiford was leading a combo. A bassist of prodigious technique, all of which was needed to keep his passions in some order, Pettiford could be volcanic—with his fists as well as his instrument. He was bristlingly proud of his Native American ancestry, and after enough libations he sometimes looked and sounded as if he were about to go after John Wayne in revenge for all of Oscar's relatives shot from their horses in Duke's movies.

On this night a large, round young man came to the stand, carrying an alto saxophone that looked almost like a toy against his girth. I asked some of the jazz critics and musicians who he was. Nobody knew. The round young man asked Pettiford if he could sit in.

I'd known Oscar for some time, and I saw a look on his face of sadistic glee. He waved the outlander onto the stand and set off the fastest tempo I had ever heard, as the other musicians in the band grinned.

"Goddamn," I said, "he isn't even going to let the kid warm up." The big kid, an impressively confident improviser, sailed through the number without a trace of strain or sweat. Not only didn't the tempo faze him, but his solos were naturally lyrical—even at so demanding a pace—and airily cohesive.

Pettiford was so stunned that he forgot to be disappointed. He got the young man's name and announced it to us all— Julian "Cannonball" Adderley, a teacher of music at a college in Florida.

The next day, Cannonball had a record contract. He soon went on to work with Miles Davis, and then led his own successful combo until he died of a stroke in 1975.

Color was constantly on Cannonball's mind. He was like

the Jews I grew up with in Boston, who saw the city, the state, the country, the world as "They"—the goyim. "They" were our enemies. Whatever was in the news was good for the Jews or bad for the Jews, mostly the latter. When I left home, my mother's final advice—as she tearfully let her only son voyage into the vast unknown—was: "Never trust a goy."

Many of the blacks I knew, in and out of music, felt that way about whites. Some, like Malcolm, made a few exceptions. Cannonball did. I don't think I was one of them. But he talked to me with icy bitterness about the dynamics of Jim Crow. He particularly focused on the music business, because that was *his* business. Over time he had learned how to read contracts more carefully, and he stayed away from those jazz record companies that had what he called "a plantation owner's attitude" toward black musicians.

One player, who was not well enough known to escape the plantation record companies, told me, "I get whatever advance I can talk them into, but that's it. I know I'll never see any royalties. They keep many sets of books, and I can't afford some accountant to go and look at those books."

I wrote about these and other unfair labor practices in *Down Beat*, but nothing much changed. Cannonball and other black musicians kept saying that the only way up was for musicians to form their own record companies and booking agencies. A few tried, but nothing much came of that either.

What did work, to some extent, was a rebellion against what was called "West Coast Jazz." Mostly white, this well-mannered, technically skilled music was generally low in soul and high in pretensions. Among its leading players were Shorty Rogers, Shelly Manne, and Dave Brubeck. In recordings and club and concert dates, these white sounds attracted large audiences—as did the predominantly white Stan Kenton Orchestra, which was massively devoid of wit, grace, or genuine warmth. In contemporary terms, the Kenton band sounded like a giant synthesizer operated by Arnold Schwarzenegger. It did not swing.

So attractive to white listeners was this manufactured "West Coast Jazz" that some of the players appeared in ads for colognes and other genteel merchandise in the fashion magazines. I don't recall a single black face in those ads.

In New York, Cannonball and other musicians were furious. Here were these white guys appropriating black music, stripping it of its soul, and making much more money than the deep swingers in the jazz capital of the world.

One afternoon I went to what turned out to be an event of some historic consequence for what, decades later, would be called Afrocentricity.

Pianist Horace Silver—usually a gentle, good-humored man—had just joined drummer Art Blakey to form a group called the Jazz Messengers, and they invited me to the combo's first rehearsal. Both Silver and Blakey were in good, revengeful spirits.

"We're going to be playing," Horace told me, "tunes white guys can't play—not so it'll sound authentic. Anyway, they won't be comfortable with this music. We're going to play jazz with the beat and the sounds of where we grew up—in black churches, in black neighborhoods."

There was soon a resounding hit, Horace Silver's "The Preacher," which would have been wholly at rocking ease in Daddy Grace's church in Harlem or any of thousands of black meeting houses. Cannonball Adderley, also with gleeful revenge, included in his combo's repertory "Better Get in Your Soul." And other leaders also went back to their black roots.

What made the job at *Down Beat* so pleasurable was the contact with musicians. I have since worked in other fields, covering education, politics, police work, the courts (including the Supreme Court), the First Amendment, and the rest of the Bill of Rights. I find those areas continually intriguing, but, with exceptions, the players in those areas are less energizing than the jazz musicians back then.

For one thing, jazz players are often widely knowledgeable. Having traveled a lot, they are the least parochial of professionals—including secretaries of state, who do not get a chance to walk beyond the palaces or other grand meeting places. And by working with musicians from many parts of the world, jazz players become easily multicultural without having to take courses in cosmopolitanism.

They also engage in far fewer euphemisms. The music is spontaneous, and so, in most of their conversations, are they.

They have much more varied experiences than the rest of us. Duke Ellington once told me about the learning life of the itinerant improviser:

"What I'm involved in is a continuing autobiography, a continuing record of the people I meet, the places I see and then, years later, see change. Furthermore, what is music if it isn't communication? I like to *know* firsthand what the response is to what I write. And it's by playing all these one-nighters that I can hear reactions from all kinds of audiences. You get real contact when you play a phrase, and somebody sighs."

I had known Ellington since I was a teenager, and I was always more than somewhat in awe of him—the scope and depth of his compositions and of his orchestra. Only Charles Ives came close to Ellington as an original American composer.

But I wasn't constantly in awe of Duke. When I was New York editor of *Down Beat,* he called one afternoon from Boston. "You know," he said in a silken voice, "Barry Ulanov and Leonard Feather have discovered singers, and that's how they themselves became more famous. Therefore, Nat, I'm going to give you a chance to make a discovery that will make *you* famous." He had a new singer, and I was to be given an exclusive interview with her and then continue to speed her career. I had heard the singer, and I knew she would be no more famous as a *jazz* performer than Margaret Truman as an interpreter of lieder. I figured that Duke wanted to impress her with his star-making press contacts. To what end was none of my business.

I declined as artfully as I could. I felt it must have been like turning down Beethoven when he asked for a favor.

During those years, there were also Charles Mingus, Miles Davis, Paul Desmond, Rex Stewart, Billie Holiday, Henry "Red" Allen, Ben Webster, and many more musicians with whom I spent my working nights. Each distinctive, and never quite predictable. They were continually surprising themselves—in the rhythms of their lives, and therefore in their music. As Fats Waller used to say, "One never knows, do one?"

Margot has pointed out, and I think she's right, that the musicians of Ellington's era were as much literary as musical figures—like larger-than-life characters in a novel. They had absorbing stories to tell—off the stand as well as on.

And sometimes I actually saw one of those stories being enacted, as happened once when Mingus was playing at the Five Spot, on the Lower East Side. When he finished a set, he joined me at the bar. I was telling him about Jewish cantorial music—deep Jewish blues—in which the cantor improvises, like a blues singer, and continually uses melisma—a series of different notes sung to a single syllable. It's powerful soul music, I told Mingus.

He was starting to ask me more when a young black man—very black—who had been listening to us, said contemptuously to Mingus, "You're not black enough to play the blues."

Indeed, Mingus's color was not as black as his accuser's; but in his music there was no one blacker. Never a pacifist, Mingus raised his fist, but suddenly put it down. Instead, he leaped onto the stand, grabbed his bass, brought it down to the bar, and played a blues. Mingus had the most speechlike and penetrating sound on bass of anyone in jazz, and his thunderstorm of a blues that night reverberated through the room and into the street. It was a blues on which Bessie Smith could have improvised. It told a story centuries old, and still new.

The very black man, without saying another word, hurried out into the night.

Going to work to hear music, and to talk with those who made it, came to an end in 1956. For some time I had been urging the Chicago office—*Down Beat*'s headquarters—to hire someone black there and in New York. Here we were, I said—to the growing annoyance of the front office—making money out of what was essentially black music. And there were no blacks on the magazine's staff.

There was only a mumbled response, and no change in the hiring rule that nobody could be hired for the New York office without prior approval from headquarters.

We needed a secretary in the New York office, and a dark young woman applied. Her résumé was better than the salary she was going to get. She was bright and pleasant. I hired her without calling Chicago.

The boss soon made a visit to New York, and the next Monday I came in with a lot of record and nightclub reviews to be sent to Chicago. I started to go to my desk, but was told that would not be necessary. I had no desk anymore.

Headquarters never gave me a clear reason for my last chorus, but employees there told me—not for attribution—that I had been insubordinate. I had not cleared the hiring with Chicago, especially so historic a hiring.

Several years later I found out that the secretary at issue was not black, but Egyptian. Of course, these days, the creators and practitioners of Afrocentricity would rule that, being Egyptian, the new secretary was, of course, black. Either way, I would still have been fired.

A FANTASY COME TO LIFE

After being defenestrated, I still covered the jazz scene, picking up occasional gigs at the *Saturday Review* and other magazines. And, wholly unexpectedly, I had a chance to begin to fulfill a fantasy I'd nurtured from the time I was eleven and started working after school to finance my jazz record habit.

The fantasy was common to most jazz buffs, as we used to be called. Someday, somehow, I would have my own record label and record my favorite musicians. The releases would be pure jazz, and therefore would last for generations. Untold numbers of people all around the world would remember my name gratefully.

In the late 1950s, a limited version of that fantasy first came true. Les Koenig owned Contemporary Records in Los Angeles—a small, often adventurous label. He was the first, for instance, to record Ornette Coleman—a bold, uncategorizable alto saxophonist and composer whom many of the older players regarded as an arrant con man—not a real musician at all. I was present at that session to write the liner notes. Startling as Coleman's playing was, it had at its core the cry and cadences of the human voice. If he'd come from another background, he could have been a Jewish cantor.

When Koenig asked me to put together some sessions in New York, I was delighted but also apprehensive. I had been at recording sessions of Bob Dylan, Sarah Vaughan, Miles Davis, and an agonizing Stan Kenton date during which Kenton, as mechanical a person as his music, forced a hapless trombonist to do seventeen consecutive takes before he could master a passage to Kenton's liking. I kept that scene in mind when I started to supervise my own sessions.

I was apprehensive because I wasn't sure I had the right stuff to be a jazz A&R man. I was not a musician. Although I could read music, I couldn't, listening, name a chord, any chord.

Walking down the street, brooding, I saw Gil Evans. A continually original arranger who wove the subtlest of colors into his orchestrations, Evans was respected by just about every modern player and composer in jazz.

I told him that aside from jumping into this minefield, I had also long been uneasy about reviewing jazz recordings, though I had done it for *Down Beat*, the *Chronicle of Higher Education*, and other publications.

"I thought you knew better than that," Gil said. "The listener—and obviously he's the one all of us are trying to reach—doesn't have to be able to 'analyze.' He doesn't have to know, from a reviewer, how it's put together.

"But if we can reach him *emotionally*, the music becomes part of him, and that helps keep the music alive. I mean, the music is out there, moving into so many different people's experiences in ways the musicians can't possibly conceive. Reaching people is what counts, not whether a reviewer or an A&R man can tell what the chords are. I read you. Clearly, you've been listening a long time, and you know what music lasts—because you get inside it."

Among the albums I did for Les Koenig in New York was a session by two venerable Harlem two-handed stride pianists,

Willie "the Lion" Smith—whose business card announced that he spoke Yiddish, which he did—and Luckey Roberts, as much a master of his idiom as Artur Rubinstein was of his. Each had a side of the album to himself, and I have rarely heard such long-lined lyricism and joy in creation.

I made a big mistake at that session, and have regretted it ever since. In Los Angeles, Les Koenig started the tapes rolling from the moment a musician walked in the door. He didn't want to miss anything that might be worth preserving. I forgot to do that. While the studio was being set up and before the recording began, the Lion and Luckey swapped stories for about an hour about the "ticklers"—the virtuoso black ragtime pianists who traveled the Atlantic seaboard earlier in the century and were as personally singular as their music.

But the tapes weren't running, and I lost those stories.

The recordings I made for Koenig hardly established any jazz sales records, but the reviews were good, and I was contacted by Archie Bleyer, who conducted the band on Arthur Godfrey's radio show and was also the owner and chief A&R man for Cadence Records, a label that focused on well-crafted popular music and had been quite successful. Bleyer had somehow decided that he ought to make a contribution to jazz, a music he didn't know much about, but that he considered an important, though rather neglected, part of the culture. He was setting up a new jazz label, which would not be expected to bring him a splendid rate of return on his investment, but which would have integrity.

I would head the new label, and could record anyone I wanted. That guarantee was never broken, Archie being a man of integrity. I called the label Candid. After a while Bleyer sometimes puzzled over some of my releases, but he never said a word to me—until a year later, when he closed down the label and me.

People who have never run a recording session are some-times curious as to what an A&R man does. What I did, aside from choosing the leaders of the dates, was provide plenty of sandwiches, soft drinks, and beer. I wrote down the times of the takes, and when the music began to stammer, I'd make non-abrasive suggestions. And if the gridlock still continued, I'd ask the musicians—without any arrangement at hand—to just play the blues. The blues, the common language of jazz, always broke the tension.

From the sessions I did for Les Koenig, I'd also learned the necessity of finding an engineer who did not think that the placement of his microphones was more important than en-abling the musicians to interact freely. For instance, at the time, it was standard practice to confine vocalists in what amounted to an isolation booth in the studio—with the result that communication between the singer and the instrumental-ists was fragmented.

I took the booth away, remembering, years before, having seen Ernest Ansermet, at a recording session, conduct a full symphony orchestra—with just one overhanging microphone gathering it all. The musicians weren't even aware of the mike, and the sound was vibrant and full.

My friend Charles Mingus once knocked out a prominent engineer who had made it clear that the music was secondary to *his* sound, which was his unmistakable signature on all his recordings. Mingus figured, however, that he came to record *his* music, and when the engineer refused to give way, Mingus finished the argument decisively.

On my sessions for Candid, I used a young, knowledgeable engineer, Bob d'Orleans, who, like me, knew his place. He could even operate in near darkness when he had to, as I dis-covered when Mingus, on his first session for Candid, wanted the feeling of a nightclub, and so most of the lights were turned off. Mingus introduced the numbers and the musicians as if the rather small studio were crowded with listeners at tables jammed close together. It was a powerful session, a spiraling conversation in which all the voices were equal and urgent. Mingus said it was his best recording, which made me feel good, though I had nothing to do with the music—except get out of its way.

For me, being in the same studio with jazz musicians—some of whose recordings I had played over and over again from boyhood on—was like being in the same courtroom with Louis Brandeis, William O. Douglas, John Harlan, and Oliver Wendell Holmes. I had been so in awe of Coleman Hawkins, for example, that I had always imagined him as physically big—because his sound was so huge. But close up, in the studio, he was rather short. I was amazed.

One of my deepest pleasures was recording Otis Spann, a Mississippi-born blues singer and pianist. He had long been with Muddy Waters, who had received much more attention from reviewers than had the chubby pianist and auxiliary singer. Spann was a natural rolling force as both pianist and vocalist. His was the sound of a deep river of feeling, sometimes rushing against rocks and sometimes deceptively serene.

Spann just sat down one afternoon and recorded one blues after another. Practically all the tracks were first takes.

In Chicago, Muddy Waters and Otis Spann played at Smitty's Corner, on the South Side. "Most of the people who come to hear us," Otis told me, "work hard during the day. What they want from us are stories. The blues for them is something like a book. They want to hear stories out of their own experiences, and that's the kind we tell:

> *"This is my story,*
> *All I got to say to you:*
> *So long, baby,*
> *I don't care what you do."*

A 1960 session with Pee Wee Russell, the gentlest person I have ever known—and the most daring musician—provided a revealing exchange with Coleman Hawkins, who was also on the date. Finishing a glass of cognac, the magisterial Hawkins was reminiscing about a 1929 session he had made with Pee Wee. "Back then, and for the last thirty years," said Hawkins, "I've been listening to him play those funny notes. He used to think they were wrong, but they weren't. He's always been way out, but they didn't have a name for it then."

Seeing Pee Wee that afternoon, I remembered, when I was a teenager, going to hear him in a dive in Boston—a small, narrow, cheerless room. One night, at the end of his gig there, Pee Wee was confronted by a student at the nearby New England Conservatory of Music who unrolled a series of music manuscript pages.

They were densely covered with what looked like notes of an extraordinarily complex avant-garde classical composition.

"I brought this for you," the young man said to Pee Wee, who stared at him as if he were a Martian. "It's one of your solos from last night. I transcribed it."

Shaking his head, Pee Wee looked at the manuscript. "This can't be me. I can't play this."

The student assured Pee Wee that the transcribed solo—with its fiendishly difficult and startling turns of invention—was indeed Pee Wee's.

"Well," the shy clarinetist said, "even if it is, I wouldn't play it again the same way—even if I could, which I can't."

Listening to Pee Wee on the record we made with him and Coleman Hawkins—*Jazz Reunion*—was like listening to him anywhere. He could move into a chorus in such a way that he soon seemed to be in a cul-de-sac, with no way out melodically or harmonically—except to throw the clarinet away. But always he extricated himself and went on to further stone walls.

I never thought, back then in Boston, that I'd be contributing to the legend of Pee Wee Russell.

I also recorded a rebellion. A group of musicians had become indignant at the growing commercialism of the Newport Jazz Festival, and—right there at Newport—they created a counter-festival. The rebels included Charles Mingus, Max Roach, Eric Dolphy, Roy Eldridge, and "the man who played like the wind," drummer Jo Jones.

The music of the Newport rebels, there and in the recording studio, was spirited and contagiously swinging. A dividend—for me—was the playing out between takes in the studio of several pieces of jazz history.

When Mingus was in the high school band in Los Angeles, word came that Roy "Little Jazz" Eldridge was coming as a guest artist with the band. A black kid in the band told Mingus that Eldridge was one of those older jazz guys who couldn't play in tune, couldn't play in a section, and weren't trained at all. Mingus was advised to pay attention to the white jazzmen because *they* had the essential techniques.

When Eldridge came to the high school, young Mingus told him what had been said about him. Mingus told me Eldridge's answer: "You see this horn? I play what I feel on it. That's jazz. You'd better find out about the music of your people. Someday you're going to thank me for talking to you like this."

Actually, Eldridge could and did play in tune and in a section, but he wanted young Mingus to dig into the roots of black music.

Knowing about that exchange, I was watching to see what they would have to say to each other on the *Newport Rebels* date after all these years. They had never recorded together, and Mingus was rather apprehensive. When the session was over, I heard Eldridge say to Mingus, "I'm glad I made this. I wanted to find out what bag you were in. Now I know you're in the right bag. I'm not naming names, but a lot of the young ones are so busy being busy on their instruments, they forget the basics. They don't get all the way down into the music. You did, baby. It's good to know. There are very few of us left out here."

Mingus was in a state of exaltation.

Standing in the studio, just watching and listening, was a young modern trumpeter from Detroit. He had come thinking Eldridge was old-timey. But at the end of the take, his mouth open, he stared at Roy.

Roy laughed and said to him, "We're still trying, aren't we?"

I greatly enjoyed that year of being closer to the music than I had ever been before. It came to an end because, according to Archie Bleyer, the recordings were not making a profit. I reminded him that when we'd started, I'd told him the albums wouldn't break even for some time, since they weren't in the least commercial. But Bleyer hadn't had much commercial success himself lately on Cadence, and it was time to cut his losses. I was grateful to him for letting me run up Candid's losses that long. Since then, musicians traveling through Europe and in Japan tell me the Candid sets are still available, still selling. I guess they've broken even by now.

More than thirty years later I was asked by a British record owner to go back in the studio again. But most of the musicians I had held in awe had died, and not enough of that larger-than-life quality was in their successors. So I declined the return to the control room. I had shown I could put together sessions that would last. I didn't want to show that I could turn out clinkers too.

HUCKLEBERRY DRACULA

From time to time I've been asked by college journalists what I consider my greatest accomplishment—so far. My answer is always the same. A CBS television program in 1957 called "The Sound of Jazz." I didn't write the script and it wasn't based on any of the books I've written about jazz. But I helped select the musicians, and it turned out to be the truest and therefore the most exciting jazz program in the history of television. Nothing has come close to it since.

Just to be in the same studio with Billie Holiday, Count Basie, Lester Young, Roy Eldridge, Pee Wee Russell, Henry "Red" Allen, Thelonious Monk, Ben Webster, Vic Dickenson, Jo Jones, and Jimmy Rushing was like being among the immortals. When I was a kid, listening to the recordings of these players beyond category, I'd never thought I'd be in their presence, all at once. And then to be directly involved in sending their music to millions across the nation—that was a natural high.

A few minutes after six that Sunday afternoon, when "The Sound of Jazz" had ended, Billie Holiday found me in the wings and kissed me. A few days before, at the first camera-blocking session in the vast CBS television studio on West 57th Street, Billie had called me a motherfucker. She had just discovered there was to be no set—only the studio space, the television cameras, and the cameramen. And all the musicians were to dress as they did at rehearsals, including the hats that many jazzmen in those days wore continually in the daytime, as if they were Orthodox Jews.

"I just bought a goddam five-hundred-dollar gown," Billie had glared at me during the blocking session. "You said this was going to be a *network* show!"

What I should have told her was that it would indeed be on the CBS network, but the producer, Robert Herridge, was unlike any other television producer in history. One of the abiding joys of working on "The Sound of Jazz" was getting to know Herridge, and a resultant friendship that was to lead to my working with him on a number of other programs.

He became a kind of mentor to me. In some ways Herridge was like a jazz musician. He had learned his craft and kept learning, so that he knew television as thoroughly as a jazz player knows his instrument. Because of that depth of knowledge, he was a fearless improviser.

What has stayed in my mind—along with his work—was his mantra, which I heard him shout going into, and all the way through, every program he did. "Keep it pure, *Partisan Review* pure." This was not the wistful cry of an academic. Herridge was an untenured barroom boozer, womanizer, and exemplifier of what Thomas Wolfe (the one not in the white suit) called the "goat cry." He had a lust not only for life but also for lifegiving literature (from Dostoyevsky to Melville). He was a passionate intellectual and an insatiable imbiber of music. Colossally stubborn, he took more risks in his work than a trapeze artist.

Herridge is part of this book because of what he meant to me, and because hardly anyone mentions his name any more.

In 1981, the year of Herridge's death, 150 public television stations were showing *The Golden Age of Television*—

kinescopes from "Marty," "The Days of Wine and Roses," and other widely praised programs. Among the honored writers, producers, and directors were Fred Coe, Paddy Chayefsky, J. P. Miller, Delbert Mann, and John Frankenheimer.

Looking over the list, I called a coordinator of "The Golden Age of Television" and asked her, "Where's something about Robert Herridge?"

There was a pause. "I'm sorry. I don't know the name. Could you clue me in?"

I told her that doing the series without a Herridge show was like producing a celebration of jazz and leaving out Charlie Parker.

"Oh," she said. "Well, in all the materials I've been reading about 'the Golden Age,' I've never come across Mr. Herridge's name."

In creating the single most original body of work in television history, Herridge found for television its own forms and rhythms. He thought it was dumb "to make a small-scale motion picture and call it television," or to shoot a play as if it were on a theater stage, the only difference on television being more close-ups. And he hated—I mean *hated*—the kind of naturalism represented by *Marty* and its clones of the period. Herridge called that "kitchen writing," because there was at least one scene set in a kitchen that, by God, had real pots and pans. With remnants of food in them.

Herridge stubbornly believed that television could create its own ways of telling a story, not only in drama, but through music. He cared and knew more about music than any other television writer or producer or director I've known, and I've met a lot of them. In his music shows like "The Sound of Jazz" and an exhilarating hour with Eugene Ormandy and the Philadelphia Orchestra, Herridge refused to do what he called "reporting"—that is, just shooting what the musicians would be doing in a concert hall or club. Instead, with no tricky camera work and without getting in the way of the musicians, he enabled the viewer to get inside the dynamics of the making of the music. He instructed his camera operators to improvise—to react to the emotions of the players, and their own. And so we were able to see something of the inner experiences of the musicians.

And when he brought Dostoyevsky, Joyce, Faulkner, and Melville to television, Herridge—again without the slightest distortion of the original—created, each time, a new theater of the imagination, a *television* theater.

He not only produced, but often directed and sometimes wrote. Robert Carrington, a former associate producer with Herridge, told me, "He creates a whole world—sometimes just out of light. In 'Emily Dickinson' on Herridge's *Camera Three* [a local series in New York and then on the national CBS network], her house was evoked by using the back wall of the studio and a piece of canvas representing the ceiling. The rest—corridors, the separate rooms, stairs—was made entirely by lighting." Herridge didn't need twenty-foot scenery with wallpaper.

Herridge also found out what he needed to know about cameras, investigating their depths of focus and fields. He would even push around the different kinds to get a sense of the problems a cameraman runs into with each of them when he's shooting. In addition, Herridge was involved with casting, very involved. A good many actors very much wanted to work with Herridge, even though it often meant cuts in their regular fees. (Herridge's budgets were usually sparse.)

In 1961, Nancy Wickwire told me: "He does everything with such passion that he makes it more exciting to be a part of one of his shows. Furthermore, you can trust him. I've never heard him say, 'If we can only get so-and-so [a big name], we can push up the rating.' I'm always without fear when I work with Herridge. I know that five days after rehearsals begin, an agency or network man won't come in and change everything. Herridge is in charge, and the confidence we have in him gives us more confidence in ourselves."

Oh, Herridge was always in charge, all right. In 1960, while I was working with him on a folk music show for CBS, he insisted on including a choral group that had about the same relationship to folk music as Wonder Bread has to pumpernickel. It was one of the few times we totally disagreed, and I was totally overruled. Brooding, I was taking some comfort in the fact that at least one of my choices, Cisco Houston, was on the show. Houston, who had wandered over earth and sea with Woody Guthrie, was a low-key minstrel, and thereby all the more compelling.

From the sponsor's booth, a CBS page descended with a note for Herridge. I walked over, and Herridge showed it to me. There was still a residue of blacklisting in those days; Pete Seeger was barred from two network programs—at CBS and ABC—three years later. The note said that someone (not named) had checked out Cisco Houston, and he was not suitable for this CBS folk song show. No reason was given, but it obviously had nothing to do with Cisco's choice of chords.

I gave the note back to Herridge. He took it and tore it up. That was the end of it. The rehearsal, including Cisco, went on, and for a while I felt so good I could almost stand that milky choral group.

My relationship with Herridge began as a viewer. I had come to New York in 1953, at just about the time Herridge—a former poet (published), road-gang worker, expert in nineteenth-century American literature, and dishwasher—had finally, at thirty-nine, found what he wanted to do with his life. He had just started writing, producing, and largely staging

Camera 3 on Channel 2. Every Sunday, even if I had been listening to Count Basie at Birdland until three that morning, I got up in time to watch what I had never imagined could take place on a television screen—a six-part *Moby Dick,* for instance, in which somehow four stools, some ropes, a capstan, and a platform became the consuming world of Ahab. I didn't see the white whale, but I sure knew he was there.

The marvels never stopped. There was "A Ballad of Huck Finn"; and the most extraordinary television show I have seen anywhere, a three-part *Notes from Underground.* Only one actor, a ladder, and an overwhelming intensity. I wasn't thinking about the lighting or direction. I was just stunned that so much force was coming out of that box.

In a number of ways, Herridge was like Charles Mingus, with whom Herridge had a warm, tumultuous friendship. Both were almost ingenuous in some respects, and therefore quite vulnerable; but they could also be shrewdly realistic. Both also had a wildness in them—not mean, but defiant. And until their last years, it was a wildness that sometimes got out of control, like that of a boy who gets into a fiercely stubborn state, tries to get out of it, and has forgotten how. Both were obsessed by their callings, and were world-class improvisers.

One of Herridge's problems in television was that he could not stand anyone—to use Huck Finn's word—trying to "sivilize" him. Karl Genus, a director who worked often with him, said, a few years before Herridge left commercial television in 1966, "He never plays it safe. He charged into television as if it were a vast overgrown jungle, and he kept hacking away at it instead of resting in the places that had already been cleared. He's always been an enigma to the executives in this industry."

Other powers in the industry were downright furious at the very idea of Herridge. David Susskind, for whom Herridge worked briefly in the 1950s, called him "a kook," and went on to hoot at the way he dressed: "Herridge affected being a bohemian, never wore a tie," Susskind complained to me. "He tried to substitute nonconformity of dress for talent." Furthermore, instead of meeting with writers in the office, as responsible producers did, Herridge—said Susskind—met them in bars, "those *little* bars where people pose as artists. Herridge creates anarchy. That's what he creates, no matter what he's doing."

Yet, while with Susskind's Talent Associates, Herridge produced, in 1958 for *Kraft Theater*, two of the most powerful shows ever associated with Susskind's name: versions of Ernest Hemingway's *Fifty Grand* and Robert Penn Warren's *All the King's Men*, the latter a far more gripping transformation of the book than Robert Rossen's screen version. Those two productions were the last Herridge did for Susskind. And it was on those two that Herridge demanded Susskind stay the hell out of the way until the dress rehearsal, instead of continually inflicting his artistic judgment on Herridge, the actors, the writer, and the sandwich shop.

Maybe that's why, years ago, Susskind's final word to me on Herridge—shaking his fists and shouting—was, "The Herridge legend must be broken!"

Well, I guess it was broken. Or, rather, it was forgotten. Like the PBS coordinator for *The Golden Age of Television* who'd never heard the name before, Huckleberry Dracula, being so hopelessly "unsivilized," does not fit into official Golden Ages.

That name, Huckleberry Dracula, came from S. Lee Pogostin, a writer on a number of Herridge shows. Mark Twain's incorrigibly independent Huckleberry Finn struck Pogostin as a soul brother to Herridge.

As for the Dracula description, Herridge's eyes could take on a most unsettling intensity. Pogostin once told me about a discussion he and Herridge were having at the Russian Tea Room about the "kitchen" school of television writing. Herridge let go a barrage of language in which, like Mark Twain, he cursed for thirty minutes without repeating himself. But the cursing was merely a cadenza.

"The concerto," Pogostin continued, "consisted of what seemed to be the entire classical learning of the Western world. Herridge's face got redder and redder, and he drank his whitish-green drink with such viciousness and vengeance that innocent people who just happened to be passing the table found themselves being glared at by Dracula-eyes. The women, in particular, held their necks as if thinking, 'This is it! Imagine, in the Russian Tea Room! He's going to bite us!' Like a great storm, it was over. And there was calm. But Herridge continued to glare—with those eyes."

It was Eugene Ormandy, long the conductor of the Philadelphia Orchestra, who once gently admonished a relatively calm Herridge: "What you have done with the orchestra on television, Mr. Herridge, is marvelous. But please, do not call it a 'band.' "

For "The Sound of Jazz," Herridge asked Whitney Balliett, jazz critic for *The New Yorker*, and me to select and assemble the musicians. To keep it "*Partisan Review* pure," he made sure—as Billie Holiday found out—that there would be no set. That is, the studio and the camera would be the set. And he told the people behind the cameras to improvise—to signal the control room when they had a particularly good shot.

Through the years, Herridge had kept tabs on the more adventurous cameramen at CBS, and when he had a particularly challenging project, he would somehow pick them out of whatever assignments they had at the time and bring them together for his gig.

"The Sound of Jazz," like most television in 1957, was live. That was the way Herridge preferred it all his television life.

The tension and the excitement were high. Any mistakes had to be rescued by improvisation; and the spontaneity came directly through to the audiences.

One of the many letters Herridge received after "The Sound of Jazz" was aired came from a woman in White Plains, New York, who, writing as soon as the program was over, said, "One so seldom has the chance to see real people doing something that really matters to them."

Herridge carried that letter around with him for quite a while.

After "The Sound of Jazz," Herridge wanted to do a program with Miles Davis. Davis, a man of strong views and language, had told me he would never do television again, saying, "They would fuck it up." But I talked him into meeting with Herridge, in whom Miles found somebody he could curse and respect. The result was "The Sound of Miles Davis," with John Coltrane and Gil Evans. It's still played around the world, as is "The Sound of Jazz."

The hardest time we had in persuading a musician to do a program was the very long night we spent with Duke Ellington. Duke was aware that he was the most original composer in the country—"beyond category," as he sometimes described other musicians. He despised such labels as "jazz" or "classical music." In the 1920s, Ellington had gone to Fletcher Henderson, Duke once told me, and urged him to scrap the term "jazz" and call what he did and what Ellington did "black music." Henderson refused.

Ellington was always highly aware of his payroll. The "expensive gentlemen" of his orchestra, as he used to say, were on the road with him all year long. Accordingly, Ellington was concerned with keeping his followers around the country satisfied, and adding new ones. So he left ample room for medleys of his standards and other familiar compositions during nearly every engagement, performing his longer, more ambitious works less often—and never, at that time, on television.

Ellington had appeared on *The Ed Sullivan Show* playing a couple of his songs that even people who knew nothing about jazz easily recognized. What Herridge and I wanted him to perform, however, was "Harlem Suite," an extended work that would never have been considered on any other commercial television network at the time. We were indeed doing this for a commercial network, Metromedia, but there were to be no commercials on this particular hour—and Herridge was to be in total control.

With his infinite charm masking his infinite stubbornness, Duke turned down our proposal. I tried to assure him that there were significant numbers of people who would welcome a chance to hear and see a long Ellington work. No, he answered, but he'd be glad to do a series of his standards.

The impasse went on for a long time until I finally found a word that would change his mind. Posterity. If you tape this classic work, I told him, it will be seen for generations.

Duke finally agreed. The piece, also known as "A Tone Parallel to Harlem," was one of Ellington's favorites among his longer works, and the Ellington orchestra that night gave it the most evocative performance I've ever heard. A tour of Harlem, it tells of people at work, in church, celebrating, parading, mourning, picketing. It all came vividly, compellingly alive.

Duke was pleased. Herridge and I were much more than pleased. Herridge was supposed to pick up the tape after it ran, but he forgot to for a while. By the time he remembered and showed up at Metromedia for "Tone Parallel to Harlem," it had been erased so that the tape could be used for something else. We had promised Duke posterity, and we had failed him. But I never told him. Of course, he was connected to posterity anyway.

Herridge left commercial television in 1966 because he felt that, at last, the forces of what he called the "ABM" (the American Business Machine) had become far too strong at all the networks for him to keep trying to survive there on his own terms. He was to learn later that the ABM had also enveloped public television. In 1980, for instance, Herridge entered a competition for a jazz series to be shown on PBS. He lost. "You see," a PBS power told Herridge, "it wasn't that your entry failed [tapes of "The Sound of Jazz" and "The Sound of Miles Davis"]. Yours was easily the best of the lot. It's just that the winner came in with a lot of money from an oil company to help finance the series."

From 1966 to 1969, Herridge had tried Hollywood, which found him even more uncategorizable, and therefore more unusable, than television had. He then wrote two plays on commission for Arena Stage in Washington, D.C., and a novel. But he had to find a way back into television. That's where he had discovered his true calling, and where his body of work had been created. Writers, he used to say, experienced rebirths. Why couldn't a television producer?

So, under a grant from the National Endowment for the Humanities, he worked with some academics on a projected series of television dramas based on American history. It was not a salubrious mix. The professors fed on facts; Herridge heard voices. But he persevered, because this could be a way back *in*. Maybe, he felt, he could be born again on PBS— despite the oil companies. The American history series never materialized.

Finally there was an opening. Herridge was asked to be something called the creative producer for "A Salute to Duke Ellington" on PBS, a show done in conjunction with WQED in Pittsburgh and the Kennedy Center for the Performing Arts in Washington. The months before the broadcast were very vexing for the man who always before had been in control of every element of a show that had his name on the credits.

The concept at PBS, Herridge found, was that "creative" thinking had to be done by a hive of executives. And not only executives. There were swarms of lesser young functionaries who also got themselves nibbles of power. "They all have college degrees," Herridge told me one morning on the phone, "and they think that makes them experts on everything. But they don't *know* anything about someone like Duke Ellington, about where his music came from. I don't know *what* they really know anything about."

He resisted many of the hive's ukases, but yielded on some. He so needed to be back on television, to prove he still had the magic, that he allowed two performers to be pushed into that program whom he in no way wanted. But his only other choice would have been to lose the show—the pressures were that imperious. Somehow, Herridge pulled it off. "A Salute to Duke Ellington" was not a total astonishment, as his other jazz programs had been, but there were gloriously illuminated passages, like a Sarah Vaughan–Joe Williams duet in which Sarah, for once, forgot she was on television.

I called Herridge right after the program to tell him I thought it had worked. He was pleased, but tired, very tired. Maybe cable television, he said. Now that cable was opening up to "the arts," he had some ideas for a series there.

Robert Herridge died of a heart attack on August 14, 1981. He told me once: "We never did have a 'golden age' of television, although some very good things were done in the late 1940s and early 1950s. But if there is a 'golden age,' it's ahead of us."

He *was* the "Golden Age." All by himself.

. . .

Herridge was responsible for the single most memorable musical experience I've known. It was on "The Sound of Jazz," and involved Billie Holiday—the most honest jazz singer in the history of the music—and tenor saxophonist Lester Young, who was chronically original ("The way I play, I try not to be a repeater pencil").

At the start of that hour, Billie, wearing slacks, her hair in a ponytail, made her entrance, walking merrily through the ranks of a band composed of nonpareil jazz players with Count Basie at the piano.

Off the studio, in an austerely furnished room, sat Lester Young. He looked lost. He was ill, and so weak that we had to remove him from the big-band section of the program. His only remaining assignment in the hour was in the combo that would be accompanying "Lady Day," as he had named Billie long before. (And she had called him "Prez," as jazz players did ever after.)

Once Billie and Lester had been very close, but years before, something—none of the musicians knew exactly what—had caused them to stop speaking. Until "The Sound of Jazz."

For Billie's number, "Fine and Mellow," she was perched on a high stool facing a semicircle of musicians who were all standing—except for Lester Young. I had told him he could keep sitting, including his solo.

Slumped in his chair, his eyes were averted from Billie, and she looked past him. It was one of the few blues in her repertory, and this time she was using it to speak not so much of the troubles she'd known, but rather of the bittersweet triumph of having survived—with some kicks along the way.

Despite the myth that toward the end of her life—she died less than two years after "The Sound of Jazz"—Lady invariably sounded like a cracked husk of what she had been years before, when she wouldn't sing without a gardenia in her hair, that afternoon she was in full control of the tart, penetrating, sinuously swinging instrument that was her voice.

It was time for Prez's solo. Somehow he managed to stand up, and then he blew the sparest, purest blues I have ever heard. Billie, smiling, nodding to the beat, looked into Prez's eyes, and he into hers. It was as if she was looking back, with the gentlest of regrets, at their past together. Whatever had blighted that relationship was forgotten in the communion of the music. Sitting in the control room, I felt tears, and saw tears on the faces of the others, including Herridge.

"The Sound of Jazz" has been shown in many countries, sometimes as a whole or in excerpts. The excerpt most often shown is the reunion of Lady Day and Prez.

Off camera, after the show, they left the studio separately.

Years later, the Museum of Broadcasting in New York had a showing of "The Sound of Jazz." Some of us who had been involved in the program were there.

During the discussion following the show, a young man asked me, "How were you able to get so many great players in one place at the same time?"

"They could all use the gig," I said.

Most of the musicians in "The Sound of Jazz" are now dead. Since then, a number of skilled young musicians have made their reputations, but only a few are likely to become legends. The CBS studio that Sunday afternoon was filled with legends. In their own time as well as now.

Herridge, however, did not become a legend. Except to me.

MENTORS: GEORGE SELDES,

I. F. STONE

Herridge, though not a journalist, was an influence on me. He was uncompromising, decisive in his judgment; as much at home in a bar as in a concert hall; and he enjoyed combat. I approved of—and tried to live up to—all these characteristics. And he was easily enraged.

I was once asked by a journalism student what most impelled me to go after a story. Without having to hesitate, I said, "Rage." And I told her of a tribute that Tom Wicker, then a columnist for the *New York Times*, paid I. F. Stone, one of my mentors, years ago. "What keeps on energizing Izzy," Wicker said, "is that he has never lost his sense of rage."

That is true, to one degree or another, of a good many journalists—for example, Jack Newfield of the *New York Post* and Colman McCarthy, formerly with the *Washington Post*. Some of the others become accustomed to the bitter fruits of injustice and are no longer startled by such stories.

I've always been attracted to the perennially indignant chroniclers of our time.

When I was fifteen, I picked up a copy of a four-page weekly called *In Fact: An Antidote for Falsehoods in the Daily Press*. The solo practitioner was George Seldes, who had worked for a number of news organizations, including the

United Press and the *Chicago Tribune*. As a foreign correspondent, Seldes had interviewed Lenin and Hitler, among
other insatiable predators. He resigned from the *Tribune* because its autocratic owner, Colonel Robert Rutherford Mc-
Cormick, censored those of Seldes's dispatches that strayed
from the Colonel's choleric ideological agenda.

Growing up in Boston, I read most of the daily newspapers—there were eight of them—but I had never seen anything like *In Fact* for ceaseless, fearless muckraking. Seldes
attacked the powerful National Association of Manufac-
turers and individual corporations, as well as the American
Legion. (He somehow obtained—and printed—a letter from
the Commander of the American Legion ordering the legion-
naires to no longer wear their uniforms when engaged in
strikebreaking activities.)

In Fact, which charged its readers two cents a copy, attacked the established press for refusing to print a 1938 report
by Dr. Raymond Pearl—head of the department of biology at
Johns Hopkins University—that was among the first to link the
smoking of cigarettes to cancer. For his accusatory independence, Seldes was punished across the board. No mention of
him was allowed in the *New York Times* for years; he was listed
by congressional Red-hunters; and he and *In Fact* were boycotted by the Communist Party, which was outraged by a
Seldes article applauding Tito's removal of Yugoslavia from
the embrace of the Kremlin.

Seldes's writing had a verve, an immediacy, a delight in
risk-taking that reminded me of the jazz musicians I so respected and marveled at. Like them, he was his own man: "I
belong," he said, "to no party, no group, society, or faction."

Ten years after it was founded in 1940, *In Fact* died. Only
three years before, it had reached a circulation of 176,000; but
it was too controversial to survive at a time when people were
becoming very careful about the magazines they subscribed to

and the papers they bought—in plain view—at a newsstand. Even labor unions—which had been subscribers to *In Fact* from its early years—canceled their subscriptions. And the mainstream press, which devoutly wished that Seldes would disappear, provided, of course, no support.

Three years after *In Fact* was no more, George Seldes was subpoenaed to appear before Senator Joseph McCarthy's committee. The confrontation was behind closed doors, and the chief accuser was Roy Cohn, the senator's highly imaginative and ruthless confidant. Cohn, with his customary contempt, asked Seldes about the Communist cell he was purportedly building in Vermont.

"What a crooked little son of a bitch Cohn was," Seldes fondly recalled the occasion for me years later.

Joe McCarthy then asked Seldes why Martin Dies's House Committee on Un-American Activities had listed him as a Communist.

Seldes told the senator, who had scared much of the nation, "If the President of the United States and the nine members of the Supreme Court came in here, pointed their fingers at me, and said I was a Communist, I'd say, 'You are ten liars!' And so I would say to Congressman Dies."

At the end of the closed hearing, Senator McCarthy left the room and told the waiting press that Seldes had been cleared.

"How many people do you know," Seldes asked me thirty-five years later, "who can go around the country saying, 'I was cleared by Joe McCarthy'?"

I still miss *In Fact*. Although there have been a number of magazines since then that specialize in press criticism, none has had the flair—or brimstone—of *In Fact*'s assaults on the mainstream dailies.

Seldes went on to write books, but he slipped so far from press—and thereby public—attention that by the early 1970s he was listed as deceased in *Webster's Biographical Dictionary* and *Bartlett's Familiar Quotations.*

I first found out that George Seldes had not left us when I received a note from him in 1982. I had written an article for *Lithopinion*—a quarterly published by Local One, Amalgamated Lithographers of America—in which I cited George Seldes and I. F. Stone as recommended state-of-the-art models for any journalist concerned with keeping his or her self-respect in this business.

A few months after the piece appeared, Seldes wrote me from Hartland Four Corners, Vermont. He had seen the article, and wrote, "I wonder if you realize that this is the first favorable mention I've had since 1940 when I started publishing *In Fact* and criticizing the press."

The statement was an exaggeration, but not by much. Although certain reporters admired Seldes and contributed anonymously to *In Fact*, he was not beloved of publishers or most editors. For instance, the blacklisting of Seldes by the *New York Times* lasted some forty years. He was banned not only for what he'd written about the *Times* in *In Fact*, but also because he had testified in 1934 in a hearing before the National Labor Relations Board when the Newspaper Guild was trying to organize the *Times*.

Heywood Broun, a much-respected journalist and president of the Guild, asked Seldes if he'd testify about the wages of journalists. With customary gusto, Seldes did bear witness to the abysmal salaries of journalists at the time.

During the First World War, Seldes became a close friend of *Times* correspondent Edwin James when both were covering American forces in Europe. James—later known as "King James" to the *Times* staff—became managing editor of the *Times* in 1932.

"The day I testified for the Guild two years later," Seldes

told me, "Edwin James came up to me on the steps of the courthouse and said, 'Well, George, I guess your name will never again be mentioned in the *Times*.' And let me tell you"—Seldes pointed a finger at me—"that order was obeyed!" Once, when Seldes tried to buy an ad for *In Fact* in the *Times*, the ad was rejected.

The books Seldes began writing after *In Fact* died were far from blockbusters, but in 1985, Ballantine published Seldes's *The Great Thoughts*, which sold very well and made Seldes visible again, canceling his obituaries.

The book was a collection of what he considered to be "the greatest thoughts of the ages." From 1960 to 1984, Seldes told me, he did little else but research *The Great Thoughts*, compiling 10,000 filing cards and reading or rereading many of the books involved.

One of the *Great Thoughts*—by John Stuart Mill—could be George Seldes's signature: "If all mankind minus one were of one opinion, and only one person were of the contrary opinion, mankind would be no more justified in silencing that one person, than he, if he had the power, would be justified in silencing mankind."

I went to see George Seldes in the fall of 1985 for an article on his book—and on him. It was about nine in the morning when I came into his New York hotel room. He was reading the newspapers—underlining some pieces and clipping out others. At ninety-four, he was no longer in the journalism business, but he couldn't stop. He looked at me and, without saying hello, handed me some of the clippings. "You ought to look into these stories," he said.

As he spoke animatedly, I remembered that first issue of *In Fact* I'd read when I was fifteen. And here before me was the peerless muckraker himself. He sort of smiled at me. "I'm getting old, yes," he said, "but to hell with being mellow."

We talked of *In Fact*. "Remember," Seldes said, "*In Fact*

was the first regular publication in the whole world that was devoted to press criticism and to publishing news that had been suppressed by the press."

And the press responded by trying to kill *In Fact* with silence. But it took a very long time for its influence to die.

I. F. Stone once stated that he'd followed in George Seldes's footsteps. *"In Fact,"* he said, "was independent, it was radical, it got to the roots of things. It exposed big business malpractices a lot of papers were afraid to touch. It was antifascist and upheld civil liberties."

Izzy, too, delighted in being a muckraker, but he was more of an analyst than Seldes. And he was more fascinated by ideas than by scoops, though he reveled in those he came upon.

I knew Izzy for many years, and whatever forces were gnawing at the Bill of Rights, getting me down, he was always a brightening presence. A prodigious autodidact—Izzy was not a college graduate—his reading had taught him that the struggle for individual liberties, while often seemingly lost, always started up again. To be part of that resurrection, one had to have courage—sustained courage.

To the end, Izzy regarded it as a privilege, as he put it, "to spit in the eye" of the illegitimately powerful. When most journalists took cover in the time of Joe McCarthy, Izzy kept nailing his lies and was accordingly ostracized for years in Washington lest he infect his colleagues with his courage.

Izzy never lost his sense of joy, however. I've never known a journalist—or anyone else—who took so much delight in his work.

As Izzy said in Jerry Bruck's 1973 documentary *I. F. Stone's Weekly*—and I often heard him say it in conversation—"I really have so much fun, I ought to be arrested. . . . To be able . . . to do what you think is right, and report the news, and have enough readers to make some impact, is such a pleasure. . . ."

Izzy took pleasure in practically everything he did. One

summer night on Fire Island, we were in the presence of Artur Rubinstein, via television, playing Beethoven. I've been around music all my life, and I've never seen anybody as totally immersed in a performance as Izzy was that evening. When he talked about it afterward, he was glowing.

Another day, Izzy, who started learning classical Greek in his seventies, arrived in a state of excitement. He had been able, for the first time, to read a poem by an ancient Greek author in the original. And he had discovered more than he ever knew existed in that poem. He couldn't have been happier if he'd found a new, bottomless lode of corruption in the Pentagon. To Izzy, everything was contemporary.

The joy could also come from a love of beauty—in the curve of a phrase, a whisper in a chord change, or a deserted beach in early evening. All of this would have been a surprise to the high officials he so often disrobed in the public prints. They, who never met him, saw Izzy in their dreams as a grim zealot.

Izzy was best known—until his unexpectedly successful book, *The Trial of Socrates*—as the owner, publisher, editor, and reporter for *I. F. Stone's Weekly* (and then *Bi-Weekly*) from 1953 to 1971. His wife, Esther, handled everything else—and there was a lot—from the kitchen table in their Washington apartment.

The *Weekly* was always full of surprises, and nearly all of them came from government documents or, sometimes, from middle-level bureaucrats whom hardly anyone else in the press bothered to search out. After all, James Reston could get to see the folks in charge anytime, and the folks in charge would tell James Reston only what they would like to see in the *New York Times*. Among the subscribers to *I. F. Stone's Weekly* were Albert Einstein (a charter subscriber), Bertrand Russell, Eleanor Roosevelt, and Norman Thomas. They wanted more than they could find in the *New York Times*.

Izzy had a hearing problem, but that wasn't the reason he never went to press conferences. They consisted, he said, of government propaganda—or the propaganda of anybody else holding a press conference. Instead, he would read voluminous committee reports, Pentagon documents, transcripts of congressional hearings, and—that trove of serendipitous revelations—*The Congressional Record.* With their daily deadlines, most other reporters had no time for such extensive reading, and besides, it could be boring.

It should be said that Izzy was not above a certain degree of derring-do in getting the news. In his early years in Washington, he had an old-fashioned hearing aid that, if he put the receiver to a door, enabled him to hear what was going on inside. This was how Izzy, on occasion, monitored certain closed-door committee hearings.

He used to tell me, and many other journalists, that the first thing a reporter has to remember is that "all governments are run by liars." This knowledge didn't make him a cynic; it made him a hell of a good reporter. He also emphasized that any government "reveals a good deal if you take the time to study what it says."

Or, as he told Andrew Patner for his book, *I. F. Stone,* "The bureaucracies put out so much that they cannot help letting the truth slip [in] from time to time."

Among the marvels of *I. F. Stone's Weekly* were the boxes—short epiphanies of deceit, hypocrisy, official contradictions, and sometimes sheer governmental lunacy. These succulent items encompassed not only the White House and the Pentagon, but a range of disreputable governments around the world.

I had no idea what went into finding these boxes until the first summer we lived on the same street on Fire Island. Izzy would come back from the post office every day hauling a wagon full of mail. Most of it consisted of periodicals in a number of languages. Izzy would pore over them with intense anticipation, and then—like a gull sighting an evening meal— he'd pounce and capture a box for the next issue of the *Weekly*.

He made enemies because of some of those all-too-illuminating boxes, as he did with the rest of his work. Izzy was no friend of ideological orthodoxy, including that of the left from time to time, although he was a man of the left. And I think the obituary line that might have pleased him most was Peter Flint's in the *New York Times*: "He annoyed some people all the time and all people one time or another."

Among the early supporters of the *Weekly* were some who were still dedicated to the delusion that the dream of an eventual classless society had not died in the Soviet Union. Izzy traveled there in 1956, and wrote on his return that "the worker is more exploited than in Western welfare states. This is not a good society, and it is not led by honest men." He lost four hundred subscribers with that one.

In later years, writing for the *New York Review of Books*, Izzy refused to join wholly in the general round of tributes to Mikhail Gorbachev. Underneath all the earnest humanistic rhetoric, he said, the head of the USSR was a hypocrite when it came to human rights.

Izzy saw one idea in the Soviet Constitution that he liked. As he told his friend, editor Erwin Knoll, in the July 1984 *Progressive*: "When Stalin's constitution was promulgated in the 1930s, he claimed it was better than the American constitution on freedom of the press because it provided that printing presses and other necessary materials should be made freely available to anyone who wished to express himself. Of course, he never obeyed it."

Izzy was a true believer in freedom of the press here, but recognized that he himself was free because he *owned* his paper. In his preface to *In a Time of Torment: 1961–67*, a collection of columns from the *Weekly*, he wrote:

> In an age when young men, setting out on a career in journalism, must find their niche in some huge newspaper or magazine combine, I have been a wholly independent newspaperman, standing alone, without organizational or party backing, beholden to no one but my good readers. I am even one up on Benjamin Franklin—I have never accepted advertising.

Being free of any ideological or institutional ties, he came under fire from his readers as well as from the government— any government. One of the fiercest and most extended attacks on Izzy by his readers concerned Israel. He had reported firsthand on the underground struggle to establish a Jewish state, and in 1946 he joined hundreds of Jewish Holocaust survivors in successfully running the British blockade of Palestine.

Years later the Jewish state, for which Izzy had great hopes, was, he felt, losing its Jewish ethos in the way it treated the Palestinians. In the late 1970s Pantheon reissued his 1946 book, *Underground to Palestine*—which was used by the Israeli army to indoctrinate its troops—with a new section that contained "Confessions of a Jewish Dissident" and "The Other Zionism."

Izzy characterized "the other Zionism" as the credo of key pioneer Zionists in Palestine a half-century and more earlier. They recognized "that two peoples—not one—occupy the same land and have the same rights."

And in lectures and broadcast appearances, Izzy would say, "How can Israel talk of the Jewish right to a homeland and deny one to the Palestinians? How can there be peace without some measure of justice?"

The mainstream Jewish press, and many of the leaders of the Jewish Establishment, responded by trying to read Izzy out of the Jewish people. "There is hardly a Jewish paper that has not attacked me," Izzy said.

I was present in 1968 at Izzy's sixtieth-birthday party at Town Hall. The tributes and songs, and Izzy's own stand-up piece, were followed by a poisonous attack on Izzy by a claque in the audience that claimed to have a chokehold on "true Zionism," which they defined as allowing political rights only for Jews in the Occupied Territories—and never permitting an independent Palestinian state. Izzy fought back with his perennial weapon—facts—but the evening had soured.

In matters of domestic human rights, Izzy was also well ahead of most of his colleagues in the American press. He scooped them not only in reporting but also in basic decency. A story he liked to tell was how he had been expelled from the National Press Club—the Washington shrine to the free press—in 1941. The club, which worshipped the First Amendment but scorned the Fourteenth—booted Izzy because he had brought a black man to lunch there—William Hastie, the first African American federal judge. In 1956, when he reapplied for admission, Izzy could get only nine of the twenty-five required sponsors. Five years later, the National Press Club finally let the incorrigible troublemaker back through its doors.

In 1987, in a radio interview, Erwin Knoll asked Izzy about the state of the public's awareness of what goes on in its name.

Izzy, characteristically, was not gloomy. Not at all. "There is an awakening," he said.

For example, when Lincoln raised his voice against the Mexican war, he was a lone figure. In the 1920s, as a boy, I knew all about American imperialism and about the good journalists who were exposing what we were doing in Nicaragua and elsewhere, but nobody cared.

However, there has never been a period in American history, as there is now, when so many Americans became aware of injustice—and of malpractice on our part in the name of democracy—in Central America. A time, moreover, in which the clergy—particularly the Catholic bishops—have played an honorable role. All that's to the good.

What Izzy didn't say is that part of the reason for what he calls "an awakening" is those scores, indeed hundreds, of journalists who have been influenced by Izzy's lessons in basic reporting through the years:

"You can't be a prisoner of your preconceptions."

"Look it up. The facts have to be facts."

"You can't be a prisoner of stereotypes. You can't be a know-it-all smart-ass, starting out a story thinking you know all about it."

Then there was the other Izzy, the one who was not directly teaching, the one who used to go out dancing at night whenever there was a place to dance. He was disturbed that there were fewer and fewer such places in an allegedly civilized society. And there was the Izzy quoted by Andrew Patner:

"A friend asked me how it was going with my Greek. I said, 'I do all right.' He said, 'Can you really understand it?' I said, 'I do my best. I get by.' 'Well, Izzy,' he said, 'if Pericles came back, could you talk with him?' I said, 'Sure. If he spoke Yiddish.'"

In 1971, on the night *I. F. Stone's Weekly*—a paper that packed a remarkable amount of information and analysis into four pages—closed, I was with Izzy at McDonald's Printers in Washington. Our conversation was filmed for the public television program *Behind the Lines*.

Izzy talked that night about being a dissenter. He had been

so persistent and principled a dissenter that he was still largely ignored, if not shunned, by the "stars" of journalism in Washington. (And he never, of course, got a Pulitzer Prize. Neither did George Seldes.) "For me," he told me that night, "Washington has been a very lonely place."

But he hadn't been surprised:

> It's hard to uphold the right to dissent and the right to speak freely in any society. In any group. It takes many, many generations to develop the tradition of letting the other side speak. There were the terrible civil wars in history—seventeenth-century England and the American Revolution—and those other great high points in the development of this tradition. But the struggles of a lot of lonely and often forgotten men in between those peaks made the freedom to dissent possible.

Izzy did not, in any sense, feel sorry for himself. He considered himself part of a scrappy and necessary band of heretics, with forebears far back in time:

> The only kind of fights worth fighting are those you are going to lose because somebody has to fight them and lose and lose and lose until someday, somebody who believes as you do wins. In order for somebody to win an important major fight one hundred years hence, a lot of other people have got to be willing—for the sheer fun and joy of it—to go right ahead and fight, knowing you're going to lose. You mustn't feel like a martyr. You've got to enjoy it.

That kind of joy didn't win Izzy any invitations to the White House during any administration. Of course he wouldn't have gone anyway, because he believed that reporters became corrupted by allowing themselves to become "insiders."

Mary McGrory said to Izzy that he was the quintessential outsider. She was right.

FREELANCING

After being fired from *Down Beat*, what I should have absorbed from Izzy Stone and George Seldes was what it took to be in total charge of what you write. I thought hard of starting my own newsletter on jazz or press criticism or violations of free speech. On the salary I'd been getting from *Down Beat*, I didn't have much money in reserve, but I could have borrowed enough to start an independent weekly that was no fancier than Izzy's or Seldes's.

But I didn't have the courage to bet on independence paying the rent and the other basics. So I tried freelancing. In those years, there were still general mass-circulation magazines that paid large sums to writers: *Look, Life, The Saturday Evening Post, Collier's.* I sent ideas to some of them, but didn't connect until I got an assignment to profile the Smothers Brothers for what turned out to be the last issue of *Look*.

I had no reservations about writing for a mass audience. I just didn't know the way. A friend of mine, Richard Gehman—"Dick the factory," his friends called him—was spectacularly successful and spectacularly fast. He once wrote almost an entire issue of *Cosmopolitan*. Once, when we shared a hotel room at the Newport Jazz Festival in Rhode Island, we lurched in at about two in the morning, so drunk that the beds seemed to be trying to get out of our way.

At six, I heard an alarm. Soon afterward, Gehman was sitting at a table with a typewriter and three cardboard boxes in front of him. He typed a page and put it in one of the boxes. He typed another page and put it in the second box. And so on.

He was writing three articles for three different magazines, he later told me, and each of them was on deadline.

I felt like a kid trumpet player in a high school band watching Dizzy Gillespie at work.

Not being in the big time, financially, I wrote for special-interest publications, mostly on jazz, but sometimes on non-musical subjects. The most prestigious was *The Reporter*, which specialized in first-class investigative reporting—domestic and foreign. It also had a section, at the back, concerned with music, theater, and diverse arts.

The magazine's founder and editor-in-chief was Max Ascoli, a brave antifascist in his native Italy, who left the country before acolytes of Mussolini considered him too troublesome to be endured. He left the country to stay alive. Ascoli didn't care much about what happened in the arts pages. I expect he didn't know the difference between Guy Lombardo and Duke Ellington, except maybe that one was darker.

There was no criticism from the often ferocious Ascoli when I wrote, up front, a long piece on the Nation of Islam and Malcolm X. But a storm blew me out of the magazine when we disagreed on the Vietnam War. Ascoli was a devout believer in the political and moral necessity of defeating the Communists in the North, lest they overrun Southeast Asia, and more. He hated an authoritarian state, having lived in one, and therefore any of the arguments against the war in Vietnam paled by contrast with the possibility of a victory by insatiable Communism.

I was just as devoutly opposed to the Vietnam War as Ascoli was supportive of it. I had no illusions that the North was a populist agrarian society that only wanted to be left in peace. It was clearly a classic Communist state in which dissent often turned out to be a mortal disease. But the government in the South that we were supporting was incurably corrupt and just as cruel as its enemy.

It was senseless for Americans to kill Vietnamese, children included, and to die themselves in this obscure civil war. And I wrote that, often, in my column in the *Village Voice*. In one of those jeremiads, I referred to Max Ascoli as having become one of the nation's leading enthusiasts for American involvement in this horrifying war, with its mounting corpses on both sides. I added that Ascoli brought comfort to Lyndon Johnson at the White House by persistently encouraging him in his bloody pursuit of victory.

A few days later I called my editor at *The Reporter* to go over the galleys for a folk music review. On hearing my voice, the editor began to whisper.

"We're not running it," he said.

"Why?"

"We're not running anything of yours anymore." He was still whispering.

"Why?"

"Mr. Ascoli saw what you said about him in the *Voice*."

In the land of the free and the home of the brave, Max Ascoli, himself an unbending dissenter in Italy and here, could not bear too much free speech.

Some years later I was talking on the phone to a brilliant, resourceful lawyer on the staff of the American Civil Liberties Union's headquarters in New York. He had seen a pro-life column of mine in the *Washington Post*, and he too began to whisper, so softly that I could barely hear him.

"I agree with you," he said. "I'm pro-life. But *please*, don't ever quote me. I'll lose my job."

Even at the American Civil Liberties Union, there are limits to free speech.

I FIND A HOME, SORT
OF, AT THE *VILLAGE VOICE*

My main problem as a freelancer—aside from the economic uncertainties of that rollercoaster way of life—was that I had been largely stereotyped by most of the editors who would never answer my calls. The years working for *Down Beat* and the books on jazz I'd written had pigeonholed me as a specialist in jazz. What could a jazz specialist know about education or civil liberties or politics?

I broke through the stereotype occasionally, but not often enough to be able to stop scrambling to make the rent. At last, and unexpectedly, I was given a chance to break through.

In 1955 a small weekly New York newspaper—the *Village Voice*—was started by Ed Fancher, a psychologist, and Dan Wolf, a writer for encyclopedias. Fancher was the publisher, Wolf was the editor, and Jerry Tallmer, a staff writer specializing in drama criticism, went on to invent off-Broadway theater.

I read the paper from its start. It brought news of Greenwich Village, including long, meandering articles about neighborhoods and people in whom the daily papers would have had no interest because, though singular, they were neither mainstream nor bizarre.

In 1958 I began writing a column for the paper. During those years the *Voice* reflected the credo of Dan Wolf: "Those of us who started the *Voice* had long since been left cold by the dull pieties of official liberalism with its dreary, if unspoken, drive to put every family in a housing development and give its child his own social worker."

At the beginning, there was no party line in the paper. Staffers criticized each other in print, and readers had—in addition to the fractious letters page—"The Press of Freedom" space in which to express their dissonant obsessions. The paper resonated with so many different views that once, when I was lecturing to the Nieman Fellows at Harvard, a professor of government sitting in told me how exasperated he was with the *Voice*.

"I never know what the *Village Voice*—as the *Village Voice*—believes. I never know what it stands for."

"That's the point," I said. "You can read all kinds of views in the *Voice*, and then make up your own mind. We don't tell you what to think. That's why there are hardly any editorials."

Dan Wolf despised cant and anything that had the prim self-righteousness of what later came to be called "political correctness." Some *Voice* writers in the early years were more radical, to say the least, than he was. But he also encouraged writers who were more conservative than he. What he did not encourage was boilerplate thinking. While he was there, the writers' passions in the paper were personal, not group-think.

That was then. The *Voice*, alas, was to become largely monolithic in its politics—and much else—especially after Dan Wolf was forced to leave in 1974 by a new commander-in-chief, Clay Felker (of whom more anon). By the 1980s the paper's basic constituencies were considered to be liberals, radicals, blacks, gays, Latinos, and pro-choice feminists. None were to be unduly offended.

Over the years, the *Voice* righteously distanced itself from Dan Wolf's intent that it not be predictable, and became an unabashed paper of the left. Or, in view of the rigid orthodoxies of many—not all—of the writers, it could be called a paper of the "religious left" because it was, at times, as unbending in its revealed truths as the Christian Coalition.

I have stayed at the *Voice* all these years because the successive editors have never tried to tell me what to write—or what not to write. And, indeed, the views of the writers of "the religious left" are also entirely theirs. In that crucial respect, the *Voice* is an uncensored paper. Accordingly, there is also freedom for a new writer to come along and shake the shibboleths of his or her colleagues. There have not been many.

One of the pleasures of writing for the *Voice*, at its beginning, was that it reached—as Margot put it—"a particular community of consciousness." Though based in Greenwich Village, it had readers, in small numbers, from Wyoming to Virginia, who welcomed the paper's independence and corollary surprises. Meeting some of them, in various parts of the country, was like meeting jazz musicians for the first time. We had a common language.

Those readers also had uncommon persistence. The paper's makeup was such that the long, serpentine pieces could inch their way through page after page, skipping some pages, while the reader tried to pursue them. Izzy Stone used to tell me, "I'd like to read you in the *Voice*, but I can't find you."

When I started at the *Voice*, it was for no pay. Only the very few full-time staffers at the *Voice* received more than psychic income—and that just barely enough to live on. As an unsteady freelancer, I could hardly afford to write for free, but since I was being stereotyped elsewhere as solely a jazz writer, I couldn't afford to turn down this chance for liberation.

As Dan Wolf put it later, "Nat Hentoff, a major jazz writer, initiated 'Second Chorus,' which is about anything controversial—except jazz." That was my nonnegotiable bargaining position. I would agree to accept no pay, and they would agree not to ask me to write about jazz.

I soon discovered how easy it is to be regarded as an expert by nonexperts. Having written about education for the *Voice*, I began to be invited to conferences on education—and to be paid for coming. So, too, with other issues I often wrote about: civil liberties, politics, euthanasia, the First Amendment, the disintegrating relationship between blacks and Jews.

But I still was working for the *Voice* for nothing, and I was acutely aware of the increasing number of ads in the paper. Surely, enough revenue was coming to pay me *something*. One morning, my anger rising, I called the publisher, Ed Fancher, and said I would resign unless I started getting twenty dollars a column. Fancher flatly refused, and I hung up.

On ten seconds' reflection, I decided it would be foolish for me to lose my weekly chance to say whatever I wanted about anything (except jazz). I called Fancher back and unresigned. He then decided to give me and all the other nontenured regular writers ten dollars an article.

I was right about the rise in the paper's fortunes, and in 1974 the New York Magazine Company bought control from Wolf and Fancher for $4 million. As Jules Feiffer noted, "At least Wolf and Fancher could have given us a bottle of champagne." They didn't even give us a going-away present of an extra ten dollars.

The new editor was Clay Felker, who had successfully created *New York* magazine—which became the model for other slick "city magazines" around the country. Felker had no patience for the serendipitous nature of the *Voice*—the long, rather eccentric pieces that were not in the least newsworthy, except to the writer. Nor did he agree with Dan Wolf's conviction that the *Voice* ought to be a writer's paper, with only the most necessary editing.

Felker, a burly man given to bursts of temper, decided to remake the *Voice*, and in the process came close to destroying it. What seemed like platoons of editors were brought in, and more and more of the paper was written according to their dictates—rather than the writer's priorities. Many of those articles were shallow but glitzy, and the *Voice* became known for brashly inviting headlines that were not always substantiated by the stories inside.

Some of us veterans of the paper were profoundly dissatisfied, but—abandoning the *Voice* tradition—none of us said so in the paper.

One day, riding in the car as my wife drove and my two young sons bickered in the backseat, I was reading aloud a letter I had just opened. It was from a *Voice* reader who said that in the old *Voice*, which was far from faultless, at least "the banality of chic was relatively minimal." The new *Voice*, he charged, had "spiffy packaging," but often, "when you open the box, all you find is more packaging."

He went on to say that before I next criticized the *New York Times* or any other outside publication in my *Voice* column, I must, at long last, "look sternly at what had become of this paper."

From the backseat, my younger son, Tom, then ten, heartily agreed. "Aren't you going to write about that?" he said accusatorially.

My older daughter had called me a few days before to ask if I was now writing for the *National Enquirer*. And when I spoke at colleges, no matter the subject of the talk, I would often be asked, "What the hell's going on at the *Voice*?" So, expecting to be fired, I wrote a column that I titled "What's Become of the *Voice*?":

Voice journalism is becoming increasingly formularized to fit the overall circus barker tone of the paper. As this happens, there is inevitably more input—from gestation on—by the editors. Only certain kinds of pieces will fit into this staccato format. And the editors know which ones. Experienced writers can more or less handle these constant windstorms, but I would no longer advise a young writer that the *Voice* is a desirable place to break in. You could burn out fast.

As rushing patterns of editor-controlled *Voice* journalism have developed, gone are the unpredictable, unfashionable, sometimes rambling, often idiosyncratic (but not "streamlined") pieces that were integral to the old *Voice*. This kind of writing usually cannot be assigned. It gropes into the light from one writer's insistent obsession.

Dan Wolf, the *Voice*'s founding and only previous editor, encouraged such writing. Clay Felker, who is now in command, does not. Felker's preferred style of journalism is sharp-edged; tightly written and designed; trendy; and certainly not confusing. People have only a limited attention span, and you got to grab them on their way to *TV Guide*. . . .

Where all this begins and ends is in a difference in conception. The clearest distillation I know of what the old *Voice* was about is in an as yet unpublished memoir by my wife, Margot Hentoff:

"The old *Voice* always spoke with an authentic voice. There was never the sense of a manufactured story in which too many editors had had their hands. Instead one understood that the *Voice*'s writers spoke out of their own nutty concerns rather than on assignment to fill a predetermined space."

This is not to say, nor did Margot intend to say, that every issue of the old *Voice* was so resplendent in its authenticity that it had to be read all the way through before life could continue. After all, there are writers who are authentic schmucks, and the old *Voice* printed a goodly number of them.

But that paper was handmade. . . . Dan Wolf respected

writers. Not in their persons necessarily, or he would have paid them a lot better. But he did respect their work.

My sense of Clay Felker is . . . that he sees writers as Balanchine sees dancers—they exist to be bent to fit, and so they are interchangeable.

So what more can I tell the exasperated reader pining for the old *Voice?* . . . Well, as Clay Felker has said, money and control are the basic roots of all disagreements. He has the money and he has the control.

My editor at the time, Audrey Berman, was stunned when I gave her this column. With extreme reluctance, she put it through. "Don't you ever do that to me again," she said with cold fear.

Clay Felker was not amused either. Some of my colleagues looked as if they were about to figure out an appropriate going-away present for me. Indeed, Felker really was about to fire me; I learned that from, as we say, an informed source. But two *Voice* staffers, Jack Newfield and Karen Durbin, somehow persuaded him not to. "It worked," Newfield told me years later, "because Felker had such a short attention span."

I was surprised at the reprieve. But I knew that in any case, Felker considered my column "too serious" and was angry that I had been among the organizers of an attempt to bring a union into the *Voice*. Despite the reprieve, I expected that sooner or later I'd be defenestrated.

But Felker eventually left the *Voice*, moving back to *New York* magazine, which, after all, he had created. He still was an owner of the *Voice*, but later he lost both publications to Rupert Murdoch in a corporate putsch.

Before Felker left, insubordination, subtle rather than confrontational, became chronic—although once, at a staff meeting, writer Richard Goldstein, acutely frustrated at what

Felker was doing to the paper, punched him in the stomach, to the approbation of just about everyone on the *Voice*.

Always the staff, no matter how much they disagreed with one another, have regarded the paper as *theirs* and resented any attempts by management to make it into something else. This proprietary attitude by the rank and file by no means guarantees first-class journalism on a regular basis—as has been evident at the paper through the years—but it does ensure a drifting level of paranoia whenever a new owner or editor takes over.

After Felker, there was a short, calm period—except for me—when Tom Morgan became editor. A successful freelance writer and former press secretary to Mayor John Lindsay, Morgan was blessedly free of Felker's volcanic temperament and had a more substantial notion of journalism. (The paper began to look less feverish.)

Some months into Morgan's reign, the *Columbia Journalism Review* asked me to write something about the "new" *Voice*. I had a few criticisms, none of them severe. When the issue appeared, however, Morgan invited me to lunch. I asked about the possibility of a raise. Morgan looked at me with an anger that seemed motivated by something far beyond a request for more money. He had read the *Columbia Journalism Review* article, and he informed me that he had no use for anyone who "pissed in the tent." The *Voice* was the tent, and I made what passed for my living there. Accordingly I had no business publicly criticizing the paper I worked for. Even Judas Iscariot hadn't done that.

For the rest of his tenure at the paper, my relations with Morgan were less than cool. I no longer regarded him as the paladin of free expression I had thought he was. And he regarded me as a troublemaker. Both of us were accurate. And there was no raise.

The next editor-in-chief was exhilarating. Marianne Partridge had been an editor at *Rolling Stone*, which was all I knew about her when she came. She almost disappeared before I did get to know her.

By then the *Voice* had a new owner, a man feared by his newspaper employees in many cities, here and abroad. The news of his coming so terrified the workforce at the *Voice* that he turned out to be the most effective labor organizer in the history of the paper.

For years, Jules Feiffer, Howard Smith, and I had been trying to organize enough of the *Voice*'s employees so that we could begin to get a labor union to represent us. Most of the workers, however, were relatively young, and politically on the "pure" left. Therefore they viewed organized labor as an enemy. The AFL-CIO was supporting the war in Vietnam, and many of its member unions were defiantly racist. Accordingly, *Voice* workers would not soil themselves by associating with Big Labor; they could take care of themselves.

In January 1977, soon after Rupert Murdoch, the Australian Citizen Kane—notorious for strikebreaking and for unashamedly shaping his papers to promote his political views—bought the paper, there was a mass conversion to organized labor at the *Voice*.

A long line of workers from all departments—not only editorial—walked down to the offices of District 65, Distributive Workers of America, a catchall union that included factory workers, clerical employees, and other kinds of office workers at places like Columbia University.

To our surprise, Murdoch did not resist the union, and we had a contract fairly soon. He did, however, cause a near-mutiny concerning another matter.

Someone had convinced Murdoch that whatever virtues Marianne Partridge might have as an editor, a woman could not decisively run a newspaper in a tough city like New York. A woman didn't have the necessary combativeness—the killer instinct—to duke it out with the other newspapers in the city.

Actually, Marianne turned out to have more energy and determination than any other editor the paper had ever had to that point. And no one could intimidate her. She was so vivid that I went to all the editorial meetings—something I had not done before, or ever have since. Most important, she put out a lively, unpredictable paper.

We didn't know about the impending termination of Marianne—before she even started—until Jack Newfield got a call from Michael Kramer, then with *New York* magazine and, in later years, a columnist for *Time*. Kramer cheerfully announced that he was to be the *Voice*'s new editor, since Murdoch was about to fire Marianne. Newfield liked what he had seen of Marianne—her spirit and independence. He told Kramer, with a certain amount of hyperbole, that he would kill Kramer if he were to take the job.

Alexander Cockburn entered into the campaign to rescue Marianne. The *Voice*'s press critic, he was a full-fledged radical, but with a wit—often savage—and a grace of polemical language that made him entertaining to read. He is the most charming aspiring revolutionary I've known.

Cockburn and Newfield arrived at the Murdochs' apartment on upper Fifth Avenue at nine one evening.

Murdoch opened the door—he knew they were coming— and said, "I'm going to take the wind out of your sails. Have a drink, mates, we're back to square one."

Having won the battle without firing a shot, Newfield and Cockburn spent the rest of the evening listening to Murdoch tell stories about himself as a young man of the left—Red Rupert—at Oxford.

From then on, Murdoch did not express any doubts, as far as we knew, about a woman having the fortitude to run a newspaper on the predatory playing fields of New York City. Bill Ryan, the *Voice*'s publisher, however, did have large and growing doubts about her future at the paper. The *Voice* was doing well, but Ryan was a man of tradition and propriety— so far as relations between men and women were concerned. The daily sight of this striding, dashingly irreverent woman personifying the *Voice* to the outside world struck him as going against the laws of nature. Certainly against his nature.

In May 1978, Bill Ryan fired Marianne Partridge—or thought he had. In a sudden revival of the sit-in strikes of the 1930s, we took over the building—"we" being most of the staff. Every morning we escorted Marianne and her dog to the *Voice*, lest some hired guard try to keep her out. And every evening we escorted her and her dog from the *Voice*.

From our redoubt we kept putting out the paper as we fed news of this defiance of our publisher to the local dailies. Ryan capitulated, and Marianne stayed for the remainder of her contract, until January 1979.

Some time later, Murdoch held a meeting of the publishers of his various newspapers and magazines. Bill Ryan was there. Murdoch was interested in their advice on a complex problem affecting part of his empire. At one point Ryan started to speak, but Murdoch interrupted: "You weren't able to fire that editor and make it stick. I don't think there's any advice we need to hear from you."

Not too long after, Bill Ryan left the *Voice*.

Murdoch had never coveted the *Voice*; he'd bought it as part of a package that included *New York* magazine. But he appreciated the profits the *Voice* brought him, and that explained—we found out when he sold the paper—why he had never openly punished any of us for writing views that collided with his own. He had summarily quashed dissent at a number of his other publications, but never did so at the *Voice*.

On selling the *Voice* at a handsome profit, Murdoch told a *New York Times* reporter that while he often hated the paper, he had decided to avoid interfering with its contents. The essence of the *Voice*, he explained, was its irreverence, and had he compromised that quality, the *Voice*—as a piece of property—would have had less value.

What Murdoch did not say publicly as he departed was that he had, from time to time, called the editor of the *Voice* in a state of rage. The one thing he could not bear was to be criticized personally in a paper he owned. Shortly after he bought the *Voice*, I interviewed him for a story I was doing in the paper on grievances some of the reporters at the *New York Post*—also owned by Murdoch—had against him. As he got the direction of my questions, Murdoch looked at me as if about to condemn me to the everlasting fires. "You cannot criticize *me*," he roared.

Actually, I had intended to criticize him anyway, but was talked out of it by some of my colleagues who, along with me, were covertly planning to establish our own newspaper. If Murdoch saw himself criticized, I was told by my co-conspirators, he would fire the editor, Marianne Partridge, who was to be in charge of the new paper. But we were many months away from setting up that worker-owned weekly, and we needed Marianne to keep her job until then. So did we. As long as she kept her job, we would keep ours—until we could collectively resign.

So, with some guilt, I refrained from attacking Murdoch in my story. But, after our plans for our own paper fell apart—owing to the presence of a quisling among us—Murdoch was criticized by name on occasion in the *Voice*. So far as I know, it was the only time so bold a thing happened in one of his worldwide possessions.

THE CONTINUING CIVIL

WARS AT THE *VOICE*

During Marianne Partridge's high-spirited reign, I caused a near–civil war at the paper because of my involvement with the perennial troublemaker Joan Baez, and with a remarkable worldwide protector of human rights, Ginetta Sagan.

I had known Joan since shortly after she became an instant icon at the Newport Folk Festival in 1959. She was eighteen, and transcended all the other earnest performers with her "achingly pure soprano," as one writer put it, and her equally pure presence. It was not that she was sexless; quite the opposite. It was that she was unattainable, or so it seemed.

The next year, when Robert Herridge wanted to do a folk music program on the CBS TV network, I suggested Joan. Herridge took the suggestion seriously, but I had to bring Joan to meet him. She told Herridge she would perform only by herself, and that she must have total control of the music in her section, as well as of the setting. There were other nonnegotiable demands.

Once he heard her, Herridge could not bear being without the sound of her voice on that show, though he would have preferred it to be disembodied, so irritated was he at her demands—to which he grumblingly yielded.

Later, in the control room, turning to me, who had brought him this iron maiden, Herridge muttered, "The bitch is nineteen years old, and she thinks she's Thomas Mann!"

The nineteen-year-old apprentice Thomas Mann stunned the crew—and Herridge again—when she sang. He more or less cooled down.

Elsewhere in the studio, John Lee Hooker, a blues singer who sounded as if he were channeling centuries of black history, was so impressed with Joan that he asked her out. She demurred. His music was so deep, she feared she might have fallen through.

Baez and I saw each other over the years, and I followed—and agreed with—her public heresies. She worked with Cesar Chavez, gathering support for the Farm Workers Union, and during the Vietnam War she was arrested with 118 others for blocking the Armed Forces Induction Center in Oakland. She got some brief prison time for that.

During Christmas 1972, Joan was in Hanoi, in time for the first American use of B-52 bombers against the North Vietnamese. In the *New York Times* an American military officer said those raids were "the biggest aerial operation in the history of warfare." Joan was under the American bombs for twelve days.

"If I started worrying about getting killed, I'd quit doing most of everything I do," she said.

Those were years of both rhetorical and sometimes actual devotion to violence by some antiwar activists as a way to end the violence in Vietnam, but Joan never wavered in her commitment to nonviolence. At times, however, she was so convinced of her purity of motive and perspective that she sounded like the lady in the manor trying to civilize the rude commoners below.

But on human rights, anywhere in the world, Baez was utterly consistent and sometimes astonishingly brave. In Brazil, for instance, before the then-authoritarian government banned all her concerts and said she could not perform anywhere in the country, Joan went to Federal Police Headquarters in São Paulo, where, in front of the building, she sang with her customary force and clarity.

The only other person I've known who is as unhesitatingly brave as Joan Baez is Ginetta Sagan. During the Second World War, Ginetta was a member of the Italian Resistance. Through an underground railroad that she helped run, many Jews and other targets of the Italian fascist government escaped. Then, when she was nineteen, secret police captured her. She was viciously tortured.

Ginetta survived and has since spent most of her life trying to rescue what Amnesty International describes as prisoners of conscience. She was one of the founders of Amnesty International U.S.A., and she has helped save the lives of hundreds of political prisoners in Greece, Chile, Poland, Czechoslovakia, and Vietnam. In 1996, Ginetta was awarded the Presidential Medal of Freedom by Bill Clinton at the White House.

Once, in a very minor way, I helped her free a journalist from a prison in Czechoslovakia. No risk was required of me—just some letters to certain people in certain places.

Ginetta did not engage in rescue operations based on political partisanship. She took her risks on the same basis as Joan Baez. Their credo, as Joan put it, was, "To be consistent, you have to be able to recognize repression in left-wing countries and in right-wing countries and in Third World countries. Repression is repression. A rubber hose is a rubber hose. The beating must feel the same whether a Socialist or an imperialist is doing it."

In the 1970s and after, they came to me, these two relentless humanists, with stories of how the victors in the Vietnam War were doing very cruel things to people who disagreed in conscience with the government. The same woman who had been one of the more visible and persistent protestors against American involvement in that war was now—along with Ginetta Sagan—accusing the Communist government of suppression of dissent, and much worse.

This kind of consistency in defense of human rights was considered abhorrent by many Americans who had, like Joan, worked to end the war. No American, they said, had the moral right to criticize the government of a nation that had been bombed so devastatingly by us. (Because of American bombing during Christmas 1972, when Joan was in Hanoi, thousands of children in Hanoi and Haiphong alone—British journalist John Pilger wrote—became permanently deaf.)

Baez and Sagan, however, kept bringing the news of the "reeducation camps" being set up by the rulers of Vietnam. Herded into them were writers, pacifists, Buddhists, Catholics, trade-union and women's leaders, lawyers, scholars, musicians, painters. Some of the prisoners were shoved into small Convex boxes—metal or wood shipping containers left over from the war in Vietnam. As days went by and the sun made the temperature inside the boxes rise higher and higher, prisoners died.

Denunciations of Baez mounted at home from liberals and radicals who were infuriated by Joan's saying, and saying often, "As in the sixties we raised our voices so that the people of Vietnam may live, so now some of us are raising our voices so that the people of Vietnam may live."

Baez talked about the reeducation camps during her concerts, and paid for newspaper ads in the *New York Times*, the *Washington Post*, the *San Francisco Chronicle*, and the *Los Angeles Times*. And she wrote an "Open Letter to the Socialist Republic of Vietnam," which was sent to the President of the Socialist Republic of Vietnam and the Secretary General of the United Nations. I was one of the signatories of that letter.

In working to get the word out, Baez and Sagan sent to me, among others, their research—a good deal of it from Amnesty International. And I conducted some of my own fact-checking from sources abroad. I also asked various anti–Vietnam War activists for reactions to the rising number of prisoners of conscience in Vietnam. Most waved the issue aside as they indignantly reminded me of the horrifying things America had done to Vietnam. And William Kunstler, the bold civil rights lawyer, told me proudly that he would never criticize a socialist country. Ever.

About to write the first in a series of articles on the thought police in Vietnam for the *Village Voice*, I was confronted by a fierce campaign inside the *Voice* to exercise terminal prior restraint on those articles.

The leader of those outraged by my appalling insensitivity to the suffering of Vietnam at the hands of Americans was Alexander Cockburn. In a previous exchange with me in the paper, Cockburn had insisted that the responsibility of newspapers and journalists on the left was to trumpet their points of view—without regard to "balance" or "fairness." My rebuttal—which sounded pietistic even to me, but which I believed—was that a paper ought to present a forceful diversity of views and let the reader decide among them.

Though we disagreed on that and other fundamentals of life and journalism, I have always found it hard to dislike Cockburn personally. He has a keen and merry eye for the preening whited sepulchers among us, and he is a wickedly clever storyteller.

When we joined battle over whether the *Village Voice* should compound the cruelty of Lyndon Johnson and Richard Nixon by indicting the government of Vietnam then rising, with great difficulty, from the destruction of the war, neither Cockburn nor I gave any quarter.

He presented his case to Marianne Partridge, and the editor not only dismissed it, but also gave most of the cover of the *Voice* and four pages inside to my story, "Vietnam 1977: Is It Any of Our Business?" It was more space than I'd ever had before. Marianne thought it bizarre for a newspaper to exempt *any* person or any government from exposure, particularly when a government broiled dissenters alive in Convex boxes.

Some of my other critics at the *Voice* questioned the credibility of my sources. The government of Vietnam, of course, denied everything—furiously. So, I was asked—as Joan Baez has been—"What if it's not true? What if it's anti-Communist propaganda?"

In answer, I quoted Joan: "I would rather make a mistake in unintentionally offending government officials anywhere in the world than offend one political prisoner whom I might now conceivably help and whom later I may never be able to reach."

My opponents at the paper were not won over. This, after all, was the workforce that—despite abysmal pay—would not join a union for years because the AFL-CIO backed the war in Vietnam.

Of the editors of the *Voice* after Marianne, the one who had the rockiest—indeed, the most hostile—start was David Schneiderman. He had been a protégé of Harrison Salisbury at the *New York Times*, working on the op-ed page. A. M. Rosenthal, the autocrat of the *Times* in those years, regarded Schneiderman as a young radical; but because his territory did not include the editorial pages, Abe could not get rid of this stripling on the left.

Actually, then as now, Schneiderman was a skeptical liberal, with emphasis on "skeptical." He had a wide range of knowledge and curiosity, and a stubborn streak that was to be necessary to his survival at the *Voice*.

When he was hired, however, he was decidedly not welcome at the raffish paper downtown. Management's plan was for him to replace Marianne Partridge. Our plan was for Marianne to stay.

So a delegation of us marched up to the hushed precincts of that floor at the *Times* where editorials are conceived and birthed. The place was so quiet that I—coming from turbulent Greenwich Village—wondered how anyone could think in such deafening silence. The secretaries and the editors, dressed like tenured professors, eyed our grim, tieless caravan with apprehension and barely concealed disgust.

Schneiderman, so calm that he left our indignation stranded, listened to our demands and said he would prefer not to accede to them. He would indeed become the paper's editor, he assured us, but Marianne could finish out her contract.

During the waiting period—from June to December 1978—Schneiderman, in an office uptown, read an alarming number of back issues of the *Voice*. He also interviewed every member of the staff during that period. That he still wanted to be the paper's editor reflected, I thought, either a reformer's zeal and optimism or the sensibility of a Hollywood stuntman.

During the years Schneiderman was indeed the editor—he later became publisher, a post that required only limited dealings with unruly journalists—he was more than competent. Actually, after Dan Wolf and Marianne Partridge, he was the most astute editor the paper has had up to now.

Knowledgeable in a number of fields, he was curious to learn more. And he was cool under Rupert Murdoch's fire, as when—in August 1983—Murdoch, furious about something Alexander Cockburn had written about him, called Schneiderman and demanded that Cockburn be fired. Schneiderman refused—thereby, of course, angering Murdoch even more, since he had hardly ever had to deal with a mutiny in any of his other properties. The owner of the *Voice* ended the conversation by threatening dire, very dire, consequences to Schneiderman if he did not sack the contemptuous Cockburn. The direst consequence, Murdoch thundered, would be: "I'll sell the paper to someone worse than I am."

Cockburn stayed, and Murdoch never delivered on his threat. Cockburn did leave later, but that event had nothing to do with Murdoch. Alex was widely regarded in much of the Jewish community as being anti-Israel and, for that matter, anti-Semitic. He was not anti-Semitic—as I told unbelieving, hostile Jewish audiences at the time. He was, however, sharply critical of Israel's treatment of Palestinians in the Occupied Territories.

A pro-Israel group sifted through Cockburn's garbage one night and discovered that an organization of Arab-American students had offered him an advance of a fair amount of money to write a book on Israel, the Palestinians—and justice in the Middle East.

The *Voice* being a paper without any written code of ethics, if Cockburn had simply said in his column that he was writing the book—and mentioned the funding source—nothing much would have been made of the deal.

He did not, however. And he made one other mistake. The garbage-explorers first offered the story to muckraker Jack Anderson in Washington. A lowly member of Anderson's staff—a fan of Cockburn's—tried to alert Alex that he was being pursued. He left a number of messages at the *Voice*, but since Cockburn didn't recognize the name, he did not return any of the calls. Accordingly, he wasn't alerted to what had been found in his garbage.

I absorbed the lesson, and since then have returned all calls, including those of people I don't know. Well, nearly all.

Jack Anderson did not pick up the story, but others in the press did, and it was played as a minor scandal. Cockburn had conceded being paid by a group whose interests he wrote about. Alex was himself a critic of the press, often a very wounding one, and so some in the press took considerable glee in getting revenge.

Schneiderman was embarrassed. It looked as if the *Voice*— or at least one of its prominent columnists—were for sale. An act of contrition by Cockburn might have helped, though it was so far out of character as to be unlikely. But in any case, for a few days, Cockburn was not to be found. He wasn't hiding; he was just elsewhere, out of reach.

During that time I suggested a reasonably short suspension—with a specific expiration date. Schneiderman, however, decided to make the suspension indefinite. Cockburn, a most impatient man in any case, found this indeterminate sentence to be humiliating, and he never came back. It was a loss for the paper.

If Schneiderman commendably resisted pressures from Murdoch—and not so commendably left Cockburn hanging, who then refused to hang—he bore up remarkably well when confronted with the occasional unpleasant surprises delivered by some members of the rank and file.

From the time of my arrival in 1958, the *Voice* has been fertile ground for conspiracy theories among its warring tribes. And in the weeks leading up to contract negotiations with management, all the tribes unite against management. There are ominous auguries of civil war—with bellicose internal bulletins to fire up the masses, and benefit events to swell the strike fund. Actually, there never has been a strike at the paper, but we enjoy the war games.

As might be surmised, there have been periods in the history of the paper when the editor, even in Marianne's time, must have felt like a lion tamer in a too small cage. The tensions are not only collectively stirred, but there have been individuals who have posed formidable challenges to the editor.

Howard Smith, for example. A longtime, imaginatively irreverent columnist, Smith was smoldering one evening. He felt he had been treated unjustly, and to make his point, Howard leaped onto Schneiderman's desk. There he stood, continually making his point, for a very long time. Schneiderman did not call for a security guard or the police. He waited for the volcano to exhaust itself.

Since then, in interviewing candidates for the job of editor, Schneiderman the publisher has often asked what each would do if the top of his or her desk were invaded by a greatly aggrieved member of the staff.

For a time we finally had an editor who was as given to conspiracy theories as were members of the staff. Jon Larsen had a credible background as a journalist. He had been editor of a serious, though not somber, magazine, *New Times,* and had been *Time* magazine's bureau chief in Saigon during the hostilities there. (His father, Roy Larsen, was for many years president of *Time* and held other key posts from the beginning of that magazine.)

The Jon Larsen we knew, however, could have stepped into the role of Captain Queeg in a road company of *The Caine Mutiny.* He did bring in some new writers and nurtured others, but he acted as if various members of the staff were out to overthrow him. Of course, he wasn't entirely wrong. The atmosphere of suspicion that he created fed the very paranoia of which he accused his real and imaginary enemies. Not since the reign of Clay Felker had the *Voice* been so unpleasant a place to work.

My only direct difficulty with Larsen had to do with a "package"—an array of pieces by various writers on the same subject. The focus was on Anita Hill and Clarence Thomas.

My contribution was the only one in the package that did not venerate Anita Hill. I thought Clarence Thomas had lied, but not as viciously as she did. Also, her continued if intermittent relationship with Thomas after the alleged sexual harassment belied her charge of hurt and harm.

Larsen killed my piece. I pointed out in my next column in the *Voice* that his explanation was that my piece had not been of the same quality as the others. Since the other authors in that package, I wrote, were Montaigne, Mark Twain, and Charles Lamb, among others, Larsen may have had a point.

Larsen did not find this modest satire amusing. For the rest of his tenure, we had as little to do with each other as possible, much to our mutual satisfaction.

His successor, Karen Durbin, had been at the *Voice* years before as both a writer and an editor. Her particular strength as a writer lay in her willingness and ability to explore herself— the most difficult kind of reporting because it too easily slides into sentimental solipsism.

As editor-in-chief, however, she lasted only two and a half years. She lost the confidence of some of the staff because her concern with hard news and political analysis was secondary to such lifestyle features as diverse sexual relationships. Sometimes very diverse.

Also, Karen, as a member of the rank and file years before, had been the shop's most militant union activist. But as editor, at the behest of the administration, she summarily fired staff members under a bizarre interpretation of the union contract that, she said, allowed her to fire people at will as a matter of taste. As I wrote in the *Voice* at the time, that could mean political affiliations or manner of dress. The union would become irrelevant.

While Karen was still editor, the *Voice* became a free paper in Manhattan, but still had to be paid for in the outer boroughs, where circulation was slight. We were stunned at the change because—fairly or not—we regarded writers for free papers as of lesser status. Wayne Barrett, the *Voice*'s combative chief investigative reporter, said when the internal news came, "I haven't worked for a free paper since I was in college."

The free-paper strategy may work. The paper's circulation has more than doubled, and as of the spring of 1997, has come close to 300,000. When a newspaper is free, the circulation is the number of copies you print. But the advertisers remain, and there are more readers, because the free papers do quickly disappear from their various containers.

A more important change took place in October 1996, when, for the first time in the history of the *Voice*, an editor-in-chief was appointed who had extensive hard-news experience, disdained "political correctness," and was considerably older—sixty-four—than all but a couple of people at the paper.

Don Forst had worked for the late *New York Herald Tribune*, the *New York Times* (cultural editor and assistant metro editor), the *New York Post*, the *Boston Herald American*, and *New York Newsday* (which won two Pulitzer Prizes during his tenure as editor).

"I've never been in a place like this," Forst told me shortly after his arrival at the *Voice*. "They're bright," he said of the largely young staff, "but they have to learn to write shorter and to be a lot timelier. Thirty-five hundred words is too long."

"I thought of the *Voice* as a magazine," one of the editors said to me, "but I guess, according to Forst, we're a newspaper."

At one staff meeting, Forst deliberately shook up the reporters and editors: "Why not have a fascist, a real bastard, as a columnist? So long as he can write and has ideas."

Another time, he presented the staff with a challenge: "There is this guy on the subway. He didn't get a raise. He's been flirting with his secretary and she's not giving him the time of day. His wife is pissed off at him. What do you have in the paper this week that he'll want to read?"

"We don't want him," a reporter muttered. "He's not a *Voice* reader."

The future of the paper may depend, in part, on that guy on the subway becoming a *Voice* reader.

PRIVATE LIVES

I n all the years of the *Voice*, the one writer who was "beyond category"—the phrase Duke Ellington used for only a very few musicians—was Margot Hentoff.

She was one of Dan Wolf's favorite writers. They were much alike; both skewered hypocrisy and were in no one's camp, political or otherwise.

Often, when I'm on a college campus for a lecture, a professor of a certain age tells me he still has *Voice* columns of hers. So do I. An accurate description of her presence at the paper was given by Kevin McAuliffe in his often acerbic *The Great American Newspaper: The Rise and Fall of the* Village Voice (Scribner's):

". . . an independent, and most entertaining, neoconservative, with an honesty about her that was refreshing: she was openly, frankly bourgeois, under no illusions about it. And when she dissented from the rest of the staff, as she frequently did, she made them think."

For example, she reported on the premiere of *Battle of Algiers* at the New York Film Festival. An intensely popular movie, including at the *Voice*, in those romantic "revolutionary" years, *Battle of Algiers* chronicled the coldly violent liberation of Algeria from the coldly inhumane French. Margot wrote the following:

> From the beginning of the film, it was obvious that a number of parallels could be drawn between the French position in Algeria and our own policies both abroad and at home, between the rebels in the Casbah and our nationalist leaders in our own "Arab quarters."
>
> And, as the film rolled on, the audience drew every one of them. Waves of applause broke out at scenes of terrorism against the French colonials, at individual acts of murder. At times there were cheers. "Saigon next," a man shouted as the Algerians blew up a crowded café in the French quarter.
>
> "What do you people want?" a French officer asked on screen. The audience laughed in understanding and waited for the next bomb blast.
>
> They really loved the movie, those people in Philharmonic Hall, many of them dressed in dinner clothes and holding invitations to a post-performance champagne reception. If it was the intention of the festival's program committee to épater the bourgeoisie with its choice of an opening film, then it entirely misread the temper of the bourgeoisie. It doesn't épater these days, it just has fun. Has there ever before been such a time when the oppressors themselves sit and applaud their own symbolic murder?

In another column, she listed "People I am not speaking to next year": "Jimmy Breslin, because he once called my house at two in the morning and used obscene language. And it wasn't even me he wanted to speak to. . . .

"[Also] two of my children, and Nat Hentoff. Maybe."

Margot is my third wife.

The first marriage ended in less than a year, although we had had more than a passing relationship for several years before. Her name was Miriam Sargent and her forebears were among the first arrivals in the Massachusetts Bay Colony. She was remarkably honest without being combative; she flowed naturally into jazz and was just as natural with its musicians. Miriam was truly color-blind.

Miriam's father, a Unitarian minister in rural Maine, was far less judgmental about the human species than many atheists I have known, including me. Her mother was mild of manner, but intensely interested in undoing injustice—insofar as she could, from her post in Maine. She cherished a book of letters by Sacco and Vanzetti, and she gave me the book because her daughter thought well of me.

Miriam and I met through jazz, and got to know each other in a Boston jazz club, the Savoy. For a couple of years we were the closest of friends, as well as lovers, until we were married and became merely polite acquaintances. What went wrong, and why, was a mystery—and still is.

There was no preliminary conversation between us about a divorce. She simply told me one night that she was going to California to enroll in the University of California at Berkeley. No return ticket. I was not surprised, because we had not been in real contact for some time, but I grieved. For a long time. In California, Miriam became a social worker and a union organizer in that field. Like her parents, she had no patience with injustice.

My second marriage lasted five years. Her name was Trudi Bernstein. She was a painter. Paul Desmond, the effortlessly lyrical alto saxophonist with Dave Brubeck, sent her to me. But he didn't mean any harm. As it turned out, the only thing she and I had in common was our acute dissatisfaction with each other. But there were two children—Jessica and Miranda—and they were certainly worth the otherwise bleak marital journey.

I stayed longer in that parched marriage, for the sake of

the children, as desperately unhappy people say; but fortunately I met Margot, and left. And that led to my third marriage, which has lasted, as of this writing, more than thirty-seven years.

Margot Hentoff is the only person to whom I can say and reveal anything, no matter how foolish—or worse—it makes me seem. She is my most perceptive and irritating critic—and the most piercingly intelligent person I have ever known. She is also ceaselessly desirable. Although an atheist, I know I have been blessed.

THE MARK OF THE BEAST

While we often disagree—as on abortion—Margot and I were as one in our opposition to the Vietnam War, though she went further than I did; for example, she committed civil disobedience, alongside A. J. Muste, in the entrance to an Atomic Energy Commission office.

We also shared disgust at those prestigious antiwar liberals who supported an end to violence in Vietnam while simultaneously nodding in approval at violence committed at home by antiwar activists. Some of these whited sepulchers, for instance, appeared at a sentencing hearing for a student who—in his zeal to show how opposed he was to the war in Vietnam—had bombed a University of Wisconsin building, killing a researcher inside.

This was the revolting underside of the antiwar movement.

On August 24, 1970, the University of Wisconsin's Army Mathematics Research Center was bombed. It happened at around four o'clock in the morning, and resulted in the death of thirty-three-year-old Robert Fassnacht, a physicist, who, unfortunately for him and his family, was working very late.

After the bombing and death, the Marion Delgado Collective—who "accepted the terrible responsibility" for the act—declared in an unsigned pronunciamento: "While the major pure research center of the Army was demolished, a man was killed and others injured when the blast went off four minutes early. For this death, there can be no rationalization. But while we mourn an unnecessary death, we celebrate the blow to U.S. imperialism. . . ."

In the September 10, 1970, *Voice,* I wrote the following:

> These young men—having grown up during a time when the normative public speech in America has been newspeak (anti-human speech that has caused so many deaths)—have themselves become so infected by this murderous corruption of meaning that they too are executioners.
>
> "We accept the terrible responsibility"—What does that *mean*? In what fundamental sense does it differ from all those statements by all those American spokesmen who also accept "the terrible responsibility" for all those deaths in Vietnam but then go on—in each next sentence—to "celebrate" each new blow to what they call "Communist aggression"?
>
> A man has been killed. What do his executioners have to say to his wife and children? We goofed. The blast went off four minutes early. But we will not rationalize. We mourn. We mourn and yet we celebrate.
>
> How easy. How terribly easy. Our official leaders have always been expert at mourning in the abstract. They also do what they have to do for the greater good of some other abstraction. But because of them, specific people die. Now, because of a set of "revolutionary" abstractions, one more man has died. In the name of humankind, of course.
>
> Lyndon Johnson and Richard Nixon, meet the members of the Marion Delgado Collective.

More than three years later, Karl Armstrong, one of the bombers for peace, was in court in Madison, Wisconsin. He had pleaded guilty to reduced state charges of second-degree murder and arson. And he pleaded guilty to several federal charges.

For some days, a mitigation hearing, based on Armstrong's character, was held before a circuit judge in Madison. On the basis of that hearing, Armstrong's sentence would be determined.

In the mail I received exculpatory literature from the Karl Armstrong Defense Fund. Its thrust was that the Math Center bombing, in a year that had witnessed the American invasion of Cambodia, came about because "we had been protesting against this war for so long and it seemed then that the government just wasn't able to listen to its own citizens, to those of the world."

What about citizen Fassnacht? The Karl Armstrong Defense Committee said: "A life was lost in the attack. An action carried out in the name of humanity inadvertently killed a man."

Sorry about that.

"The bombing," the Karl Armstrong Defense Committee further clarified the issue, "was a political act in which the government is the victim."

But the government survived. The committee's justification continued:

In Madison, on September 28 [1973], Karleton Armstrong assumed the responsibility for the bombing: he has acknowledged that it was, in fact, he who attacked the building," the Defense Committee continued. "He does not by himself assume the responsibility for the death of Robert Fassnacht. Though sorrowful, Karl, with other anti-war activists here, realizes that the loss must be shared by those who carried out the war in Indochina, setting the context and the imperative for acts of resistance against their policies. . . . Far from being a criminal, we feel Karl to be just one of many who took actions when they saw the results of our acts.

A gentle and courageous man, Karl is admitting the facts to avert the example he feels that the government would make of the case and, most importantly, he is doing it so that at his hearing to determine sentence, the facts of the war will themselves be put on trial.

And the facts of the war were put on trial. On October 16, John F. Naveau, a thirty-eight-year-old former Marine Corps sergeant, testified that he had been responsible for the deaths of twenty-four Vietnamese schoolchildren. A former army man, after testifying that brutality against Vietnamese civilians had been commonplace, pointed toward Karl Armstrong and said, "I feel a lot more criminal than him."

On October 19, former Senator Ernest Gruening of Alaska, who, with Wayne Morse, had been alone in the Senate against the war for a long time, testified for Karl Armstrong. Gruening, now seventy-six, told the judge that war resisters deserved not "castigation, but an accolade. . . . All acts of resistance to this war are fully justified—in whatever form they take."

Or, as the Karl Armstrong Defense Committee put it, "Karl deserves your continuing support not only because his actions were motivated by deep feelings of love and sorrow, but because he is continuing to resist the government now and in the coming weeks and years."

On the day of Gruening's appearance, Professor Richard Falk of Princeton, also a longtime and knowledgeable opponent of the war, cited, according to the *New York Times*, "the Nuremberg trials as precedent for defense assertions that private American citizens had 'a right, and perhaps a duty' to actively oppose the war by any means. . . . Scientists who worked at the mathematics center are 'indictable for war crimes conspiracy, depending on the extent of their knowledge and involvement.'" Professor Falk's authority for that statement was the Nuremberg code, which, he said, "was formulated with the assistance of the United States government."

Robert Fassnacht, it turned out, was not working on anything to do with the war. But what if he was?

On October 22, six former students who had become radical activists at the University of Wisconsin in the late 1960s agreed (as one of them, Billy Kaplan, said tearfully) that the bombing of the Math Center came from the "highest motivation." The bombing, he explained, was intended as an "affirmation of life" to "hinder" the Vietnam War.

Philip Berrigan, the former priest, said that "Robert Fassnacht's death is mourned but I believe very profoundly that it was accidental and has to be balanced by the calculated deaths of millions."

Is that the profundity we have as a legacy from this branch of the peace movement? That you can "balance" one death against those of millions? And that you can do this balancing in the name of humanity?

The corpse of Robert Fassnacht ought not to be explained away so glibly on the thesis that because the United States government criminally took life wholesale, an individual American had the right—and perhaps the duty (according to Professor Falk)—to oppose that war actively by any means, even if his actions resulted, however accidentally, in one retail death.

The taking of a life—any life, on any side—should not be so glancingly dismissed as the death of Robert Fassnacht has been dismissed (with routine expressions of regret) by those who consider themselves to be affirmers of life.

The literature of the Karl Armstrong Defense Fund, for instance, said that the bombing took place "between semesters at 4 a.m. on a Monday morning, with a warning telephoned into the police."

The Karl Armstrong Defense Committee somehow neglected to mention that the warning was telephoned just *three minutes* before the explosion. Obviously that gesture of "warning" was perfunctory, as perfunctory as Philip Berrigan's fleeting reference to such "sad happenings" as the death of Robert Fassnacht.

Then there is the primary excuse by Armstrong and his supporters for this unfortunate accident. Peaceful demonstrations had not worked. The destruction of draft-board records had not worked. Nearly every witness at the Madison hearing implied or stated explicitly that Karl Armstrong had been driven to bomb the building because he felt so keenly the frustration of the continuing war and the continuing research-for-death at the Army Mathematics Research Center.

In his frustration, Armstrong fulfilled the prophecy of Father Daniel Berrigan: "The mark of inhuman treatment of humans is . . . the mark of the beast, whether its insignia is the military or the movement."

And:

"A revolution is interesting insofar as it avoids like the plague the plague it promised to heal."

Consider, by contrast, Cesar Chavez and his long, hard march—in the context of the "revolutionary" act of Karl Armstrong. Chavez wrote:

> I was talking to a teamster in Coachella. He said, "Don't be such a coward. Take the women and kids out of there and you men stand up and let's fight it out." And I said, "Why? Do you want to beat us up? We're game. Beat the women and kids too. What's the difference?" And he started complaining, "Ah, we don't even know who in the hell we're fighting when we fight you guys. If we fight the worker, we've got to fight with his wife and his kids and his grandmother and his grandfather and the first, second, third, fourth, and fifth cousins!"
>
> And I said, "That's right! Plus millions of other brothers and sisters throughout the country in the labor movement, the religious communities, the blacks, the whites. You'll have to fight everybody. And we make it that way. . . .

"Farmworkers everywhere are angry and worried, but we are not going to fall into the trap that you have fallen into. We do not need to kill or destroy to win. We are a movement that builds and not destroys."

Chavez and the United Farm Workers, of course, never did anything quite as exciting as blowing up buildings, with or without people in them, but Chavez and the UFW certainly avoided like the plague the mark of the beast.

The killing act of Karl Armstrong did not particularly surprise me. I have known a number of people who have believed in the necessity of violence—for personal revenge, for historical revenge, to shock the populace into recognition of a horrifying injustice that must be paid for.

What did somewhat surprise me was the testimony at Armstrong's sentencing hearing of such self-satisfied liberals as Daniel Ellsberg, Professor Richard Falk, Senator Ernest Gruening, and Philip Berrigan. I wondered if any of them had read Arthur Koestler's novel *Darkness at Noon*, a chillingly illuminating exploration of ends so infected by means that they bore the mark of the beast. It was based on fact, on Stalin's facts on the ground.

I knew, and interviewed, Daniel Ellsberg during those years, and respected him for his liberation of the Pentagon Papers. I never doubted the seriousness of his commitment to finding a way to end the war in Vietnam. But, at Karl Armstrong's sentencing hearing, Ellsberg—as reported in Tom Bates's valuable book *Reds* (HarperCollins)—said, "However misguided, the bombing by Karl was a conscientious action."

To which the prosecutor, Michael Zeleski—a Wisconsin assistant attorney general—replied:

"Let's look at his act. He saw cars parked there. He saw bikes parked in the rack. He saw lights on. What did he do? He lit the fuse and walked away."

MY INTIMATE RELATIONSHIP

WITH THE FBI

My own antiwar activities brought me, directly and indirectly, into contact with J. Edgar Hoover's Federal Bureau of Investigation. In one sense, I owe the FBI some gratitude.

While I was writing *Boston Boy* (Knopf), a memoir of my earlier years in Boston, the FBI provided some useful research. My parents were dead, so I had no way, I thought, of finding out what towns or cities in Russia they had come from. I'd always wanted to write about my first job—in a haberdashery store, when I was eleven—but I couldn't remember its name. There were other details of name and place that I had lost.

Through the Freedom of Information Act, I received my FBI file. I had expected only a record of my civil rights and antiwar activities through the years, in both Boston and New York, and that record of subversion was indeed there. But there was much more—including where my parents had come from in Russia, and the name of that men's clothing store.

As for my un-American past, there was a copy of an article I'd written for *Playboy* in 1968, "The War on Dissent." It included a most unfriendly portrait of J. Edgar Hoover. The piece was in my FBI file because a field agent had sent it to the Director with the notation, "Also, Hentoff's a lousy writer."

I thought, briefly, of suing for defamation.

That *Playboy* article began:

> Early in 1968, the superintendent of the building where I had an office drew me aside as I was going to the elevator. "Listen," he said softly, "I shouldn't be telling you this, they told me not to, but a couple of FBI guys were asking about you yesterday."
>
> It was a warm day, but I went cold. "What did they want to know?"
>
> "Oh, do you just work here or do you live here, too? Where do you go in the summer? Who comes to see you?"

Other entries in my FBI file testify to the Bureau's long-term interest in me. There are antiwar ads I signed, letters to various newspapers, an array of contentious articles, and the appearance of my name on "A Call to Resist Illegitimate Authority," which pledged support to young men who, in conscience, resisted the draft. As a lawyer explained to me at the time, the signers could be subject to a conspiracy charge, even if we didn't actually *do* anything. I doubted that would happen, but the possibility added a frisson of danger to my participation in that noble enterprise.

Not that I was actually brave in these matters. Once, in 1959, a relatively small group of us—including Dorothy Day and Norman Mailer—committed civil disobedience in a park near City Hall. It was the first act of anti–Vietnam War resistance in the city. We refused to go into a nearby shelter during an air-raid drill. The police arrested just a few of us at random—principally, it seemed, by taking in those whose eyes met theirs. I managed to evade the eyes of every cop harvesting dissenters. I felt guilty—but not enough to raise my eyes—as some of my comrades entered the paddy wagon.

I also joined, at another point, a large crowd of protesters blocking an induction center in downtown New York. We didn't block it for long, the expedition being more symbolic than practical. I felt I had done my part in sort of helping to stop the war.

Most of the rest of my not-so-arduous antiwar efforts—as my FBI file details—consisted of assorted indignant writings. Getting the package from the Bureau was like having a free clipping service.

My file continued into the Nixon administration, but—to my chagrin and my children's humiliation—I was not included in the Nixon "enemies list." My two sons and two daughters were kind enough not to upbraid me for being so insignificant a dissenter—considering how I carried on at home. But I could see their disappointment. They had been cheated of the opportunity to boast at school about their notorious dad.

Later I was told by a reporter doing some digging in Treasury Department files that there was another Nixon enemies list—much smaller but with very irritating sanctions attached. This was a list of people, some of them reporters, who had annoyed the White House and had to pay for it. My name was on that list. I then understood why our income tax returns had been so carefully audited during those years.

The most adventurous experience I had as a dissenter concerned the FBI, but that story was not in my file because it embarrassed the Bureau that they had missed a chance to nab me with stolen FBI files. Those files were in plain view in my apartment, but the men from the Bureau blew it.

In March 1971, I received a package in the mail that included a letter from a group I'd never heard of before—the Citizens' Commission to Investigate the FBI. The letter began:

Enclosed you will find copies of certain files from the Media, Pennsylvania, office of the FBI which were removed by our commission for public scrutiny. . . . All the files in the desks and file cabinets were liberated. Of these some thirty percent were manuals, routine forms, and similar procedural materials; forty percent political surveillance and other investigations of political activity. Of these cases, two were right wing, 10 concerned immigrants, and over 200 were on left or liberal groups.

As for the rest of the files, the Citizens' Commission said,

. . . one percent concerned organized crime, mostly gambling. We are making these copies available to you and to several other persons in public life because we feel you have shown concern and courage as regards the issues which are, in part, documented in the enclosed materials.

We have carried out this action in a way which does not physically threaten anyone. We intend no personal harassment of the people who work in the office from which the files were taken. . . . We have taken this action because . . . we believe the FBI has betrayed its democratic trust and we wish to present evidence for this claim to the open and public judgment of our fellow citizens.

On March 25, 1971, Attorney General John Mitchell urgently asked the press not to publish any of these stolen FBI documents. The *Washington Post*, nonetheless, ran a front-page story about the FBI files, with excerpts, and the *New York Times* followed.

In a lead editorial on March 25, "What Is the FBI Up to?," the *Washington Post* noted that the Justice Department had admitted the stolen records were indeed authentic FBI documents. In its comment about those documents, the *Post* editorial said:

We reported the substance of the records . . . because we were convinced that it served the public interest to do so. . . . We believe the American public needs to know what the FBI is doing. We believe the American public needs to think long and hard about whether internal security rests essentially upon official surveillance and the suppression of dissent or upon the traditional right of every citizen to speak his mind on any subject—whether others consider what he says wise or foolish, patriotic or subversive, conservative or radical. That is why we published the substance of the stolen FBI records.

The Citizens' Commission made a point of removing names and identifying characteristics of those who were spied on by the FBI. The reason was that identifying those persons of interest to J. Edgar Hoover would also make them targets of other "internal security" agencies.

I printed more of the material than any other reporter to whom the documents were sent, because I had more space. Pay at the *Voice* was scant, but there were no limits on how many columns I chose to write on any subject.

The files revealed, for example, the covert pursuit of a college senior described in one of the Bureau's memoranda as "known to be an inverterate [*sic*] Marxist revolutionist, and a type of person that should be watched as she will probably be very active in revolutionary activities."

But then an FBI informant struck up a conversation with this "inverterate Marxist" at a meeting and, according to the stolen files, "received no indication that she was doing anything other than the average liberal minded student that is common" on the campus under surveillance.

Did that mean the young woman's name had accordingly been struck from FBI files? On the contrary. The instructions from headquarters were that she was to be kept under surveillance for promotion to the more ominous Security Index. In the spying business, you can never be too sure.

Then there was the case file of a professor at a prestigious liberal-arts college. He was the subject of a three-page, single-spaced FBI file.

On the first page there is an indication of why he was being surveilled: "The professor and his wife and children live in a house that numerous college students visit frequently."

The chief switchboard operator at the college ("conceal identity due to position at the school") informed the FBI that the professor had been inviting "controversial speakers" without "clearing with others." Presumably the "others" involved the switchboard operator.

This operator, who knew her duty when she saw it, "will," according to the file, "confidentially furnish pertinent information regarding any long distance calls made or received by the professor."

The FBI, ever thorough, did not depend solely on one informant. Down the road from the professor's house—the one swarming with visiting college students—there lived a local peace officer. On being contacted by the FBI, he certainly wanted to help, and he told an FBI agent that "the garage to the rear of the professor's residence has been converted to a printing shop and it houses enough equipment to publish a newspaper." He had no information to indicate that a newspaper *was* being published, or would be published. But, said the file, he was keeping a close eye on that garage "to ascertain what activity takes place there."

And the postmaster in the town was told by the FBI "to remain alert as to who the professor and his family get letters from and send letters to."

There was much more, but what particularly intrigued me was a memo in the first edition of an internal FBI newsletter, "New Left Notes" (a title filched from a newsletter of the avowedly left-wing Students for a Democratic Society): "There was a pretty general consensus that more interviews with these [students] are in order for plenty of reasons, chief of which is it will enhance that paranoia endemic in these circles and *will further serve to get the point across that there is an FBI agent behind every mailbox.*" (Emphasis added.)

Actually, whether it was paranoia or a sense of survival, a good many people during those years did act as if the elevator operator or the doorman or the bartender might be an employee of Mr. Hoover.

I tell this to high school and college students to give them a sense of what it is like, in this constitutional democracy, to live in fear because of your ideas. In how many high schools is the era of McCarthyism taught?

Margot, for instance, was in college back then, and tells of buying a liberal magazine, the *New Republic,* and a recording, *Songs of the Spanish Civil War*—and putting them quickly in a brown paper bag. Others stopped buying dangerous magazines, but if they were so unfortunate as to have been subscribers, they were likely to wind up in FBI files—even if they wouldn't, under any circumstances, have had Stalin to dinner.

For years now, in telling students of that grim period, I bring with me a book that testifies to the fear at large then. The name of the author is not on the cover, for it has been taped over. Nor is there any hint of the writer's identity on the spine. Tape covers that too. The title, however, is on the cover: *The Civil War.*

Who in the FBI, during the McCarthy years, could have objected to a book on the Civil War? But when the book is opened to the title page, all is clear: *The Civil War in the United States,* by Karl Marx and Friedrich Engels.

The book had been in the library of a history professor who had no connection with the Communist Party. He did, however, have friends and acquaintances in his home from time to time, and for all he knew—during the McCarthy years—one or more of them might have been informants for the FBI, or for Senator McCarthy himself. So, he taped over the incriminating parts of the book's cover.

Still, what he had done to the book made him uncomfortable, so he sold it, as a curiosity, to a dealer in used books. The dealer—Fred Bass of New York's famed Strand Bookstore—gave it to me to instruct the young about the years of darkness.

I used to wonder what the FBI would think of some of the titles of the books in my office. I had volumes, undisguised, by, among others, Karl Marx, Adolf Hitler, Malcolm X, and Leon Trotsky.

One day the FBI did come calling, but they couldn't look at my books because I didn't permit them to pass beyond the doorway. It was a Friday afternoon in early April 1971, a month after I received the first package from the Citizens' Commission to Investigate the FBI. There were two agents, and they were cordial at first. In my experience, FBI agents usually are cordial—at first.

They wanted me to show them the stolen FBI files about which I was writing in the *Voice*. (I declined.)

My office is so disorderly, all the time, that my wife has forbidden my setting up an annex, however small, in my home. On the day of the visit from the agents, I had, as usual, piles of manuscripts and books on the floor. One pile, very near the front door, consisted of all the stolen FBI files I had received so far. I had an almost uncontrollable urge to stare at it as the agents were trying to question me. I resisted the urge. Since the pile on the floor near the door was indistinguishable from the rest of the chaos on the floor, it didn't attract their attention.

As I was looking anywhere but at the floor to my right, one of the agents opened a page of the *Voice* he was carrying to a column of mine on the files. Would I at least tell them I had actually received copies of the stolen documents? Since they didn't have a search warrant—I had asked them about that at the beginning of the conversation—I didn't have to answer any of their questions. And so I told them. Their cordiality vanished. Did I really want to be involved in a criminal act? Did I want to be subpoenaed?

I told them to see my attorneys at the American Civil Liberties Union, which was not far from where we were.

The false cordiality returned. One of them smiled, and said they'd be back. They didn't come back. I wrote about their coming, as did several other reporters who, for one reason or another, had been visited by the FBI in an attempt to turn them into sources. We all wrote that the agents had failed, and one way or another, we made fun of them.

A source in the Bureau told me some months afterwards that J. Edgar Hoover had issued an order forbidding any further visits by agents to journalists who had previously written about such visits.

I kept writing about Director Hoover from time to time, and was sorry when he died. Hoover was good copy.

The members of the Citizens' Commission to Investigate the FBI were never found, although the FBI surely did their very best to capture them.

I didn't hear—directly—from the FBI again. But I had previously become involved with other investigators of un-American activities. On October 14, 1970, Congressman Richard Ichord (Democrat-Missouri), chairman of the House Internal Security Committee, released a report listing sixty-five "radical" campus speakers. Or, as the vigilant chairman put it in a foreword to the report:

> Early this year I became concerned—as did many of my colleagues—with frequent news accounts of inflammatory speeches that were being made to large audiences on college and university campuses by the radical rhetoricians of the New Left—promoting violence and encouraging the destruction of our system of government.

I was one of the sixty-five on the list of those charged with promoting violence and working toward the destruction of our government. The committee's researchers had somehow missed the time I was shouted down at an antiwar rally in the 1960s because I criticized those on the antiwar left who were violently disrupting meetings of the opposition and preventing pro–Vietnam War veterans from speaking. I said at that rally—until I was drowned out—that those of the left who committed violence to crush dissent were mirror images of the South Vietnamese government whom they were so vigorously opposing.

Congressman Ichord explained why the dread list of radical campus speakers had been assembled. Where did "revolutionary movements in the United States obtain the financing for their activities?" It must be, he explained, from the "substantial appearance fees" these preachers of "hate for America and its institutions" often received.

Clearly it was the Internal Security Committee's "hope and expectation"—as Federal District Judge Gerhard Gesell later emphasized—"that college officials, alumni and parents would bring social and economic pressures upon the institutions that had permitted these speeches—in order to ostracize the speakers."

We were to be banished from the company of impressionable students and faculty. And the very college buildings would thereby become safe because the Ichord Report had implied that these inflammatory speakers had actually caused arson and other destruction by listeners fired up by our speeches. Campus buildings burned in our wake.

The Ichord Report listed me as being affiliated with three "radical organizations": the Socialist Workers Party, Students for a Democratic Society, and the Spring Mobilization Committee to End the War in Vietnam. The Internal Security Committee omitted, however, that my only connection with the Socialist Workers Party was an article criticizing the exclusion of that party, or any party, from the ballot in the 1969 New York mayoralty election.

As for Students for a Democratic Society, my sole connection had been a subscription to its newspaper. I like to know what's going on.

And I must have signed a good many petitions to end the war in Vietnam, including the one distributed by the Spring Mobilization Committee.

None of the exculpatory information concerning me—or rebuttals by others in the House Internal Security Committee Report—were included by the *New York Times* when it published, on October 15, 1970, the full list of the Pied Pipers of Pernicious Propaganda, including every one of our alleged affiliations.

It is one thing to be the newspaper of record, but quite another to print false records without any attempt to check them out. The Ichord Report had been legitimized by the *New York Times*.

Edwin R. Newman, later to become a model of proper word usage on the NBC television network, was at the time an anchor on New York's local NBC news. A civil libertarian, he saw the Ichord Report in the *Times* and called to ask me if I wanted to correct it on the air. Indeed I did. It struck me at the time—and since—that hardly any other TV news anchor in the nation would have thought to do that.

As for the *Times*—which, after all, has a considerable staff—nothing would have prevented it from contacting those on the list to check the accuracy of their "affiliations." Otherwise, damage could be—and was—done to some of the "subversives" by readers who had full faith in the *Times*.

I found out later that I had lost some speaking engagements because of the *Times*'s news (*sic*) article. And an editor at Harper & Row wrote me: "If the *Times* denies your claim that its report tended to confirm the Ichord report, you can use this letter to prove that at least one experienced newspaper reader was indeed misled. . . . I actually did assume you belonged to those three organizations . . . simply because of the way the *Times* presented the list."

And an editor at Agathon Press also made part of my day: "I was surprised you were a member of the Socialist Workers Party. It affected my assessment of where you stood politically. In a sense, it opened a kind of pigeonhole into which you could now fit. Notice, however, that I did not question the accuracy of the *Times*. It was there, so it must be true."

In not-for-attribution conversations, *New York Times* editors in New York and Washington told me that there had been no policy decision to print the list without checking its accuracy. They described what happened as actually having resulted from "carelessness" and "sloppiness."

This explanation, of course, was never carried in the columns of the *Times*.

Congressman Ichord and his colleagues did, however, bring me two great pleasures. One was the text of a letter to Ichord from the nine students who constituted the Oberlin College Forum Board:

"We, the members of the Oberlin College Forum Board, a student-sponsored organization which brings speakers to the campus, would like to thank you for providing us with a list of 65 of the most relevant, courageous, committed and inspiring speakers in America today. The list will be a great help in selecting future speakers."

The second boon from being on a national list of those who cause college buildings to go up in flames was a lawsuit. I had long wanted to have my name on a constitutional law case. And there it was—filed by the American Civil Liberties Union:

Nat Hentoff et al., Plaintiffs v. Richard H. Ichord et al., Defendants in the United States District Court, District of Columbia. In his memorandum opinion, Judge Gerhard Gesell wrote:

> Plaintiffs seek to enjoin the official publication and distribution of a Report of the Committee on Internal Security of the House of Representatives. . . .
>
> It is important to recognize that this litigation unquestionably presents an immediate issue of free speech and assembly. . . . Plaintiffs clearly demonstrate that they are faced with irreparable injury if publication of the "blacklist" under the auspices of Congress is allowed, and accordingly, defendants must demonstrate a constitutionally protected justification for publication. . . .
>
> These are times of stress when our most cherished institutions are threatened by extremists of many different persuasions. It is in these circumstances that the right of free speech and assembly must be jealously safeguarded by all branches of government. . . .
>
> There are undoubtedly individuals who would destroy our institutions and form of government. If any of them are listed in this Report, our Constitution nevertheless preserves their right to speak even though their acts may be restrained.
>
> It is alien to any legitimate congressional function, as well as contrary to our most established traditions, for any committee of Congress to disseminate lists designed to suppress

speech. Members of the Committee may speak their minds, and their words will carry added weight because of the great prestige of their high office. They cannot, however, by the mere process of a report devoid of legislative purpose, transform their views into official action by the Congress and have them published and widely distributed at public expense. . . .

The Public Printer and the Superintendent of Documents are permanently enjoined from printing or distributing the Report or any facsimile thereof.

But the Report, said Judge Gesell, could be introduced into or mentioned during the proceedings of the Congress— and could be printed in the Congressional Record: "The Court will take no action which limits the use that individual Congressmen choose to make of the Report or its contents on or off the floor of the Congress.

However, the judge's opinion ends: "[This] Report of the House Committee for Internal Security . . . infringes on the rights of individuals named therein as protected by the First Amendment to the Constitution of the United States, and any publication of said Report at public expense, except as herein provided, is illegal."

The *Washington Post* noted that this "was believed to be the first time in the nation's history that a judge had prevented the widespread publication of a document of Congress."

At last I was in the index of the nation's lawbooks.

The House Internal Security Committee defied Judge Gesell and printed the report anyway beyond the limits of his decision. But the precedent stands—despite that outlaw act of that patriotic committee.

THE BLUES JUMPED

A RABBIT—ME

Besides the FBI and the House Internal Security Committee, another law enforcement outfit had me in its sights. One morning, as I put the key in the lock to my office, a large hand came from behind me and stopped the key from turning. I looked into the wintry eyes of a large man who showed me a badge. I also saw a gun in a holster.

"I'm a detective with the district attorney's office," he said. "You have to come downtown."

"I'm on a deadline," I said. "I'll come down later."

"Now," he said.

"What's it all about?"

"You'll find out when you get there."

When I got there, a stern assistant district attorney sat me down and started the interrogation.

"Do you know a magazine called *Eros*?"

"Yes, I wrote an article for it on the blues."

He reached in his desk drawer for a copy of the magazine as I heard in my head a vintage blues lyric: "The blues jumped a rabbit and rode him a solid mile."

I was the rabbit. It became evident that Ralph Ginzburg, the editor and publisher of *Eros*, was about to be indicted on a charge of publishing obscene material. Among those materials was my article in the Spring 1962 *Eros*: "The Blues of Black and White," subtitled "Views of love are different in the song lyrics of negroes and whites."

The article simply underlined the honesty of black blues in matters of sex and death, among other things, by contrast with the chronic euphemisms of white popular composers—and it was not the first time this dichotomy had been written about. One of my illustrations was:

> *He's a deep-sea diver with a stroke that can't go wrong,*
> *Oh, he's a deep-sea diver with a stroke that can't go wrong,*
> *He can touch the bottom, and his wind holds out so long.*

Also:

> *Every time I climb your tree, I wonder what make you smile,*
> *Yes, every time I climb your tree, baby, I wonder what make*
>   *you smile,*
> *You want me to climb up your tree ever since you was a chile.*

I tried to explain to the assistant DA how bracing the directness of the sexual imagery was. He did not respond. He did ask me what other obscene works Ralph Ginzburg had published or was about to publish. I told him that "obscene"— being a subjective word—had no clear meaning for me. The words in the First Amendment, I said, *were* clear.

He gave me a very cold look and said I could leave— subject to recall at any time.

On reflection, I was outraged at having been pulled in—by a man with a gun, yet. My wife thought it was very funny.

Ginzburg was indicted, convicted, and sentenced to five years in prison and fined $28,000. The case wound up at the Supreme Court (*Ginzburg v. United States*, 1966). He lost there too, in a stunningly unjust decision written by Justice William Brennan, who, next to William O. Douglas, had otherwise been the most tenacious defender of free expression in the Court's history.

Ginzburg was convicted—and sent to prison—not for obscenity but for *pandering*. *Eros*, a magazine advertised as "devoted to the joy of love and sex," had been mailed from such towns as Intercourse and Blue Ball, Pennsylvania. Adding to its salacious appeal, a majority of the Court held, its ads stressed "sexual candor."

Although Ginzburg had not been charged with pandering in the courts below, Brennan found he had been "engaged in the sordid business of pandering." Justice John Harlan was appalled, writing that Brennan had engaged in "astonishing judicial improvisation." Among the other dissenters, Hugo Black noted that the First Amendment requires that "sex, at least as much as any other aspect of life, is so much a part of our society that its discussion should not be made a crime."

But what had happened to Brennan, that paladin of the First Amendment? A lawyer I knew, watching Brennan indignantly reading his opinion from the bench, told me that he saw the back of Brennan's neck get redder and redder as he dispatched Ginzburg to a prison cell. "You see," the lawyer told me, "Brennan has a daughter, and while he is a libertarian in other matters, he becomes a censor of materials that might harm the purity of his daughter."

Reading the decision, I felt that it had also been directed at me. After all, I had been a contributor to that pandering magazine mailed from Intercourse, Pennsylvania. Worse yet, I had been betrayed by one of my heroes of the Bill of Rights.

I did not forgive Brennan for a while, but then I got to spend a considerable amount of time with him while I was writing a profile of him for *The New Yorker*—and after. He told me of the struggles he'd had through the years in trying to figure out where the First Amendment ends and punishment of obscenity begins.

In his chambers early one morning, Brennan told me, "I put sixteen years into that damn obscenity thing. I tried and I tried, and I waffled back and forth, and I finally gave up. If you can't define it, you can't prosecute people for it. And that's why, in 1973, in my *Paris Adult Theatre* dissent, I finally abandoned the whole effort." (Seven years after his Ginzburg decision.)

"I reached the conclusion that every criminal-obscenity statute . . . was necessarily unconstitutional, because it was impossible, from the statute, to define obscenity. Accordingly, anybody charged with violating the statute would not have known that his conduct was a violation of the law. He wouldn't know whether the material was obscene until the court told him."

I asked Brennan about sending Ralph Ginzburg to prison for pandering, when *Eros* itself was protected by the First Amendment. He brushed my question aside. The customarily self-confident justice was uncomfortable with that memory.

Ginzburg aside, Brennan's abiding faith in the resiliency of the First Amendment continued after his retirement. One afternoon I asked him a schoolboy's question: What was his favorite part of the Constitution?

"The First Amendment," he said. "Its enforcement gives us this society. The other provisions of the Constitution merely embellish it."

"But," I said, "a future Supreme Court can greatly reduce the powers of the First Amendment."

"Look, pal," Brennan answered, "we've always known— the Framers knew—that liberty is a fragile thing. A very fragile thing." He smiled, and did not seem apprehensive.

MR. SHAWN'S *NEW YORKER*

y appearance in the files of the FBI and the House
Internal Security Committee did not affect me
economically as a writer. The citations from pursuers of subversives might, however, have led to my being ter-
minated from some publications. At the *New York Times*, for
instance, some of the staff who refused to testify before committees testing patriotism were dismissed.

But at the *Voice*, any writer being stalked by agents of the
government's thought police was honored. At *The New
Yorker*, where I also became a regular, a couple of years after
joining the *Voice*, there was no danger of being set adrift because of the attentions of J. Edgar Hoover and Richard Ichord.

Aside from that similarity, *The New Yorker* was unlike any
other place I've worked. And that was because its editor,
William Shawn, was utterly singular. He was more open to the
needs and anxieties of writers than other editors I'd known,
but he was also so formal and distant in manner that even a
trace of familiarity was out of the question.

Although he was respectful of writers, which extended to
paying them generously, Shawn was less attentive to the economic needs of some of the lower-level workers.

Most of the time, I was almost in awe of Mr. Shawn. A dismaying exception had to do with an attempt by some staff members to form a union. The writers involved—and some were not—particularly wanted fairness for employees in the library and in clerical and other low-paid positions. In a number of cases I was surprised at how low the wages were, as were what passed for pensions for long-term employees.

The drive for a union among all divisions of the staff was gathering considerable momentum. At one meeting I went to, I was impressed by the determination of the organizers to persevere despite what they knew would be Mr. Shawn's appalled and determined opposition.

But Mr. Shawn prevailed. In a letter to the staff, and in talks, Shawn made the classic management pitch against unions. *The New Yorker* was a family. The management and the workers knew each other well, he said. The door was always open to complaints and suggestions by the workers. Bringing in outsiders would create and escalate tensions and destroy the family feeling and familiarity that already existed.

The vote went to Shawn, and I was disgusted. Having organized my first union—in a Boston candy store—when I was fifteen, and then having helped bring a union into a radio station four years later—I knew the disingenuous strategies of bosses. And in this case, Shawn—still unfailingly courteous, soft-spoken, even gracious—was very much the manipulative boss.

Still, my regard for Shawn as an editor remained boundless.

Once in a while, from 1960 to 1986, the phone would ring and I would hear a familiar soft—very soft—voice.

"How are you, Mr. Hentoff?"

"Fine, Mr. Shawn. How are you?"

"Fine."

I would wait with acute apprehension. Was the piece accepted, or had I failed to meet the standards of *The New Yorker*, which meant the standards of Mr. Shawn?

"Mr. Hentoff, the piece worked out well, very well. We'll run it soon."

"Soon" could mean in a few months, in a few years, or when the Messiah came. But what mattered was that once again Mr. Shawn had said the piece worked. I'd be on a natural high for some time after that.

Every writer is insecure, fearful that his or her most recent piece may be rejected—whatever the writer's track record up to then. And if the piece is turned down, that, in the writer's nightmare, begins the slide into oblivion. Shawn knew this.

I was a long-piece writer at *The New Yorker*, and yet Shawn would call within a few days after I'd turned in a profile or a reporter-at-large piece, no matter how long. With everything else he had to do—he read everything that was printed in each issue, and he supervised nearly everything else, from covers to cartoon captions—Shawn also read new submissions as they came in. He didn't want the writer's suspense to last any longer than it had to.

He also edited some of the pieces himself. My first profile was a two-parter on Gerry Mulligan. (I had been at the Newport Jazz Festival, along with Lillian Ross of *The New Yorker*, and she'd suggested to Shawn that I might do something for the magazine.) Mr. Shawn edited the Mulligan profile.

On a Sunday, he tracked me down in Connecticut (I have no idea how he found out where I was). Would it be all right, he asked, if he changed a word halfway through the piece? The change was so slight that I would not have noticed it in print. But no change was made at *The New Yorker*—by Shawn or any of the other editors—without the writer's being asked. And the editors made it clear that all changes were suggestions. They were not mandatory. But most of the time the suggestions made such immediate sense that I found nothing to argue about. That was not my experience elsewhere.

For many pieces, there were no deadlines. No pressure to get a piece in fast because it was topical. It was not that kind of magazine.

I knew readers, including me, who would put aside issues of *The New Yorker* because there was no time to read them when they came out. But when I picked one up six months later, time had not overtaken a fair number of pieces. *The New Yorker* was written and edited for a longer span of relevance. Or, as a longtime staff writer, Whitney Balliett, puts it: "Shawn's *New Yorker* had its own sense of time."

Without the pressure of deadlines, you could do as much research as you felt the piece required. Profiles of John Cardinal O'Connor and Justice William Brennan took me two years each. Others went faster. But it was up to me.

In 1987, after Mr. Shawn had been removed by S. I. Newhouse Jr., the ultimate boss of *The New Yorker*, I remembered the song "When Cootie Left the Duke." Cootie was Cootie Williams, a trumpeter with a sound—or rather, sounds, including an unrivaled growl—that were so integral to Duke Ellington's wondrous, complex mosaic that it was inconceivable Cootie would no longer be there. Much of the jazz world was in stunned mourning, and so, years later, were many of the writers and editors of *The New Yorker* when Mr. Shawn— himself stunned—was forced to leave.

The *New York Times*, in an editorial amid the shock waves, said, "For several generations of [writers], winning the chance to work with William Shawn was like being asked to dance with Fred Astaire."

I had never fantasized dancing with Fred Astaire, but I had dreamed of two utterly unattainable desires. I used to play clarinet and soprano saxophone, and I fantasized—during classes at Boston Latin School—of sitting alongside Johnny Hodges, Ben Webster, and Harry Carney in Duke Ellington's reed section.

During those years and later in radio, where I had long stretches of reading time, I read practically everything in *The New Yorker* each week. I was writing then, mainly for *Down Beat*, and I imagined one day being a staff writer on *The New Yorker*. But that was impossible, just as I would never take over for Johnny Hodges in "I Got It Bad and That Ain't Good." My horns remained in their cases, but the call did come from Mr. Shawn.

It turned out that he was very fond of jazz, and knew a lot about it. I'm told—I never heard him perform—that he played swinging piano. Once, when he telephoned, I had an Ellington recording on as loud as it would go. "I wish I could be there to listen with you," he said. The way he said it, it wasn't jive.

It was always *Mister* Shawn. A very few editors and writers who'd known him a long time called him Bill. But even among the veterans, there was a staff writer—who'd been at *The New Yorker* since the days of Shawn's predecessor, Harold Ross— who told me he'd never thought of calling him anything but "Mr. Shawn."

His office was as formal and orderly as he was. There were different-colored sheets of note paper, for instance, for different purposes. And while you were in that quiet place, there were no interruptions. He gave you his concentrated, unfailingly respectful attention.

I've never met anyone with so wide a range of knowledge. For twenty-six years I proposed a considerable variety of subjects to him, some quite recondite. Invariably, Shawn knew a lot about each one, sometimes more than I did. He had enormous, ceaseless curiosity—one of the key characteristics of a first-class editor.

Another Shawn characteristic was described by Elizabeth Drew in a superb appreciation of him in the *Washington Post*:

"Early in my years of working with him . . . I told him that I was thinking of trying something or other—I don't recall it now, but it was something I'd never tried—and he replied, 'Take a chance on anything, Mrs. Drew.' "

When I came to *The New Yorker* in 1960, Shawn knew of me primarily as a writer on jazz. But he never indicated any limits on what I could write about. That gave me the confidence to write about homicide detectives; principals who actually knew how to give kids the confidence that they could learn; a brilliant storefront psychiatrist, Marie Nyswander, who was the first in the city to treat heroin addicts on their own turf; an ageless writer of books for children, Maurice Sendak; and even a piece that involved months of going through the municipal archives to find records of slavery in New York in the early nineteenth century and the actual clothes Abe "Kid Twist" Reles wore when he sort of fell out of a window while in police custody, waiting to testify against the Mob.

The other editors there were also extraordinarily civil, considerate, and knowledgeable about all sorts of things. Elizabeth Drew recalls Shawn saying to her, "We tell our editors not to *improve* pieces."

That is, like Shawn, they did not become the writers. They did point out soft spots as well as clinkers of grammar and usage, and words that should be retired as verging on clichés. But the editors did not attack a piece; they let it breathe on its own.

Many writers at *The New Yorker* have said that Shawn and the other editors brought out the best in their work. One of the reasons was that the magazine had no editing by committees. Nor were there staff meetings. Nor did Mr. Shawn try to figure out what the magazine needed to stay "hot"—that is, what would most effectively attract readers that particular week. Or what writers *The New Yorker* must recruit to be "with it."

The New Yorker, by contrast, was a *writers'* magazine. To be sure, Shawn decided which writers to print, but those writers were free to pursue their own interests, their own compelling interests. Shawn believed there were enough people out there who wanted to read writers unconstrained by any priorities other than their own.

And maybe the readers wanted to be educated, whether they knew it or not. In E. J. Kahn Jr.'s. *About The New Yorker & Me*, he notes that "Bill Shawn heard Hannah Arendt give a lecture on the subject of Thinking, and asked her to put her views in print. Miss Arendt . . . said that she couldn't believe the magazine's readers would be interested but Mr. Shawn said that didn't matter, it would be good for them."

Critics of *The New Yorker* would say that such high-mindedness, together with very long pieces driven by writers' curiosity—rather than anticipated readers' curiosity—helped account for lagging advertising and circulation in Shawn's last years there. But circulation was still around half a million, and *The New Yorker* was not losing money, during that period.

In any case, Mr. Shawn—to his writers' consternation, and certainly to his own—was fired. As Elizabeth Drew and others have said, Mr. Shawn "never got over his having been ousted."

Hearing of his death in 1992 and recalling those phone calls—which were like milestones in my life as a writer—I remembered another place that had some of the characteristics of *The New Yorker* under Mr. Shawn.

I spent six years at the Boston Public Latin School, which reverberated with high expectations of its students and teachers. We students came from widely varying backgrounds—the children of Russian Jewish immigrants (like me) and of upwardly mobile Catholics (Joseph Kennedy Sr. had once been a pupil), and the scions of some Brahmins.

None of that mattered to the headmaster and his colleagues. All of us were expected to do well, and so most of us did, in large part precisely because that was expected of us. So, too, at *The New Yorker*, Mr. Shawn expected us to produce our best—and then some. He never lectured us to that effect. It was simply in the air. And we wrote for and to him—even if other editors there were actually going to work on the pieces. We knew he would see whatever we did anyway. He saw everything.

Some considered this a highly undemocratic way to edit a publication. No input from internal black, Jewish, women's, gay, lesbian, or disability rights caucuses. No sense of collective orthodoxies or identities.

Well, not all publications have the same reason for being. As for *The New Yorker*—ranging from John Hersey's "Hiroshima" to Rachel Carson's "Silent Spring" to many more still-resounding articles in the time of Shawn—it's accurate to repeat what John Leonard wrote in 1975. Mr. Shawn, he said, changed *The New Yorker* "into a journal that altered our experience instead of just posturing in front of it."

In 1985, on the death of E. B. White, Mr. Shawn wrote, "Because of his quiet influence, several generations of the country's writers write better than they might have done. He never wrote a mean or careless sentence. He was impervious to literary, intellectual, and political fashion."

This was also an epitaph for Mr. Shawn.

Months after Mr. Shawn had been removed from *The New Yorker*, I found out—to my deep regret and guilt—that I had inadvertently been one of the causes for the selling of *The New Yorker* to Samuel Irving Newhouse Jr., who went on to dismiss Mr. Shawn.

Before either of those alarming events took place, I was at a party in Greenwich Village. The host was a friend of mine, a lawyer, and he introduced me to one of his clients, Philip Messinger. I did not know then that Messinger was a member of *The New Yorker*'s board of directors or that much of his net worth was tied to *The New Yorker*, where he had made a considerable amount of money. Nor did I know—until I read Gigi Mahon's 1988 book, *The Last Days of* The New Yorker (McGraw-Hill)—that Messinger had been a persistent critic of the magazine's management practices.

In her book, Gigi Mahon told, in considerable detail, how that first and only meeting I'd had with Messinger helped bring down Mr. Shawn. Had I known who Messinger was, I would have kept my mouth shut. But, as Mahon reported, I didn't:

> At a party Messinger met author and *New Yorker* writer Nat Hentoff. The two men discussed *The New Yorker*, and Hentoff expressed his exasperation at how difficult it was to get published in its pages.
>
> The magazine paid him for stories he had written, but they hadn't published one for ten years. It was nice to receive a check, but it would be nicer still to see the prose in print occasionally.
>
> The conversation was light and even humorous, but it riled Messinger. He knew that writers at *The New Yorker* were paid for stories that were not published. Worse, he knew that some were allowed to draw a paycheck every week even though they never wrote a word. All of that bothered him, but there had been an abstractness to the stories in the past. Now, here was a firsthand account, an immediate, in-the-flesh description of payment without publishing. In Hentoff's case, it wasn't that the writer didn't produce, but rather, that Shawn paid for stories he never ran. As far as Messinger could determine, Shawn was accountable to no one.

There were mistakes in Mahon's account of that conversation. There was never a period as long as ten years during which one of my pieces hadn't run in the magazine. But a couple of times, two years had gone by, and some of my pieces were never published. Also, I did not draw a paycheck every week.

As for Shawn's being accountable to no one, that's why *The New Yorker* was not reflective of current trends and fancies. Sure, I was frustrated that I wasn't in more often, but that was because it meant so much to be in those pages.

In her book, Gigi Mahon noted the results of the conversation at that party: "Messinger repeatedly broached the subject in front of the board and at audit committee meetings. In 1984, *The New Yorker,* in its financial filings, valued unpublished articles and art at $3.7 million. Messinger wanted to know how they arrived at that figure, and how they kept track of what was likely to be published."

There were other reasons Messinger was decidedly unhappy at how *The New Yorker* was run, and not only on the editorial side. But Messinger did not forget that conversation. As Mahon put it, "His argument about Hentoff, he says, fell on deaf ears."

Finally, Messinger, tired of speaking to deaf ears, sold his stock in the magazine to S. I. Newhouse. Having acquired the rest of the stock he needed, Newhouse took over. On first meeting the writers and editors, Newhouse said that it was "self-evident that *The New Yorker* is *The New Yorker* and it is going to go on being *The New Yorker.* What changes will go on are those that are organic to *The New Yorker.*"

In 1986, Newhouse said of Mr. Shawn, who was still there, "This extraordinary man is what *The New Yorker* itself is all about."

Not quite a year later, Newhouse fired Shawn, solemnly

saying in a public memorandum, "Recently Mr. Shawn informed me that he will retire on March 1."

Shawn was shocked and deeply saddened. Gigi Mahon wrote, "A *New Yorker* writer who spoke with Shawn said that the editor did not sound much like the man he once knew. He seemed, he said, diminished."

Some months after Mr. Shawn had been "retired," while on my way to give a talk at the YMHA, on the Upper East Side, I stopped at a nearby coffee shop. At the counter, I was reading, but the voices across from me were so loud that I looked up. I saw Lillian Ross, and sitting beside her was William Shawn.

It was a Shawn I had never seen before. Whenever we had met in his office, he had been immaculately dressed. On his person and in the office, everything was neatly, precisely in place. In the coffee shop, however, Shawn was tieless and wore a nondescript jacket. Particularly startling was his need of a shave. His voice, which had been so soft that I often had to strain to hear it, had become coarsened.

He struck me as not so much diminished as having been almost transmogrified by having lost his center of being. For thirty-five years he had been the absolute monarch of a magazine of rare integrity—and influence. Now he looked like someone in the closing pages of a Theodore Dreiser novel.

Mr. Shawn asked me what I was going to talk about at the Y, but he wasn't much interested. The conversation, such as it was, soon ended. It was the last time I saw him.

He hadn't asked me if I was still at *The New Yorker*, and I didn't volunteer that I was. Shawn's then successor, Bob Gottlieb, had edited books of mine at Knopf, and we got on well. And Gottlieb seemed intent, in his seemingly casual way, on sustaining the honesty of what had been Mr. Shawn's *New*

Yorker. He wasn't interested in a magazine's being "hot," and Newhouse fired him too.

Then came Tina Brown. I tried suggesting pieces to her through subeditors, but I did not appear again in *The New Yorker.* Around Christmastime in 1994, I received a letter informing me that I had retired from the magazine.

I'd been on the staff for twenty-eight years, but I wasn't hurt or angry. Actually, I was relieved. *The New Yorker* had become just another magazine.

Mr. Shawn died suddenly on December 8, 1992, in his apartment at Fifth Avenue and 96th Street. He was 85. There had been no auguries of death, even at that age. His calendar contained appointments for the weeks ahead, and there were unread manuscripts on his night table.

There was a long and appreciative obituary in *The New Yorker,* noting that he had been editor of the magazine from 1952 to 1987. The tribute did not mention that he had—to his astonishment and pain—been fired from that very magazine by Samuel Newhouse. That fact—and Mr. Shawn lived on facts—is likely to be part of an eventual obituary of Mr. Newhouse.

I have one footnote about Mr. Shawn and me. I have not written about it previously because of my regard for him, but I've felt guilty at not citing what I feel was a wholly unexpected departure by him from the letter and spirit of a free press.

The one piece of mine he did not print on political grounds was a profile of A. J. Muste, the often-jailed pacifist who was a key behind-the-scenes strategist in the anti–Vietnam War and civil rights campaigns. Martin Luther King once told me that "unequivocally the emphasis on nonviolent direct action in race relations is due more to A. J. Muste than to anyone else in the country."

Mine was to have been the first profile of Muste in a general-circulation magazine. I had taken more than a year to interview many of his colleagues and detractors—along with many sessions with Muste. He was a brilliantly logical intellectual; Paul Goodman called him "the most astute political analyst in America and an Authentic Great Man." Because of the quality of his mind, his creative use of nonviolence, and his skill as an organizer, I thought it made sense for *The New Yorker* to introduce Muste to readers whose lives he was affecting—even though they didn't know it.

Mr. Shawn told me the profile had worked out very well, but he had decided not to run it. This was in 1961, still early in the antiwar movement, and Shawn explained that he didn't want to take the chance that the authority of a *New Yorker* profile might give Muste accelerated legitimacy and undermine the government's credibility in this complex war.

I was astonished, and still am, that Shawn would yield the integrity of *The New Yorker* to a speculative fear of the harm that might be done to the American government by my article on a true believer in nonviolence.

MY FRIENDSHIP WITH

THE GENGHIS KHAN

OF THE CATHOLIC CHURCH

O f all the profiles I wrote for *The New Yorker*, the one I never would have imagined possible—as I was growing up in Boston—was that of a cardinal of the Catholic Church.

Much of my experience back then with Catholics, lay and clerical, was grim. Jewish boys, myself included, were beaten up from time to time by bristling Irish youths, inflamed every Sunday—on the radio—by a priest, the mellifluous Father Charles E. Coughlin of the Shrine of the Little Flower in Royal Oak, Michigan.

With his musical brogue (though he was not born in Ireland), Coughlin regarded Jews with much the same abiding affection displayed years later by Minister Louis Farrakhan of the Nation of Islam. Coughlin insisted that we Jews were both the leaders and foot soldiers of international Communism and, simultaneously, the insatiably greedy international bankers snatching the mite of countless hapless widows.

So far as I knew, there was no record of any Boston priest or bishop publicly condemning, or at least criticizing, Father Coughlin—or the deep-seated anti-Semitism among many of the local faithful. As for William O'Connell, the cardinal of

Boston at the time, he was said to consider the firebrand from Royal Oak, Michigan, to be rather vulgar and certainly beneath a man of O'Connell's cultivated tastes in art and cruise ships. But the cardinal remained silent concerning Father Coughlin.

With two exceptions, I had nothing to do with Boston priests. What would I say to these men, all in black, their lives and their vocations founded on a faith, embodied in a crucified Jew, that was wholly alien to me?

One of the exceptions was a jazz priest, Norman O'Connor, often present at jazz clubs and festivals, and at panel discussions, some of which included me. He had a subtle but savage sense of humor that I had not expected in a priest. Though not very likable, he was fun to argue with. We never spoke about his religion or my atheism.

There was another priest, also interested in jazz, who eventually left the Church because he had many more theological questions than the Church had satisfying answers.

While he was still in black, and while I was still living at home, I invited that jazz priest to dinner, much to my mother's panic. She had never spoken to a priest, had never wanted to, had been afraid to, both in the Old Country and here. She distilled her fears and her feeling that I had betrayed her by asking me, "What do those people eat?"

In New York, I did get to know some Catholics, particularly after becoming a heretic on the left by declaring myself a pro-lifer. I gravitated mostly to the left wing of the pro-lifers— people, including some Catholics, who had been active in the antiwar, civil rights, and anti-death-penalty movements. I heard of some pacifist Catholic bishops who shared this "seamless garment" pro-life approach across the board, but I didn't know any of them.

In 1984 there came to New York a Catholic archbishop

whose views on abortion created a firestorm of anger and hatred. "I am regarded," John Cardinal O'Connor said to me
later, "as the Genghis Khan of the Church."

O'Connor, in a television interview before he actually took
office in New York, had compared "the killing of four thousand babies a day in the United States, unborn babies, to the
Holocaust." He went on to say that "Hitler tried to solve what
he called the Jewish question. So kill them, shove them into
ovens, burn them. Well, we claim that unborn babies are a
problem, so kill them. To me, it is really precisely the same."

O'Connor, I was told by liberal Catholics, took a very hard
line not only on abortion but on the need to build up atomic
weapons and on other issues dear to Ronald Reagan and his
acolytes. I decided to find out if this Genghis Khan would
be worth a *New Yorker* profile. William Shawn said I could
go ahead.

Waiting for the cardinal at the Catholic Center on First
Avenue in Manhattan, I heard a loud, angry voice in the cor-
ridor. "Over my dead body," the man was yelling, "will anyone be fired because he belongs to a union and is exercising
the right of collective bargaining."

The voice was that of the Archbishop of New York.
(O'Connor was not named a cardinal by Pope John Paul II until later.) A strike was under way against thirty-one New York
hospitals and nursing homes, including diocesan hospitals.
The bargaining agent for all the hospitals—the League of Voluntary Hospitals and Homes—had instructed its member organizations to tell the unionized strikers they would be
permanently displaced if they did not come back to work.

O'Connor stood by the men and women who had hit the
bricks; he would not displace them with scabs. His father was
an ardent union member, and the cardinal remains true to his
father's faiths, secular and religious. As I got to know O'Connor, there were other surprises. He has testified in Congress

against funding for MX missiles, urging instead that Congress address "the fact of hunger in our midst, the homeless who walk our streets, the lack of access to adequate health care, even for middle-class households." He also urged then-President Ronald Reagan not to visit the cemetery at Bitburg, with its graves of SS soldiers.

And at Christmas in 1986, at St. Patrick's Cathedral, he told the faithful, "There's no point in simply talking to people about filling their souls if you don't fill their bellies."

Some Genghis Khan!

I watched him being attacked one night at a private dinner in a university club in New York to which he had been invited by a number of prominent conservative intellectuals, including William Buckley and Irving Kristol. A first draft of the American Catholic bishops' pastoral letter on the economy had been released, and O'Connor's hosts were incensed at the pastoral letter's decidedly liberal tone. Why, they asked the cardinal, did the Church have any business issuing pronunciamentos on the minimum wage, economic justice for the poor, and such other socialist heresies?

Not at all defensive, the cardinal looked at his interrogators and told them, "The Church is concerned with the life of the individual. About nine hundred thousand individuals in New York City live in substandard conditions, including overcrowding, with all the attendant evils of that kind of life. And bishops all over the country are seeing more of this. That's why we bishops are concerned with the economy.

"The question I go to bed with—and wake up with in the morning—is 'Am I failing the people in the parishes? Am I fulfilling my religious and moral responsibilities?' I would be failing if all I did was to say Mass and carry out the religious duties of my office."

The faces around the table were closed. It was as if Genghis Khan had turned into Eugene Debs. Across the table, I said to

the cardinal, "I expect you now have a somewhat greater appreciation of the value of some of the thinking on the left than
you did before you came into this club of the privileged
tonight."

The cardinal laughed, a long laugh.

During the war in Vietnam, O'Connor had been awarded a
Legion of Merit decoration for "outstanding performance of
duty" there. He wrote a book, *A Chaplain Looks at Vietnam*
(World Publishing Company, 1968), passionately defending
American conduct of the war, sounding as if he were a
spokesman for Lyndon Johnson and Dean Rusk. As in this
passage:

> We are not deliberately or systematically using unlawful
> means. We are simply not guilty of the charges of wanton-
> ness and wholesale destruction, of napalming the innocent
> and of indiscriminate bombing, of . . . torture, alienation of
> the people, corruption, inhumanity.

Yet, years before Robert McNamara confessed lethal error,
O'Connor wrote in 1986:

> Even if it was justified for the United States to enter the
> war, as I suggested in a very poor book that I wrote on the
> subject and would like to rewrite today, or hide, it is quite
> conceivable—in accordance with Catholic Just War teach-
> ing—that our using more and more unjust means in that
> war resulted in our robbing ourselves of a justification of be-
> ing in the war at all.

Still, when he was supporting the war, O'Connor characteristically gave his all. In recommending that he receive the
Legion of Merit, Lewis Walt, then commanding general of the
Third Marine Division, wrote, "It is my opinion that no single
individual in this command contributed more to the morale of

the individual marine here in Vietnam than Father O'Connor, who spent the majority of his time in the field with the men."

There are times, however, when the cardinal is not so firm of belief and purpose. In private, for one example, he is not as ringingly clear on whether women can become priests as he is in public statements.

I took advantage of him late one afternoon when he had a bad cold and was very tired. Since early morning, he had been scheduled without a stop, and he was soon going to leave for a lecture on Thomas Merton at Columbia University.

Instead of being a compassionate reporter and giving him time to take a nap, I continued the interview because it seemed to me that this was the time to press him on an issue that was—and is—severely dividing the Church. Will women ever be able to become priests?

"It's a very, very difficult question," the cardinal said. "Very difficult. And it keeps coming up. I meet regularly with the women religious [nuns and other women who have taken vows], and some of them feel very strongly about this." He started coughing, and a priest in the small room used for interviews at the Catholic Center, suggested that he end the interview and rest for a while.

The cardinal waved the priest aside. Looking past me, he was fingering the cross he was wearing. He sighed, "Could Christ have appeared on earth as a woman? I don't know why he couldn't have. Could he return as a woman?"

Twilight had come, and O'Connor's voice was hoarse and low. "Christ always referred to his *Father*." O'Connor seemed to be talking more to himself than to me. "And Christ always spoke of himself as the Son. Why would he have done that if there was any possibility that He could have been a woman and that God could have been either his Father or his Mother? This is where you run into a theological problem. You can't just wave a magic wand and say it wasn't so."

The other priests were looking at me balefully. Why did I not have the decency to stop and let the cardinal rest? But I couldn't. It was fascinating to hear the cardinal trying to work his way out of—or into—a statement he might not want to make.

I saw an opening. Since the Church does change, I said, is it entirely inconceivable that a future Pope might decide that, since women have been barred from the priesthood on traditional grounds, it would be possible to ordain women on grounds more deeply involved in the faith?

There was a long pause. The priests leaned forward. Now they were not interested in stopping the interview. "How can I answer that and be quite honest?" the cardinal asked, aloud, of himself. "This Pope will never change this decision. But a future Pope could do something totally unexpected. However, would such a change, whatever it is, be accepted by the Church? Might the Pope even be deposed?"

The cardinal looked at me and said very softly, "The Pope is bound in certain areas by divinely revealed teachings. That is, doctrines concerning faith and morals which have been defined by the Popes in the past with the divine assistance of the Holy Spirit. Such teachings cannot be changed, because they are always true. They are infallible teachings. No successor Pope can do anything about them. He can't, for instance, decide there are four persons in the Trinity.

"But," the cardinal continued, frowning, "with regard to the theological tradition, is the Pope bound by that tradition in the same way as he is by infallible, divinely revealed teaching? By definition, he is not so bound. So, could he pronounce differently if he was convinced that his new position was theologically sound?"

There was silence in the room. Intense silence.

The cardinal nodded to himself. "I guess he could. A Pope could yield to political pressures. Popes have done so in the past. I'd have to say yes." He looked at his hands, and as he often does when he is confronted with a problem he can't avoid, he pressed his fingertips together. Slowly and carefully, he said, "What are we really talking about? To my knowledge it has never been infallibly declared that women *cannot* be ordained to the priesthood. There has never been a formal, ex-cathedra pronouncement by a Pope that it is infallible teaching that only men can be priests."

I was determined to get this said as clearly as possible. "So," I asked, "is it conceivable that sometime in the future, women may be ordained as priests?"

The cardinal nodded, cleared his throat, summoned some strength, and said, "Yes, it is conceivable. But, I remind you, it will not happen in the lifetime of this Pope." The other priests in the room seemed relieved.

My contacts with the cardinal were not limited to interviews for *The New Yorker*. He has invited my wife and me for drinks in his living quarters. Quite generous drinks. I wonder on those occasions what my mother—to whom the Church was so mysterious and therefore dangerous—would have thought. Her son, whose tooth was knocked out by a brawny Catholic boy avenging the crucifixion of Christ, sitting in a room where the host was wearing a large crucifix. Could her son safely escape that place? Or would he be subjected to a blood libel and thrown in the dungeon that must surely be beneath the floorboards?

The cardinal, as always, bid us a cheerful good night.

He and I have had only one serious disagreement. He was so angry at me that I thought I would never be invited back for more of those generous drinks.

Boston in the early 1940s was the most anti-Semitic city in the country. I remember all too clearly the silence of the men in black, wearing large crucifixes. The newsreels of Nazi street games—with Jews thrown into the gutter—moved off the screen and into our own streets. Gangs of feral Catholic youth came roaring regularly into our ghetto, smashing heads and windows—and, one evening, throwing an old, bony Jew into the gutter.

We were not surprised. We knew what these invaders were being taught, and not only by Father Charles E. Coughlin in his Sunday network radio broadcasts. At this time, before Vatican II, there was a prayer in the liturgy of Holy Week that called for the condemnation of "the perfidious Jew." And in the section of the Good Friday liturgy that was called The Reproaches, we Jews were in the spotlight again, condemned by God "for what you have done to my Son."

But it was the silence that was most frightening after each of those small but terrifying pogroms in Boston. As Anthony Lukas wrote in *Common Ground* (Knopf), "When bands of Irish youths ranged Blue Hill Avenue (they called it 'Jew Hill Avenue'), harassing and beating Jews, the Cardinal [William O'Connell] was conspicuously silent."

But then a voice *was* heard. Frances Sweeney, a young, red-haired editor of a muckraking paper and a fiercely devout Catholic, attacked the silence of the cardinal and the priests. She would not let up, and she stirred other members of the Catholic laity to join her. The cardinal was furious at Sweeney. He thought about throwing her out of the Church, but he was advised that he might thereby create a martyr.

I worked for Fran on her paper. She taught me the pleasures of being out of step. And she showed me what it took to stand your ground.

All these years later, I was listening for a resounding American Catholic voice of protest in 1987, as news came that Pope John Paul II had become the first—the very first—head of state to receive the Pariah of Vienna, Kurt Waldheim, who had been trying so hard to erase his past. This Nazi *Oberleutnant* of Hitler's Wehrmacht, this intelligence aide to Wehrmacht General Alexander Lohr (executed as a war criminal)—this accomplice in war crimes—had been charged with involvement in the shipping of Yugoslav and Greek Jews to be consumed in the Holocaust.

Moreover, Neal Sher—who, as a director of the Justice Department's Office of Special Investigations, investigated Waldheim—reported in *Washington Jewish Week* (June 27, 1996):

"Waldheim participated in transfer of civilian prisoners to the SS for exploitation as slave labor . . . and he was involved in reprisal executions of hostages and other civilians. . . . A war crimes file recommended that Waldheim be put on trial for murder and other serious crimes."

Making my own protest, I wrote in the *Voice*:

In Europe, there were a few Catholic voices of protest against the Pope's welcoming of Waldheim without a single reference to his murderous past. Indeed, John Paul II, looking warmly at this remnant of the Third Reich, had actually praised Waldheim as a man "dedicated to achieving among people" and had asked him to lead Austria "in the defense of human rights." Austria, so long known for its anti-Semitism.

The spectacle of the Pope and the Nazi in consonance was too much for Albert Cardinal Decoutray of Lyons, where the trial of Klaus Barbie was held. The Cardinal, who was in charge of Jewish-Catholic affairs in France, said that "the meeting shows a complete misperception of Jewish sensibility. . . . I am still trying to understand the reasons for this visit, but I must say that I have not understood."

Jean-Marie Cardinal Lustiger of Paris, who was born Jewish, and a number of other French bishops, who were not born Jewish, signed a letter of accusation, noting that "Pope John Paul II, with his action [to receive Waldheim], has forgotten that the rationality of politics must never supersede moral obligations."

And Uli Schmetzer, in the June 28 *Chicago Tribune*, quoted the Reverend Ivan Florianc, a Yugoslav priest, who was among those in St. Peter's Square protesting the Waldheim visit: "In Argentina and in Chile, the Pope gave communion to generals and dictators, but he would not receive the mothers of the *desaparecidos* [the disappeared victims]. For me and many priests, these are gestures that cannot be reconciled with the spiritual and moral role of a Pope."

In New York, John Cardinal O'Connor was not silent, but his words were meaningless. To Jews anyway.

As when the cardinal said to Gabe Pressman on the local NBC affiliate on June 28:

". . . I am so convinced of the integrity of this Pope, his concern for human rights, that I truly believe that he determined to do this for motives that he believes to be highly meritorious, *and my suspicion would certainly be that in the private session with Mr. Waldheim he had some pretty stern things to say.*" (Emphasis added.)

"Whatever the Pope said privately in this meeting with the *Oberleutnant* was of no use at all so long as the words remain private. And anyway, there is nothing whatever to indicate that Waldheim was even mildly chastised in that private session. When he had returned from the Vatican—when the visit of state was all over—the *Oberleutnant* was asked if he had been disturbed by the protesters with their shouts and signs:

"I did not hear them," said Waldheim. "I did not see them. I only saw smiling faces and people waving to me on the way to the Vatican." The pariah of Vienna, redeemed by the Pope, had a great day!

Meanwhile, O'Connor had spoken of what could be a dangerous backlash that was building—Catholics angry at Jews for criticizing their Pope who had received Kurt Waldheim. . . . "I don't want to exaggerate," said O'Connor, "but the backlash could be disastrous."

A few days after I wrote of my acute displeasure at the Pope's meeting with the former Oberleutnant—and the memories O'Connor brought back of the silence of the Church concerning anti-Semitism in Boston when I was a boy—I received a letter from Cardinal O'Connor. The language was so unrestrained, to use a euphemism, that I figured he had written it in the small hours of the morning. He is an insomniac. There was no indication at the bottom of the letter that anybody but the cardinal had typed it. At the top, on the left-hand corner, was the credo of his office: "There Can Be No Love Without Justice."

> Dear Nat,
> Your *Village Voice* article disappointed me, not because of your criticism of the Waldheim-Pope episode, which was arguably criticizable, or your judging my remarks meaningless (although I would obviously prefer flagellation to being considered meaningless). Your article disappointed me because you cheapened it by including a shotgun attack on the Church. . . . beating the Pope over the head and shoulders for every conceivable offense (at least you didn't berate him for being Polish), and generally clouding your thesis with a squid-like venom quite uncharacteristic of your normal writing.
> By way of your own account, I was aware of and sincerely pained by what you suffered at the hands of Catholics as the Boston Boy. In that account your sufferings were no less real and moved me to no less sadness because you chose to recount them in and with good humor. Whatever the demerits of the Waldheim-Pope affair, your relating it to your childhood came through to me as more vendetta than pain. Again uncharacteristic of your writing.
> It seems to me that you had more than enough to fill a hundred articles if you had confined yourself to the meeting. I would have found your analysis interesting and important—even "meaningful." Your focused anger would have had much greater impact. Wild swings too often hit

the wrong people. As one who has come to know, and admittedly love, Pope John Paul II, I categorically deny that he deserves the black eyes being given him by a number of dissidents who don't know him, and certainly black eyes administered for a variety of other reasons that are not germane, in my judgment, to the Waldheim affair. The whole thing came through as a "Hey, here's a great chance to slam the Pope for any reason anybody can think of. Let's exploit it."

If you want to talk about the Waldheim affair off the record and why I said what I said (after carefully checking it out with some generally responsible Jews, who encouraged it), I'll be happy to. You will learn, too, of things I have attempted to do, and am still attempting, for everyone's good, as I see it.

You are a good man, a good friend, a good writer, and quite possibly a better Jew than you may have realized. I believe you missed a useful opportunity, and for that I'm sorry.

    With deepest sincerity and respect, I remain

        Faithfully,

        John Cardinal O'Connor [signature]

        Archbishop of New York

As angry as the cardinal had become, I was angrier. I had just begun to write a column for the *Voice* that would fully, fairly, and nastily focus that anger on O'Connor when another letter from him came. It was short: "Now that I have won that argument, let us proceed. You may recall how Belloc ends his *Path to Rome*: "So let us love one another and laugh. Time passes and we shall soon laugh no longer. Meanwhile, earnest men are at siege upon us all around. So let us laugh and suffer absurdities, for that is only to suffer one another.""

I couldn't help laughing at the boldness of his strategy of reconciliation, and I didn't write a column answering his first letter. Later the cardinal did give me, off the record, some information about "the Waldheim affair." It did not exculpate the Pope at all.

The most pertinent comment on the dismal affair came in a full-page ad taken out by the American Jewish Congress on June 26, 1987. It was an open letter to John Paul II, and said that Waldheim "has become the symbol not only of an evil Nazi past, but of current efforts to diminish, falsify, and forget the Holocaust." Accordingly, with regard to the Pope's reception of Waldheim, "how is one to explain so profound an insensitivity to the meaning of the Holocaust, so painful a failure of the moral imagination, by the custodian of the Catholic conscience?"

In another area of the Catholic moral imagination, O'Connor did much better than in the Waldheim affair.

In September 1987 the cardinal agreed to meet at the New York Catholic Center, on First Avenue, with a delegation from the Coalition for Lesbian and Gay Rights. When they came into the building, "the guard at the desk to their left, who knew who they were, said, 'This way, ladies—or whatever,' " according to an account in the *National Catholic Reporter*. "As they went up in the elevator, another person who also obviously knew who they were whispered, 'Good luck.' " At the meeting, no minds were changed concerning the Church's position on homosexuality.

Two weeks later, Karen Doherty, one of the participants and a member of the Conference for Catholic Lesbians, wrote a letter to the archbishop that said, in part,

We were glad for the opportunity to speak to you in person. It was very important for us that you see us as we are, very ordinary, everyday people. You impressed me as being a very straightforward, sensitive, and capable man. What I particularly appreciated was the fact that I did not feel talked down to or held at a distance because I am a lesbian woman.

I am saddened, as I know the others are, that we cannot today reach a meeting of our hearts and minds on the issue of homosexuality. Perhaps some day.

I wish you health and happiness in your future years with us in New York. I wanted you to know that, while we strongly disagree, I have a great deal of personal respect for you and the fact that you are willing to stand up for what you believe.

Three weeks later the archbishop answered:

Dear Karen:

Your letter . . . was extraordinarily kind and touched me deeply. I am indeed grateful. It is my sincere hope and prayer that through the years ahead I will be able to serve you in some way that you will consider helpful. My convictions about church teachings are very deep. I do not anticipate a change in such teachings, and neither do I see it precluding our loving one another as sisters and brothers in Christ.

Please believe that I will give deeply sincere consideration to any recommendations that can help us in that regard in accordance with the tenets of the church which I am certain we both love.

You and your associates are very much in my masses and my prayers, and I ask that you keep me in yours as well.

Faithfully in Christ,
John J. O'Connor

Some months later I called Karen Doherty to ask if she had any further reactions to the visit with the cardinal.

A businesswoman, she had just come back from a trip out of the country. She was amiable and forthright. "No, I haven't changed my mind about the cardinal," she said. "I strongly disagree with a number of his positions, but I respect him. I'll tell you something I didn't put in the letter to him. O'Connor's predecessor, Cardinal Cooke, would never meet with us. He preferred to ignore the whole issue. But one of his secretaries did meet with us, and he did not have the decency to shake our hands. But O'Connor, at the very beginning of our meeting, made a point of shaking everybody's hand."

She went on to say, "That letter of mine shocked a lot of my gay and lesbian friends, and some of the nuns and priests who support us. The tendency is to say, 'If you're with us you're good, but if you're not, you're bad.' But I couldn't have said anything different from what I said in that letter. It would have been a lie. He is a very human person, and he had a lot of integrity. I got the impression that if he was alone in an opinion, he'd go to the mat holding that opinion. That's why he's a tremendous adversary.

"He didn't have to answer my letter. He could have ignored it the way Cooke would have. It was a risk to write to me, to treat a woman who had identified herself as a lesbian the way you'd treat a human being. I'll always remember that when I first saw him coming into the room he looked grim. He'd never met with a group like ours before.

"I looked at him, and I cracked a smile. He smiled right back. I said to myself, 'Well, there's a little hope.' There are bishops toward whom I feel more warmly, or who might feel more warmly toward me than he does, but I don't see any of them with that quality of leadership. He's like a warrior bishop."

Quite another view of the "warrior bishop" came from Gloria Steinem. On being asked by *New York* magazine to list the worst things about New York, she cited AIDS and John Cardinal O'Connor.

Not sharing her appraisal of the cardinal, I continued to see him off and on. Once, at the Catholic Center, we, along with a number of other people, were watching Dr. Bernard Nathanson's film, *The Silent Scream,* purportedly the first documentary of an actual abortion during which the terminal terror of the fetus could be seen.

The narrative by Dr. Nathanson was clear and vivid, but what was shown on the screen resembled a deep fog. After a while I whispered to the cardinal, "I don't see anything he's describing."

"Neither do I," said John Cardinal O'Connor, who has trouble censoring himself.

Some months later, I was to introduce the cardinal at a pro-life event in Toronto, but first I had to give a talk on my heretical reasons for being in that company—reasons explored in the next chapter of this book.

Toward the end of the talk, I made what seemed to me an entirely logical point. A particularly effective way to reduce the number of abortions, I said, is to encourage and finance much more research on safe, effective means of contraception. Obviously, unplanned pregnancies lead to an abundance of abortions.

Before I finished that theme, several large male pro-lifers barreled their way to the microphone, and seized it. They loudly informed the audience that any form of contraception defied the will of God and the Catholic Church.

I noted amiably that, as an atheist, I had no ties to either.

At this point Cardinal O'Connor moved toward me from the back of the room. After I had introduced him, he said, smiling, "I am delighted that Nat is not a member of the Catholic Church. We have enough trouble as it is."

EUPHEMISM KILLS

Although an official of Minister Farrakhan's Nation of Islam has identified me as the Antichrist, my own self-description, if I had a business card, would indeed be, as Cardinal O'Connor suggested, "Troublemaker."

I've involved myself in many controversies through the years, but by far the most fiercely controversial position I have ever been identified with was my decision to be pro-life. It was a decision that surprised me at the time. Until then, in the early 1980s, it had never occurred to me that there was a rational secular position in opposing abortion. What little I knew personally of pro-lifers indicated they were all committed Christians. And I am an atheist.

In any case, having spent my first twenty-eight years in Boston, I had known during that period only one pro-lifer. She was the wife of a jazz bass player, and she was Catholic. I liked her a lot—she was one of the most honest people I've ever known—but I ascribed her views on abortion solely to her having been brought up Catholic. All my other friends—students, musicians, journalists, labor organizers, professors—were unconditionally pro-abortion.

In Massachusetts, in those days, there was an extra edge—

an extra libertarian impetus—to being for abortion rights. The Catholic Church was so powerful in the legislature that just about any proposed bill of which the Cardinal disapproved never made it to a vote. And above all else, the Cardinal—William O'Connell—would not countenance any measure that might in any way lead to a softening of the criminal prohibitions against abortion.

The father of that jazz bass player had, some years before, been shown by the Commonwealth of Massachusetts how harsh these criminal penalties were. He was an eminent physician in a suburb of Boston who decided, when he was in his fifties, that he could no longer bear the suffering of women who desperately wanted an abortion and had no way to get one. (There was a legendary doctor in rural Pennsylvania who performed abortions for a small fee, but he was getting old and couldn't accommodate all who wanted his services.)

So this physician in Massachusetts started to perform abortions—at no fee. It was a matter of conscience, he said, and there should be no price tag on that. Somehow the police found him out, and he was sentenced to prison for ten years and stripped of his right to practice medicine.

That story stayed with me. From the time I came to New York in 1953, I did not stray from the pro-choice creed. I was on the board of the New York Civil Liberties Union when it was a key factor in the successful struggle to make abortion legal in New York State—before the Supreme Court's 1973 *Roe v. Wade* decision. My wife, Margot, is, and was then, a ferocious defender of a woman's right to end a pregnancy, and has utter disdain for all pro-lifers, including, intermittently, me.

It was in 1983 that I entered on the path of pariahdom among most of my friends and colleagues. An infant, initially known as Baby Jane Doe, had been born on Long Island with spina bifida. This is a lesion in the spinal column, and if it is not repaired quickly through surgery, there is danger of infection that can lead to permanent brain damage. Usually there is an accumulation of spinal fluid in the skull. As soon as possible, a shunt should be inserted to drain the fluid. Otherwise the pressure on the brain often leads to mental retardation.

The parents of Baby Jane Doe decided, however, that she would not have the operation, nor would a shunt be inserted. She was to get only "conservative treatment"—antibiotics, for instance—until she died.

All the press—print and broadcast, including the CBS newsmagazine *60 Minutes*—vigorously supported the parents. They listened to the parents' lawyer and printed the alleged facts—without checking—that the infant would, in any case, not live long, would be in intractable pain for all of her brief life, and would never recognize her parents. It was an act of compassion to let the child slip into eternity.

When the press—print and broadcast—are unanimous on anything, I get suspicious. Nothing is that simple. I found the names of the three leading pediatric neurosurgeons in this country, and called them. They were aware of the infant's condition, and the particular location of the lesion in her spine. Each of them told me that if an operation was performed very soon to close the lesion in the spine, and if a shunt was inserted in the skull, the child would—at worst—have to walk with braces as she grew up. She would *not* be retarded; she would *not* be in intractable pain; and she certainly would recognize her parents.

So I began writing—some eight columns—in opposition to the parents, their lawyer, and the press. Just about everybody in the newsroom at the *Voice* thought I was balmy. This was a damaged kid who would die soon. Why waste all this space on her? Besides, it was pro-lifers who were supporting her right to aggressive treatment. Be careful about the company you keep, I was warned.

On the other hand, I was becoming uncomfortable with the company I *had* been keeping for years. I heard Janet Benshoof, then head of the Reproductive Freedom Rights unit of the ACLU, say in a lecture that this case was really an extension of reproductive freedom rights—a woman's right to choose. The mother of Baby Jane Doe had every right to make any decision she wanted about the infant's condition. By that analysis, Baby Jane Doe, though born, had no rights of her own. She was her mother's property.

The American Civil Liberties Union officially insisted that there be no interference by any governmental body in the future of Baby Jane Doe. The mother's privacy rights were at stake.

But this was not a fetus. This was a born child. And, as Harry Blackmun emphasized in *Roe v. Wade*, once you're born, you're a person under the Constitution. And that means, I wrote, that before you're killed, you have the right to due process—independent of your mother's wishes—and you have the right to equal protection of the laws.

My comrades at the ACLU thought I had taken a strange turn. Janet Benshoof told a friend that I must have become a born-again Christian. Yet I was still a Jewish atheist. To my initial surprise, people I knew—liberals and civil libertarians—including reporters, editors, and staffers in Congress, couldn't understand where I was coming from. Many of them insisted the life of Baby Jane Doe was subordinate to the priorities of the mother. To keep this damaged kid could cost a lot of money and emotional distress. It would be understandable if she was to be sent back. Not killed. Just allowed to die.

Years later it was eventually revealed that Baby Jane Doe's real first name was Keri-Lynn. (Her last name has not been disclosed.) She was not in pain; she laughed and played with her parents (whom she recognized) and other children. But she couldn't walk. She attended special classes; her intelligence was considered below low-normal but she was educable—as reported in *New York Newsday* by Kathleen Kerr.

Appalled that Baby Jane had been given no rights of her own by her "protectors," I began to recognize the zealotry of the abortion-rights movement. And I also began to question their "evidence" that the unborn were not entitled to any rights. I began to read the medical textbooks that physicians in prenatal care read—not pro-life books, but such standard texts as *The Unborn Patient: Prenatal Diagnosis and Treatment* by Harrison, Golbus, and Filly, published by W. B. Saunders Company, a division of Harcourt Brace Jovanovich.

God is nowhere mentioned in the book. Its first chapter begins, "The concept that the fetus is a patient, an *individual* whose maladies are a proper subject for medical treatment as well as scientific observation, is alarmingly modern. . . . Only now are we beginning to consider the fetus seriously— medically, legally, and ethically."

And I read about the growing sophistication of fetal surgery—operations on the fetus that remedy various defects. But the same fetus, the next day, can legally be killed by abortion.

I spoke to a number of physicians who do research in prenatal development, and they emphasized that human life is a *continuum* from fertilization to birth to death. Setting up divisions of this process to justify abortion, for example, is artificial. It is the life of a *developing* being that is being killed. The euphemisms for an aborted fetus—"the product of conception" and "a clump of cells"—are what George Orwell might have called newspeak.

What particularly helped clarify the abortion question for

me was a statement in the *Journal of the American Medical Association* (February 18, 1990) by a North Carolina physician, Dr. Joel Hylton:

> Who can deny that the fetus is alive and is a separate genetic entity? Its humanity also cannot be questioned scientifically. It is certainly of no other species.
>
> That it is dependent on another makes it qualitatively no different from countless other humans outside the womb.
>
> It strikes me that to argue one may take an innocent life to preserve the quality of life of another is cold and carries utilitarianism to an obscene extreme. Nowhere else in our society is this permitted or even thinkable—although abortion sets a frightening prospect.

As time went on, I began to understand that there is much more to abortion than abortion itself. The mindset—the ability to regard as just and necessary the killing of at least 1.3 million developing human beings a year—helps strengthen the consistent ethic of death in the nation—including the discounting of the Baby Jane Does and the rise of support for "assisted suicide."

My sense of myself as a liberal, already weakened by my encounter with Adlai Stevenson and my subsequent "protection" of Stokely Carmichael, changed even more during my involvement in trying to give handicapped infants—born infants—due process so that their parents could not summarily end their lives.

In 1984 a coalition of disability-rights groups and some prolifers began to lobby Congress to pass a bill to extend the Child Abuse and Treatment Act. One section would broaden the definition of child abuse to include the denial of medically indicated treatment, hydration, and nutrition to infants born with life-threatening conditions. Furthermore, each state, to keep getting funds for child-abuse programs, would have to put in place a reporting system that would be alerted whenever a handicapped infant was being abused by denial of treatment or food. There were documented cases around the country of that terminal form of child abuse. The *Archives of Internal Medicine*, for instance, reported that some five hundred Down syndrome infants a year were "allowed to die" by physicians.

I covered the development of that bill as a *Washington Post* columnist. It finally passed with language that was not as strong as it ought to have been; but historically, that section of the bill was potentially a vital beginning in making it more difficult for physicians to end the life of an infant and then put on the death certificate a false report of the cause of death. In the years since, however, as *Pediatrics* magazine (January 1997) reports, many physicians have figured out ways to evade this child-protection law.

During the debate in Congress, I was most impressed with a comment by Illinois Congressman Henry Hyde, a pro-life advocate much scorned by liberals. "I suggest," he said, "that a question of life or death for a born person ought to belong to nobody, whether they are parents or not.

"The Constitution ought to protect that child. . . . Because they are handicapped, they are not to be treated differently than if they were women or Hispanics or American Indians or blacks. Their handicap may be a mental condition or a physical condition; but by God, they are human, and nobody has the right to kill them by passive starvation or anything else."

And what of the passionate *liberals* in the House—the champions of the powerless? There was a parade on the floor of ardent pro-choicers who voted against the proposed law protecting Baby Does. Among them were John Conyers, Geraldine Ferraro, Ron Dellums, Don Edwards, Robert Kastenmeier, Gerry Studds, George Crockett, David Obey, Pat Schroeder, Tom Downey, Henry Waxman, Barney Frank, Charles Rangel, Edward Markey, and the then longtime chairman of the Judiciary Committee, a very effective liberal, Peter Rodino.

In a passionate speech on the floor, Geraldine Ferraro spoke for her pro-choice liberal colleagues in focusing on the parents' right to privacy to make life-and-death decisions for handicapped newborns—who, obviously, had no voice in the matter.

Increasingly, I realized again that there was more to abortion than abortion. The privacy right to kill established in *Roe v. Wade* was spreading across the land.

During the 1980s I tracked nearly every final court decision on euthanasia in the individual states—withdrawing feeding tubes or respirators—and they all cited *Roe v. Wade* as a key precedent for terminating life. The privacy right to end the life of the fetus was legally extended to a surrogate to end the life of a husband, wife, or children who were incompetent—or appeared to be.

At a conference on euthanasia at Clark College in Worcester, Massachusetts, I met Derek Humphry, the angel of death of our time. (Jack Kevorkian is only the field commander.) Humphry, the founder of the Hemlock Society, is originally from England, and he told me that for some years in this country he had great difficulty getting his message across about the many-splendored doors of death: self-administered suicide, physician-assisted suicide, euthanasia.

"But then," Humphry said, "a wonderful thing happened. It opened all the doors for me."

"What was that wonderful thing?" I asked him.

"Roe v. Wade," Derek Humphry answered.

Providing Derek Humphry with more pride and pleasure, Barbara Rothstein, chief judge of the federal district court in the state of Washington, became the first judge in the history of the nation to declare physician-assisted suicide constitutional. She likened the freedom of the terminally ill to end their lives to a woman's fundamental right to an abortion, and cited two abortion-rights decisions: *Roe v. Wade* and *Planned Parenthood v. Casey.*

Twenty or so years ago, there was a man who foresaw the effects of abortion as a constitutional right on the fundamental values of the nation:

"What happens to the mind of a person, and the moral fabric of a nation, that accepts the aborting of the life of a baby without a pang of conscience? What kind of a society will we have twenty years hence if life can be taken so casually?"

The same man said back then, "There are those who argue that the right to privacy is of a higher order than the right of life. That was the premise of slavery. You could not protest the existence or treatment of slaves on the plantation because that was private and therefore outside of your right to be concerned."

Also, he told of how he himself had almost been aborted. A doctor had told his mother to let him go, but she refused. "Don't let the pro-choicers convince you that a fetus isn't a human being," this survivor used to warn. "That's how the whites dehumanized us, by calling us niggers. The first step was to distort the image of us as human beings in order to justify that which they wanted to do—and not even feel they'd done anything wrong."

The pro-lifer I've been quoting is Jesse Jackson. He became pro-choice when he decided to run for President. He figured that was where more of the votes were. In 1994 I saw him on a train, and we talked for a while about habeas corpus and the death penalty. Finally I told him I'd been quoting the former pro-life Jesse Jackson because his writings on the subject were among the most compelling I knew.

He looked troubled, and I asked him if he had any second

thoughts on having reversed his views on abortion. He looked even more troubled, and said, "I'll get back to you on that." I haven't heard from him since.

On the other hand, not all pro-lifers have welcomed me into the fold or, in any case, have answered some of my questions as to their pro-life consistency. I've gotten to know the chairman of the House Judiciary Committee, Henry Hyde, who—unknown to most civil libertarians—is sometimes very strong on free speech issues. But he is also a supporter of capital punishment, and I asked him how he can be pro-life and also pro-death.

He told me he'd get back to me on that. There has been no subsequent word from him, either.

A more dramatic division between me and some pro-lifers became vivid during the Reagan years. I was invited to speak at the annual Right to Life convention in Columbus, Ohio. I would be the novelty of the year—a Jewish atheist civil libertarian. A pro-lifer beyond any category they had ever seen. I expected to be warmly welcomed. The welcome turned out to be very warm indeed.

The event was held in a large field outside of the city. A rickety platform faced the almost entirely Catholic Republican crowd. I told them that, as pro-lifers, they ought to practice a consistent ethic of life. They ought to actively oppose capital punishment, preparations for war, and the life-diminishing poverty associated with the policies of then President Ronald Reagan. I emphasized that he had just cut the budget for the WIC program (a federally funded supplemental food program for women, infants, and children).

Reagan and those who supported him—I said, rolling right along—gave credibility to Congressman Barney Frank's line, "Those who oppose abortion are pro-life only up to the moment of birth."

From the back of the large crowd, and then moving forward, there were growls, shouts, and table-pounding. They were not sounds of approval. At the end of my speech, a number of pro-lifers began rushing toward the platform. It was clear they didn't want my autograph. I said to the then-head of the National Right to Life Committee, Jack Wilkie, sitting next to me, "Jack, I hadn't quite made up my mind to give up my life for this cause." He smiled and moved his chair away from me.

It turned out that these souls on fire only wanted to tell me that I was in grievous error about Ronald Reagan, an exemplary Catholic President. I was in error, they made it clear, because I had not yet found God. Later, in the mail, I received several Bibles. It didn't work.

At the *Village Voice*, my pro-life heresy has not been warmly received. Three editors, all women, stopped speaking to me after my first pro-life piece there. In two of the cases I didn't feel much of a loss. The third woman became the editor-in-chief for a time, and we agreed there were other things we can talk about.

In speaking to pro-choicers on the left, I have told them about a friend of mine and her priorities of choice. Having been active in the antiwar and civil rights movements, Mary Meehan wrote an article for *The Progressive* in which she noted:

> Some of us who went through the antiwar struggles of the 1960s and 1970s are now active in the right-to-life movement. We do not enjoy opposing our old friends on the abortion issue, but we feel that we have no choice. . . . It is out of character for the left to neglect the weak and helpless. The traditional mark of the left has been its protection of the underdog, the weak, and the poor. The unborn child is the most helpless form of humanity, even more in need of protection than the poor tenant farmer or the mental patient. The basic instinct of the left is to aid those who

cannot aid themselves. And that instinct is absolutely sound. It's what keeps the human proposition going.

Agreeing with that instinct is Feminists for Life of America, my favorite advocacy group of any kind. Its founders, in the 1970s, also came out of the civil rights and antiwar movements. It keeps growing in numbers and impact, and its credo is, "We oppose all forms of violence, including abortion, euthanasia, and capital punishment, as they are inconsistent with the core feminist principles of justice, nonviolence, and nondiscrimination."

Its first president, Rachel McNair, was arrested at least seventeen times—for protesting against nuclear plants and weapons, and for passing out pro-life leaflets at abortion clinics, as well as for sitting in front of a clinic door.

Somehow, Rachel and her colleagues are not much mentioned in the press; they don't fit the stereotype of pro-lifers as looking like Jesse Helms and wanting to expand capital punishment to all those—in print, television, movies, and cyberspace—who traffic in indecency.

By contrast, the press usually treats most pro-choicers with gentle care. But largely omitted are the views of those pro-choicers who regard abortion as an essential purifier of the species. I've met a goodly number of them.

In New York, when abortion was legalized in 1971, a staff commentator on WCBS radio celebrated the breakthrough by saying that abortion "is one sensible method of dealing with such problems as overpopulation, illegitimacy, and possible birth defects. *It is one way of fighting the rising welfare rolls and the increasing number of child abuse cases.*" (Emphasis added.)

I've often heard this joyous analysis from some pro-choicers who prefer not to speak in this vein publicly, but are otherwise quite open about the extra dividends of abortions— a safer and more aesthetically pleasing society.

In 1992, Nicholas von Hoffman wrote in the *New York Observer*:

> Free, cheap abortion is a policy of social defense. To save ourselves from being murdered in our beds and raped on the streets, we should do everything possible to encourage pregnant women who don't want the baby—and will not care for it—to get rid of the thing before it turns into a monster. . . .
>
> At their demonstrations, the anti-abortionists parade around with the pictures of dead and dismembered fetuses. The pro-abortionists should meet these displays with some of their own: pictures of the victims of the unaborted—murder victims, rape victims, mutilation victims—pictures to remind us that the fight for abortion is but part of the larger struggle for safe homes and safe streets.

There's more to abortion than abortion.

Less like Robespierre than Nicholas von Hoffman is Brian Lehrer, who hosts an eminently civilized talk show on New York's WNYC, which is part of National Public Radio. He has said on the air that "We save a lot of money if we allow medical funding of abortions for women—a lot less [sic] kids will be on welfare."

What a blessing that will be for them.

On the other hand, picketing before the Clinton White House during the debate about health-care reform, a black woman held a placard reading, "Abortion Shouldn't Be Part of a Health Care Bill—Pregnancy Isn't a Disease."

This irreverence for abortion rights leads to a fear among many pro-choicers, hooked on euphemisms, that pro-lifers can have too much free speech. Near Syracuse, New York, in 1994, I saw a billboard high above the expressway that had been vandalized four times. The intensity of the perpetrators' desire to expunge its message was impressive as they found perilous ways to climb onto the billboard.

The defacers were abortion-rights activists scandalized by the effrontery of the Western New York Chapter of Feminists for Life in putting up this message: "Abortion has two victims—one dead, one wounded." A phone number was added, and it provided, as alternatives to abortion, access to agencies providing prenatal care, housing, free financial and medical assistance, parenting classes, and adoption counseling. Each time the billboard was attacked, the message and the phone number were torn out.

A student at a nearby college asked me, "Why are my pro-life posters always torn off the bulletin boards? The pro-choice posters never are. So what does 'pro-*choice*' mean?"

In *The American Feminist*, the national magazine of Feminists for Life, Barbara Newman has written: "If it is wrong to kill with guns, bombs, or poison, with the electric chair, or the noose, it is most tragically wrong to kill with the physician's tools."

But is abortion killing? Newman wrote: "Euphemism kills."

I told the student the reason her pro-life posters were always destroyed. "You make the pro-abortion people uncomfortable. You bring death into the conversation."

A corollary dimension of the American culture of death was brought into the national consciousness when two United States Circuit Courts made steeper the slippery slope of "privacy" established in *Roe v. Wade*—by ruling that doctors had a right to assist in the suicides of terminal, mentally competent patients. And under certain conditions, said the Ninth and Second Circuit Court of Appeals, doctors may also directly kill incompetent patients—that is, they can engage in euthanasia on patients who cannot take the pills to kill themselves. No federal appellate court had ever before legitimized euthanasia and assisted suicide.

Both courts gave credit to the Supreme Court's abortion decisions—again, the privacy right to kill one's fetus can be a legal basis for getting help to kill oneself. Both courts, more-over, went beyond assisted suicide. They declared that there is not a clear line between physician-assisted suicide (the doctor supplying the lethal drugs to the patient but not being there when the patient takes them) and the *direct* administration by the doctor of the final potion.

The consequences of death as a treatment of choice were underlined two years before these decisions in a report by the New York State Task Force on Life and the Law (composed of bioethicists, lawyers, clergy, and state health officials), which said, in part:

> Assisted suicide and euthanasia will be practiced through the prism of social inequality that characterizes the services in all segments of society, including health care. Those who will be most vulnerable to abuse, error, or indifference are the poor, minorities, and those who are least educated and least empowered. . . .
>
> Many patients in large, overburdened facilities serving the urban and rural poor will not have the benefit of skilled pain management and comfort care.

Many physicians are not knowledgeable about ways to con-trol and limit pain. And if pain is indeed uncontrolled, suicide is a most seductive alternative. Many physicians, moreover, are not able to diagnose clinical depression. When the bot-tomless hopelessness of the clinically depressed is not being treated, suicide can become irresistible. None of this was ex-plored in the two historic federal court decisions.

Making a point about pain, the New York Task Force on Life and the Law noted that "a recent study found that pa-tients treated for cancer at centers that care predominantly for minority individuals were three times more likely to receive in-adequate therapy to relieve pain."

I was surprised at the recklessness of the federal court deci-sions—the lack of standards to prevent abuses and the blithe assurances that the poor and minorities have nothing to worry about. But I was not surprised at the underlying effect—the transforming of doctors into killers. It started with *Roe v. Wade* and had now logically embraced patients of all ages.

Dr. Christoph Hufeland, a German physician, writer, and humanist (1762–1836), warned: "If the physician presumes to take into consideration in his work whether a life has value or not, the consequences are boundless and the physician becomes the most dangerous man in the state."

Of all the stories with which I've gotten involved—not only as a reporter—two were especially grotesque violations of fundamental human decency. The first was committed by physicians and courts in Oklahoma; the second by frightened politicians, including Mario Cuomo when he was governor of New York, along with organized groups of feminists and gays. In that second story, another shameless advocate for terminal injustice was the American Civil Liberties Union.

First, Oklahoma and its death row for infants.

The doctors involved in this "experiment" themselves told of the deaths they had caused—not as an act of confession but rather as a declaration of prideful achievement.

Their article, "Early Management and Decision Making for the Treatment of Myelomeningocele," appeared in the October 1983 issue of *Pediatrics*, a publication of the American Academy of Pediatrics. Among the authors were Drs. Richard H. Gross, Alan Cox, and Michael Pollay.

Over a five-year period, an experiment had been conducted at the University of Oklahoma Health Sciences Center. The subjects of the experiment were newborn infants with spina bifida. Each was evaluated by a team of physicians, nurses, physical and occupational therapists, a social worker, and a psychologist.

The team decided, in each case, whether to recommend "active vigorous treatment" or to inform the parents they were not obligated to have the baby vigorously treated. Instead, the family could choose "supportive care only."

Each infant in the first group was given all medically indicated treatment, including an operation to close the spinal lesion and the implanting of a shunt to drain spinal fluid from the brain. The unfortunate infants relegated to support care received no active medical treatment: no surgery, no antibiotics to treat infection, and no routinely administered sedation during the dying process that began inexorably with only supportive care as the "treatment."

Of the twenty-four infants who did not get active, vigorous treatment, none survived. The mean age at death was thirty-seven days.

All but one of the infants who received active, vigorous treatment survived. The exception was killed in an auto accident.

To determine which infants were to be given death tickets, the medical team relied in substantial part on a "quality of life" formula: $QL = NE \times (H + S)$.

QL is the quality of life the child is likely to have if he is allowed to live; NE is the child's natural endowment (physical and intellectual); H is the contribution the child can expect from his home and family; S is the probable contribution to that handicapped child from society.

Since, under this formula, it is predominantly nonmedical factors that determine whether the infant lives or dies, his or her chances of being permitted to stay alive are greatly reduced if his parents are on the lower rungs of poverty. If, moreover, the child is poor and was born—as these infants were—during the Reagan Administration, which preferred missiles to funding for the handicapped, the baby was hit with a double whammy.

The creator of this lethal formula, which intrigued many physicians around the country, was Dr. Anthony Shaw, the director of the Department of Pediatric Surgery at the City of Hope National Medical Center in Duarte, California, and a clinical professor of surgery at the UCLA School of Medicine. He was also the chairman of the Ethics Committee of the American Pediatric Surgical Association.

When I charged Dr. Shaw, during a television debate, with having created a means test for deciding which infants shall continue to live, he said he had intended no such thing. I asked him how else could one read his formula, and he said that its purpose was to help the parents. And, of course, he added, the baby. He did not make clear how this "help" took effect with poor children.

The last two elements of the formula, plainly, have nothing to do with medical judgments. Yet Martin Gerry, who was the director of the Office for Civil Rights of the Department of Health, Education and Welfare from 1975 to 1977—and who investigated the Oklahoma experiment—found that the parents of the infants involved "were told by representatives of the [medical] team that the proposed treatment/ non-treatment alternative represented a *medical judgment* made by the team. *The quality-of-life formula used was neither discussed with nor revealed to the parents*." (Emphasis added.)

An indignant reader of the article in *Pediatrics* was Dr. John M. Freeman of the Birth Defects Treatment Center at Johns Hopkins Hospital, in Baltimore. Writing to *Pediatrics*, Freeman observed that although the Oklahoma medical team did prove that it "can get the infants to die quickly," such skill hardly qualifies as "the best available alternative" for the management of babies with spina bifida.

Dr. Freeman added that the twenty-four infants who died "might also have done well and might have . . . walked with assistive devices, gone to regular school, been of normal intelligence, and achieved bowel and bladder control."

Should anyone be charged with criminal responsibility for the deaths of these infants? "The facts, just as written by the doctors themselves in the article, clearly demonstrate violation of both state and federal law," Martin Gerry said. "I think there are clearly violations of state child-abuse laws; there are violations of state criminal laws. I think what you have here is a conspiracy to commit murder." But in neither state nor federal courts have the doctors been found guilty of anything.

The doctors said that despite what they wrote in the article, no infant was denied full-scale treatment because of nonmedical factors. They also claimed that the parents could have rejected the lesser option of "supportive care"—the alleged medical decision to let the child die.

I spoke to one of the parents, Frieda Smith, mother of Stonewall Jackson Smith, whose lifespan was fifty-three days. She told me that he was one of the infants who did indeed get *only* "supportive care." And, yes, she had agreed to that course of nontreatment.

But, she emphasized, "We did not make the decision to let Stoney die. All we were ever told was that any treatment would only cause him to suffer needlessly. Like any caring parents, we wanted to spare him any pain—and so we did what the doctors recommended. But we trusted those doctors to do everything possible to save his life under any circumstances."

Also, Frieda Smith pointed out, "the doctors failed to tell us that we were part of an experiment. We were completely unaware of this until six years later, when we saw something about it on the news."

Other parents of the dead children have claimed that when their kids were separated out from those who were chosen to get full treatment, the medical team's recommendations were not clear or complete enough to be fully understood. Nor—confirming Martin Gerry's investigation—were the parents told of the "quality of life" factor in their child's getting the black spot.

Frieda Smith and other parents filed a class-action suit against this cutting-edge medical team and the University of Oklahoma Health Services Center, where these medical advances took place. Joining in the litigation were the American Civil Liberties Union, the Spina Bifida Association of America, the Association for Persons with Severe Handicaps, and the National Legal Center for the Medically Dependent and Disabled.

Some newspapers in Oklahoma published the story, but it did not appear in the national press for a long time—and then only glancingly. I wrote about it in several columns for the *Washington Post* and the *Village Voice*. To no avail. No members of Congress were sufficiently stirred to investigate these "quality of life" deaths—even though a primary cause of action for the class-action suit was the charge that the dead spina bifida children had been discriminated against because they were handicapped, and that violated Section 504 of the 1978 Rehabilitation Act passed by Congress.

The departed children were also discriminated against, the parents claimed, because their parents had low incomes, and their class status was an element in disqualifying their kids from treatments. They claimed some of the infants on the death list had physical characteristics that were identical with those of the children who were saved, but, alas, the doomed were from the wrong side of the tracks.

The lawsuit failed in the lower courts, which ruled that the parents, after all, had been involved in the treatment decisions. In 1993 the Supreme Court of the United States—without comment—refused to review what had happened to these discarded infants.

A few months later Frieda Smith told me, "We realize that life would not have been easy with our son, but we would have liked to have the chance. We wonder what Stoney would have said and done. We see handicapped children and wonder if he would have been like them.

"Finding out, afterward, that we let him die was like burying him all over again. How the doctors say they did nothing wrong is something I just don't understand."

I spoke to Richard H. Gross, one of the doctors who conducted the experiment, and he was angry that I could possibly have thought he and his colleagues had done anything wrong. But when I asked him about his use of the specific guidelines for the five-year experiment, he refused to answer.

I was especially interested in that class-based formula for life or death. He couldn't, I told Dr. Gross, deny that the formula had been used at the University of Oklahoma Health Sciences Center because the *Pediatrics* article he co-wrote with his colleagues made it clear that the formula had indeed been used to separate the condemned infants from those allowed to live.

Dr. Gross ended the conversation abruptly.

Stonewall's mother is greatly interested, she told me, in what kind of national health plan may eventually be adopted by Congress. "My only hope," she said, "is that they will make sure that everyone will be entitled to the same medical treatment—regardless of their ability to pay. There is not a doctor in this world that can either create a life or give it back after it's gone."

Still, Stonewall's mother is apprehensive that the class you belong to will determine the quality of the medical care you get—especially as "managed care" becomes the parsimonious norm.

"With the doctors' attitude toward the lives of people in low-income brackets," she wrote me, "it's no wonder people like us don't trust those in authority."

Among the doctors "in authority" whom Frieda Smith always has in mind were the members of the medical team to which she entrusted her son, Stoney.

In their article in *Pediatrics*, the team, looking back over the children who are no longer alive, wrote blithely, "The 'untreated survivor' has not been a significant problem in our experience." That is because no child who was not "vigorously" treated lived.

It would have been helpful if the American Medical Association had expressed investigative interest in the accomplishments of that medical team as they decided the fates of spina bifida infants. But I wasn't surprised that no such concern had been forthcoming, because in 1984 the AMA's House of Delegates urged that *local* committees and hospitals set their own guidelines for treatment—or nontreatment—of "incurably ill" infants.

The AMA did not disclose whether it meant "incurable" to be synonymous with "terminal," or whether it meant a condition, like diabetes, that cannot be cured during what nonetheless can be a reasonably long life.

Ignored by the AMA was the often unwelcome fact that a born infant has constitutional rights—including the rights to due process and equal protection of the laws, the same rights that the members of the AMA's House of Delegates enjoy. Instead the AMA chose to suggest that handicapped infants be deprived of constitutional protections and be given over to the mercies of local option.

If an official medical organization in Germany had recommended such a policy concerning handicapped infants, there might have been some indignation in the United States among those who felt this "quality of life" approach was an echo of German medicine some decades ago.

But when the AMA declared it was okay to have local balloting to decide which handicapped infants shall live—and when little attention had been paid by the medical establishment or the press to an Oklahoma experiment that could have taken place in the Third Reich—I became apprehensive about the future of this nation, and not only the future of health care. Again, no doctor involved in the Oklahoma "quality of life" project was convicted of anything.

HORROR STORIES—II

In the second, particularly grotesque violation of human decency that I've covered as a reporter, one of the agents of death is the American Civil Liberties Union.

Roger Baldwin, founder of the ACLU, once told me, as he told many others, that "no civil liberties battle is ever won—permanently."

Because the Bill of Rights and the Fourteenth Amendment are indeed never out of harm's way, I did not think I would ever leave their protector, the ACLU. I had been a member for some thirty-five years, as well as a member of the New York board for over twenty years and a one-term member of the national board. Although I occasionally disagreed with some of its policies, the ACLU did keep sounding the alarm that, as Louis Brandeis put it, "The greatest dangers to liberty lurk in insidious encroachment by men of zeal, well-meaning, but without understanding."

But when the ACLU itself—with zeal and without understanding—began sacrificing the lives of children and diminishing the life expectancy of their mothers by fervently opposing the mandatory identification of HIV-infected newborns on privacy grounds, I resigned in disgust in 1995.

In forty-eight states, the Centers for Disease Control and Prevention had arranged for the testing of all newborns for HIV. Newborns were also tested for syphilis, sickle-cell anemia, and other conditions. But only the results of the HIV test were kept from the parents and the child's doctor. This was not a medical decision. The political reason for this secret HIV test was that if the child is infected, so is the mother, who is then endangered by discrimination because the HIV virus leads to AIDS. So the privacy of the mother must be protected.

Some 75 percent of the 1,200 to 1,400 infants in New York State who initially test positive each year are not actually infected. They are born with maternal antibodies, having been exposed to the virus as a result of perinatal transmission from the mother. The rest are indeed infected and can be identified as such within a short time after birth—if their condition is allowed to be known.

But if the mother does not know she and her child are infected, the child will soon be attacked by opportunistic infections, owing to a weakened immune system. And those are preventable infections that otherwise can be fatal.

The experience in becoming involved in this story—after my meeting with Adlai Stevenson at the UN and, later, the mass defection of liberal members of Congress in the fight to protect handicapped infants from being summarily dispatched from this earth—confirmed my strong disinclination to call myself a liberal. A lower-case libertarian, maybe. But being without any category makes more sense.

Also, on this story, I was able to do what I have often done in the past as a journalist—share information with reporters and columnists on papers other than those I write for. I am less interested in "exclusives"—though I wouldn't turn one down—than I am in making a difference. So Jim Dwyer, then of *Newsday*—who won a 1995 Pulitzer Prize for commentary in part because of his columns on this story—and I exchanged information as the story developed.

The fierce attempt—by a spectrum of zealous, well-meaning organizations without understanding—to prevent the mandatory disclosure of the results of these HIV tests recalled the "Tuskegee experiment," one of the more repellent public health scandals in American history.

In that "experiment," from 1932 to 1972, some four hundred illiterate black men with syphilis were observed—but not treated—by Public Health Services physicians. As the targeted black men deteriorated, they were told only that they had "bad blood." And, believing that lie, they died.

The Tuskegee reference entered the HIV-infant-test debate through Dr. Arthur Ammann, a prominent professor of pediatrics at the University of California. In a Jim Dwyer column, Ammann, referring to the anonymous testing of infants for HIV, said, "The maintenance of anonymous test results at a time when treatment and prevention are readily available will be recorded in history as analogous to the Tuskegee 'experiment.' "

It was Dr. Ammann, a specialist in pediatric AIDS, who in 1983 first discovered that the HIV virus could be received through blood transfusions. Now he was appalled that despite the horrifying lesson of Tuskegee, these mothers and infants were kept dangerously ignorant.

By contrast with the ACLU—and its negligible concern for the civil liberties of the infected infants—Dr. Ammann pointed out that "the overriding principle for a physician is the duty to inform. This is both a legal and ethical doctrine to which the physician, the scientist, and the state must be held accountable."

Back in 1983, he pointed out, everyone agreed that those

who had received HIV infection from a blood transfusion had the right to know that. "If this was the conclusion for adults in 1983," he asked, "why should infants and their mothers be of a lesser status in the 1990s?"

The public battle over saving and prolonging these children's lives began with Nettie Mayersohn, a member of the New York State Assembly. She is so forceful a feminist that in 1989 the state's chapter of the National Organization for Women voted her the feminist legislator of the year. But Mayersohn soon became a pariah among many pro-abortion-rights feminists, even though she is still firmly pro-choice.

She became a heretic when she introduced a bill in the New York State assembly that would make a basic change in the testing of newborns in New York.

Mayersohn's bill would have ensured mandatory identification of HIV infants. Mothers and their doctors would be told of the baby's condition, and the Health Department would be required to see that all such infants got treatment.

Her bill was immediately opposed—with considerable money for lobbying against it—by such liberal groups as the National Organization for Women, gays, the New York affiliate of the National Abortion and Reproductive Rights Action League, and by that paladin of open information for all, the American Civil Liberties Union.

The righteous coldness of this approach was compounded by a corollary contentious issue. In November 1994, *CBS Evening News* did a report on the discovery that the drug AZT, taken by the mother during pregnancy, could prevent many infants from being born with the HIV virus. Dr. Philip Pizzo of the National Institutes of Health said that if all pregnant women had to be tested for AIDS and then, if those tested positive were offered AZT, many children's lives could be saved.

Speaking for the opposition was Dr. Ruth Macklin, a

bioethicist at the Albert Einstein College of Medicine in New York.

"It is an invasion of privacy. It threatens the women's interests," she said.

Macklin was asked, "Is freedom to safeguard privacy that important that you might allow fifteen thousand babies' lives to be poured down the drain?"

"At a certain point," she answered, "one balances freedom against lives, knowing that a certain number of people are going to die."

It has been said—by me, anyway—that many bioethicists have formed a new priesthood of death, not only in this infant-HIV controversy, but also with regard to euthanasia and its tributaries. To many of them, death has become the preferred cost-benefit way of treatment.

As for Nettie Mayersohn and her continuing fight to save lives in this war for the freedom to live, she kept saying, "Countless people tell me that I will be destroying the mother's privacy and also that she has the right not to know. They completely dismiss the fact that there is now another human life involved whose right to medical care—and indeed to life—is being violated. It's a baby, not a statistic!

"Look, the New York State Health Department and the federal Centers for Disease Control recommend that if a woman knows she is HIV-infected, she should be warned not to breastfeed the child. But these mothers are being sent home from the hospital without being told they're infected."

The child, then, is likely to be hit, within months, with devastating attacks of PCP pneumonia, among other severely damaging infections.

In columns in the *Washington Post*, the *Village Voice*, and other papers, I wrote in astonishment that liberals would withhold life-and-death information from mothers. (I became less astonished as time went on.)

"Some of those maintaining the need for secrecy spoke of the mother's right *not* to know. But she can't evade knowing her child's HIV status because, as physicians who treat youngsters with AIDS emphasized, "Sooner or later, HIV will declare itself. The goal of newborn testing is to identify infection before it is too late to prevent certain consequences."

Inevitably the mother will know—when her child begins to die.

A persistent argument against mandatory identification of HIV infants was that the mother, if she discovers she is infected, will panic and flee the health-care system. I heard this from gays, abortion-rights activists, and leading officials of the New York and national ACLU.

None of these opponents of disclosing HIV results gave a single example of a mother who found out that she and her child were HIV-infected—and then disappeared in panic.

Even if there *were* one or ten or forty who fled, was this justification for keeping all the other infected mothers and their children fatally ignorant?

During my debates with ACLU officials and state legislators, I charged them with a patronizing colonialist attitude toward those women, particularly blacks and Latinas, unknowingly infected with HIV. To claim that these women would go underground when they found out they were infected more than implies that they do not care as much about their children as do white mothers.

Jim Dwyer of *Newsday* interviewed a number of black and Latina women who were furious "that they were never told that they and their infants were at grave risk." Said one woman whose son had become very sick, "I should have known, so I could take care of myself—and him."

Many of those women from high-risk areas are poor. The awful surprises experienced by them and their children are permitted, as Dwyer wrote in his *Newsday* column, because "the black and Latino kids who die of this disease don't have the political power or money to spend on lobbyists to compete with NOW or the Gay Men's Health Crisis" in lobbying to keep the test results secret—or to compete with the resources of the ACLU.

The lobbyists against Nettie Mayersohn urged that there be mandatory individual *counseling* instead of mandatory HIV *testing* that would reveal all HIV-infected mothers. With counseling, they said, new mothers will eventually be persuaded to find out whether they're infected. The problem is that counseling has had limited effect. First of all, a considerable number of the pregnant women at issue don't show up at a hospital until it's time to give birth. So they can't be counseled beforehand. Others who are in the health-care system are often very reluctant to be persuaded by counseling.

Accordingly, said Dr. Keith Krasinski of Bellevue Hospital in New York—who works with HIV-infected children—"*Every* child *must* be identified for HIV at birth, so that he or she can be treated. To do less is discrimination in its cruelest form."

The forces against unblinding this information often cited Harlem Hospital in New York as a resplendent illustration that the voluntary approach—counseling—can work. In most other hospitals, the results of counseling are dismaying, but not at Harlem Hospital.

Yet, Dr. Elaine Abrams, director of Pediatric AIDS Care—including the voluntary counseling program—at Harlem Hospital, emphasized, "I'd like to see HIV testing as routine as syphilis testing or eyedrops at birth. *Let's treat this as a disease*—not *a political problem.*" (Emphasis added.)

A majority of the physicians on New York's Committee for the Care of Children and Adolescents with HIV Infection agreed with Dr. Abrams. This is the one committee in the state with direct, long-term experience in treating and caring for precisely the children at great risk.

The majority of the committee pointed out that HIV-specialized medical care and other interventions "improve the outcome of HIV-infected children, resulting in better and longer life. . . . The potential benefits to HIV-infected children, *identified at birth*, are sufficient to support the 'doctrine of parental override' whereby the potential benefit to the infant outweighs the mother's right to refuse consent for HIV testing."

Mayersohn's bill was killed by the New York State assembly leadership in the 1994 session—with Governor Mario Cuomo cravenly staying out of the debate because he was facing a difficult reelection campaign and did not want to alienate such of his liberal constituencies as pro-choice feminists, gays, and civil libertarians.

But Cuomo did accidentally acknowledge to Jim Dwyer of *Newsday* that the life of a child is more vital than even privacy. After all, I kept writing, these are not fetuses. *Born* children have the due-process and equal-protection-of-the-laws rights that all persons under the Constitution have.

Nettie Mayersohn never gave up. Before the 1994 assembly adjourned, she went to the floor of that institution and spoke of

> . . . powerful groups who have a determination that they own [AIDS]—and there can be no changes in health law without their approval. As a result we will continue to send thousands of newborns home from the hospital to suffer the miseries of preventable opportunistic infections—and a premature death. . . .
>
> Last week, with great fanfare and a slap on the back for ourselves, we passed a much-needed domestic violence law. I submit to you that our failure to pass a mandatory testing bill makes us accomplices in the cruelest and most obscene

violence—the abuse and neglect of the most neglected children in our state. . . .

We protect newborn infants from a whole host of diseases by doing mandatory testing. This is considered enlightened public health policy. . . . Why do we not do the same for babies with AIDS? It is because the Religious Left has declared that there is something different about the disease, and if babies have to be sacrificed on the altar of confidentiality, so be it. . . .

Meanwhile, a dissident chapter of the New York State affiliate of the National Organization for Women—in Ulster County—supported Nettie Mayersohn and her bill, noting that "NOW should be leading the fight on this public issue. If the well-being of women and their children is not the concern of NOW, who will speak for them?"

The Mayersohn bill was killed again in 1995 although the state senate had already passed it, and a majority of the assembly was ready to vote for it. The all-powerful Speaker of the Assembly, Sheldon Silver, a Democrat, refused to bring it to a vote because of the pressure from gays and pro-choice feminists in his district.

Among those incredulous at the resistance to disclosing the test results was Dr. Arthur Caplan, director of the Center for Bioethics at the University of Pennsylvania. "It seems to me," he told the *New York Times*, "that despite all the rhetoric, this isn't such a complicated moral call. . . . To give a kid a . . . case of AIDS in the name of civil rights seems wrong."

Or in the name of civil liberties.

For many of the readers who angrily wrote me to protest my position, the moral imperative was to keep the mother's privacy inviolable. But there also came a letter from Laura Smith in Brooklyn:

Incredible that the issue of the *mother* knowing her *own* HIV status hardly seems to matter! What about the importance of her knowing so she can take responsibility for (1) not passing the virus to sex partners; (2) not having another baby; (3) getting treatment for herself. Yes, these tests should be unblinded for both the baby's and the mother's sakes!! Is it socially responsible to allow people who have the virus to remain ignorant of the fact? How can it be?!!!

Dr. Arthur Ammann was similarly puzzled: "No human research committee would allow such an experiment [blind testing of infants for HIV] at this time. . . . What loud cries for justice would be heard if we failed or refused to tell adults that they had received an HIV-infected blood transfusion?"

None of these logical points—in terms of civil liberties as well as medical priorities or human decency—made any impression on the ACLU, nor on the so-called pro-choice groups like NARAL. The latter informed the New York State legislature of its opposition to unblinding the tests with this remarkable argument:

"This legislation goes against everything that NARAL/NY strongly stands for—the most important being that we believe the full range of reproductive health choices must be available to all women, regardless of age or income level." The full range includes letting the infant—and the mother—die.

As Jim Dwyer noted, "They are talking about abortion after the child is born, which is a little late. This is the left-wing version of the right-wing militias."

A bizarre irony in the alignment of forces against the opening of the HIV tests came in promotional literature from the Gay Men's Health Crisis ("First in the Fight Against AIDS")—one of the most persistent opponents of the Mayersohn bill. In a fund-raising letter, GMHC said: "Far too many children with AIDS must face their illness without the kind of love and support they need."

There is no indication that GMHC sent sympathy cards to

the mothers whose children died of AIDS because no one had told the mother that she and the child were infected.

Also bizarre was the decision of a California organization to oppose a bill in that state's legislature that would disclose the results of HIV tests of infants. The organization calls itself "Caring for Babies With AIDS."

While this dance of death was going on, I received a note from former U.S. Surgeon General C. Everett Koop. While in office, he had presented me with a medal—the only one I've ever gotten—for my reporting on handicapped kids. Koop now said, "I cannot believe that people take the stand they do on unblinding the HIV test results when we now know that the administration of medication [for AIDS] is more effective with these patients than with any other age group."

A vivid illustration of why I resigned from the ACLU is the following story, of a mother who found out for the first time that her fifteen-month-old very sick child was HIV-positive. It first appeared in Jim Dwyer's column. The story made it impossible for me ever to return to the ACLU unless it reverses its policy, but that is as unlikely as the Christian Coalition deciding to campaign against prayer in the public schools. When the greatly distressed mother called the hospital, she was told, oh yes, her child had certainly been tested at birth. But the hospital had not been permitted to automatically give her the results at birth.

"My child," the mother told Dwyer, "could have gotten treatment from the first day or week of her birth. But there are plenty of children whose parents only find out their kids are infected when they are on [sic] death's door. Yet the hospital says it couldn't routinely give me those test results because that would violate privacy."

"Jackie, the mother," Jim Dwyer said, "also told me that she remembers being counseled at Harlem Hospital to voluntarily find out whether she was infected. But [at the time] she completely dismissed the possibility that she had the infection because her health was excellent, and she didn't suspect the child's father." So the counseling didn't work with her.

Dr. Stephen Nicholas, a New York pediatrician, is the medical director of Incarnation Children's Center, a residence in New York State for children with AIDS. He also treats kids at Harlem Hospital and Columbia Presbyterian. "The earlier the diagnosis," he says, "the longer the children live. The parents and kids I kept in ignorance are pawns to somebody else's game."

And the silence is the silence of the grave.

I found out from the Centers for Disease Control and Prevention that among children one to four years old, AIDS had become the sixth or seventh leading cause of death. The CDC predicted it would rise higher on the chart in the years ahead.

When I was young, I visited an ancient jazz musician in Harlem. "You know," he said, "or maybe you don't know, from the moment you wake up in the morning, everything is politics. Everything."

Including who lives and who dies.

Rarely, thanks to politics, lives can be saved. Nettie Mayer-sohn still kept on keeping on. "I get up with it in the morning," she told me, "and I go to sleep with it."

At last, in June 1996, her bill passed both houses and was signed by Governor George Pataki. In the assembly, Nettie was given a standing ovation. Not included among those applauding were the alleged civil libertarians and feminists who still opposed her.

The new law was the first in the country to require unequivocal mandatory testing of all newborns, disclosure of the results, and treatment. (A bill passed by Congress in the same year had many preliminary stages and was not due to kick in until the year 2000.)

"Every infected HIV baby," Nettie Mayersohn says of her law, "will finally be able to access health care that really can prolong and enhance their lives. And infants who are not infected will be protected from getting infected through breastfeeding."

Because infected newborns will now receive the quality of treatment that adults with AIDS rightfully demand, one would think that AIDS activists would have fought for the infected infants all along. But they hadn't.

In a congratulatory editorial on the Mayersohn bill, which, she believes, will set a national standard, the *Buffalo News* thought it might also help achieve the mandatory testing of pregnant women.

And indeed, at the end of June 1996, the American Medical Association did endorse mandatory testing of all newborns for the AIDS virus, as well as all pregnant women, because it had been established that pregnant women who were tested and treated cut the risk to the unborn child by two-thirds.

Meanwhile, the privacy-obsessed ACLU expressed no re- grets to certain grieving mothers. As one of those women put it, "We should not have been protected to death."

In covering this story, I was like the Ancient Mariner. For three years, in just about every lecture I gave around the coun- try—whatever the announced subject—I brought up the scan- dal, to say the least, of newborns and their mothers being kept ignorant of their HIV infections as official *policy*, not only in New York but in forty-four other states.

On call-in radio shows in many states—and on television— I indicted the ACLU and the other "liberal" groups involved in keeping the test results secret.

During a stop at Northern Illinois University, I was asked to speak to the law faculty before I talked to the student body. I explored a number of Supreme Court decisions made during that year, and then, when the session was supposed to be over, I brought the death of HIV-infected newborns into the conversation.

There were some twenty-five faculty members around the table. As had been clear from previous exchanges, they ranged from Scalia-like libertarians to traditional conservatives to professors still mourning the passing of the Warren Court and not yet recovered from the retirement of Justice William Brennan.

After I laid out the facts of the case and the arguments on both sides—and my own conclusions—I asked the faculty how they would come out.

First of all, none of them had heard of the issue, even though Illinois was one of the states where the results of HIV tests on newborns were not being disclosed. (There had been no Nettie Mayersohn in Illinois to blow the whistle.)

No member of the faculty disagreed with my conviction that the failure to inform the parent of a child's life-threatening disease—and her own condition as well—was an egregious violation of medical practice, and of fundamental fairness as well.

In other states I spoke to board members of some of the ACLU affiliates. They said they agreed with me and would try to organize a dissenting position before the national board. It never happened. They decided it would be too uncomfortable to break ranks. This reinforced my view that great harm is done by the tradition of being a team player.

Not a single officer of the national ACLU—including the president, Nadine Strossen, and the executive director, Ira Glasser—publicly questioned the ACLU's policy of elevating secrecy over life. Nor did any ACLU board member anywhere in the country express any public dissent.

I understood why some feminists had opposed the mandatory testing and disclosure of the results: they feared that the resultant breach of privacy—the testing of the infected newborn—would also reveal the mother's HIV infection without her having consented to be tested. This, they felt, could lead to the erosion of the protection of privacy at the core of *Roe v. Wade*.

Some of the gays on the same side as the feminists told me they feared that the privacy of adults' HIV tests would eventually be endangered by the mandatory testing of newborns.

I could follow the self-serving logic of those concerns, though not the resultant deaths of children. The ACLU's only special interests, however, are supposed to be the living Constitution and particularly the Bill of Rights.

While the ACLU strongly supports abortion rights, it had not until now decided that the lives of born infants, and their mothers, could also be discounted to further a higher principle.

THEY SHOOT COMMENCEMENT

SPEAKERS, DON'T THEY?

While exchanging views with the law faculty at Northern Illinois University, I was, however briefly, acting out a long-term fantasy of actually being a lawyer. When I was quite young, I searched out books about lawyers—in fact and fiction—and intended to be a defender of the accused.

Over the years I was sidetracked by working in radio and by my passion for jazz, which led to my writing about the music and then to full-time journalism—including reporting on the law and on those who become ensnared by it.

Still, the fantasy persisted. One morning, sitting in the press section at the Supreme Court, I was listening with alarm to the astonishingly uninformed arguments of a lawyer representing several high-school students in a pivotal free-press case that, if lost, would have substantially cut back the rights of high-school journalists around the country.

Watching, I was seized with the urge to leap out of the press section, station myself before the justices, and ask that "in the interests of justice," I be allowed to replace that stumbling lawyer and represent the students. I remained in my seat and the students lost (*Hazelwood School District v. Kuhlmeir*, 1988). Owing to the incompetent lawyering of the students' attorney, many public-school principals—not all—were delighted to take advantage of the decision and have greatly circumscribed the student press in public schools.

There have been other times when I wished I had a law degree so that instead of writing about raids on the Bill of Rights, I could directly repel the invaders.

In the 1980s I did get a touch of fleeting stature as an illusory lawyer when Northeastern University, where I had gone to college, awarded me an honorary doctorate of laws. The doctorate didn't allow me to take clients, of course, but it was better than being a wholly unadorned clubhouse lawyer.

What I enjoyed even more than the degree was its source. There was a time when Northeastern University devoutly wished that I had never enrolled. In the early 1940s, as a columnist and then editor of the *Northeastern News*, my goal was to create as much muckraking trouble as I could. And for that I was eventually banished as editor by the highest authority.

Indeed, my passion for freedom of speech—and the press— first took root when I was censored out of that newspaper at the age of nineteen.

The staff and I believed that the only journalism worth doing was investigative, and we broke stories of unethical behavior, and worse, on campus and in the city itself. Anti-Semitism was in full poisonous flower in Boston at the time, and we exposed some of the financial sources of that pestilence. It was a hell of a lively and focused staff. One of its members, years later, became editor of the *Boston Globe*.

The president of Northeastern, Carl S. Ell—whose life was the university that he had built from very small beginnings— was not a fan of the *Northeastern News*. We were controversial, and the president was convinced that any controversy connected with Northeastern could only do harm to his life's work.

At last the president, his fury cresting, struck. He sent his enforcer to tell me that unless we limited our coverage to positive stories on sports teams and all else connected with the university, we would be sacked. I said I was resigning, but I couldn't speak for the staff. We had a meeting, and in about fifteen seconds the staff rejected the ultimatum—except for one reporter who was silent. He became the new editor. There's always a scab.

Leaving was painful. We had become a family and we no longer had a central place to argue, to play cards, to send urgent weekly messages to the world. Above all, we missed the excitement of going after stories, of tracking their effects, of seeing our bylines.

Years later a reporter for the *Northeastern News* called me. He had been looking for a story printed during my editorship, but couldn't find it. Indeed, he couldn't find any of the bound volumes of the issues I had edited. They were no longer in the library, and nobody in the administration knew what had happened to them—or so they said.

A few years after that, the bound volumes mysteriously reappeared.

After President Ell died, his successor asked me to come back to the university and accept an award as a sort of prominent alumnus. My acceptance speech was devoted entirely to what had happened to me and the rest of the *Northeastern News* staff at the heavy hand of the revered Carl S. Ell and his accomplices.

During my return to Northeastern that year, the students seemed to enjoy these tales from the crypt. Most of the administrators on the dais listened without expression.

As time went on, I seemed to appear less and less troublesome to the university. In the summer of 1994, however, I again became the center of controversy.

Leslie Dickson, a member of the law school class that would

be graduating in 1995, asked me if she could nominate me for commencement speaker. Why sure, I said. In July, Leslie placed the nomination in the *WE Newsletter*, a journal of and for Northeastern's law students. Among other reasons she gave in *WE* for putting my name on the ballot was my advocacy "for the protection of the most unpopular speech."

"For this reason," Leslie continued, "he has supported free-speech rights of the CIA, the Nation of Islam, KKK, antichoice and pro-choice groups, Andy Rooney, Black Panthers, Anita Bryant, the National Gay Task Force, and many artists and activists of every persuasion. Please consider him as a viable candidate for class speaker."

I was grateful to Leslie because I much admired Northeastern's School of Law. In 1994 it was named the nation's leading public-interest law school. That is, in their three-month co-op work periods between three-month classes at the school, most of the students get work experience in organizations that represent the powerless. It's the only co-op law school in the country.

Students earn credits by working with, for example, the Welfare Unit of Greater Boston legal services; the UN high commissioner for refugees; the ACLU's National Prison Project; the People's Legal Services in a remote corner of a Navajo Indian reservation in Utah; New England Gay and Lesbian Advocates and Defenders; the section of Rhode Island Legal Service that fights for people who have been denied Social Security, Medicaid, and welfare benefits; and the public defender's office in Johannesburg, South Africa—as well as a two-woman firm there that focuses on police brutality and other human-rights abuses.

I was honored at being asked to address this kind of graduating class. It was my fantasy of a law school. Alan Dershowitz used to tell me that when he initially meets first-year students entering his class at Harvard Law School, he looks around the room and tells these prospective corporate lawyers that in ten years, ten percent of them will be indicted for corporate crimes.

In ten years the Northeastern Law School graduates might be making less money than teachers or journalists, but they won't be defendants.

I eventually found out some of the other commencement speaker choices of the graduating class: Janet Reno, Ruth Bader Ginsburg, Stephen Breyer, Hillary Rodham Clinton, Robert Reich, Cornel West, Angela Davis, Nina Totenberg, Judge Leon Higginbotham, Michael Moore, Senator Carol Mosley-Braun, and former Texas governor Ann Richards.

The four finalists were Reno, Ginsburg, H. R. Clinton, and me. When the top three declined the invitation, I was left. But not without resounding opposition.

In *WE*, one graduating student wrote, "It would probably be impossible to find a speaker who doesn't hold a belief that many of us find reprehensible, and I don't advocate scouring a candidate's private life for 'objectionable' views. However, Hentoff's opposition to reproductive choice is not a personal, privately held conviction, but a central tenet of his legal/political message. In a one-year period in the 1980s, he wrote 548 columns opposing legal abortion."

In the history of *daily* journalism, I doubt if any writer has ever produced 548 columns a year, let alone 548 columns on a single subject. Actually, in any one year, I write forty-eight weekly columns for the *Voice* and roughly the same number for the *Washington Post* (the latter are syndicated by United Media). About three or four of the total columns for both papers are about abortion.

The student continued: "We have no more legal *duty* to invite Hentoff to speak his mind than we do David Duke or

Phyllis Schlafly." Or, she might have added, Jesse Helms, Newt Gingrich, or Bill Clinton.

Said another student: "There's nothing that Nat Hentoff can say that would possibly interest us."

Some of the law school students charged that I approved of the killings of two women employees in the abortion clinics in Brookline on December 30, 1994, as well as the murders of doctors performing abortions elsewhere in the country. Yet, in the *Voice*, on radio and television, and in lectures, I had unequivocally said that it is impossible to be simultaneously pro-life and support, in any way, the killing of anyone.

A reporter for the *Northeastern News* called to ask my reaction to these denunciations. Well, I said, the debate about my qualifications to speak at graduation was what free speech is all about. And I certainly understood the intensity of pro-choice views, since they were directed at me sharply by my wife, almost on a daily basis.

But I was disappointed, I told the *News*, that not one of the angry law students had called to find out my actual views on abortion—for instance, that I am against any criminalization of abortion, either of the women who have them or of the doctors who perform them.

As an atheist, I said, I look to biology and the increasing discoveries of the nature of the fetus—as in fetal surgery—to persuade people that the "choice" in "pro-choice" is to kill developing human beings. Criminalizing abortion, on the other hand, creates martyrs—not an understanding of the indivisibility of human life.

In any case, the accuracy of fact patterns, I added with a touch of pomposity, is as important to a lawyer as it is to a journalist. A reporter who doesn't get his facts straight loses his or her credibility. A lawyer who doesn't verify facts can lose the life of a client. The law students who wanted to bar me, I told the reporter, never tried to find out what I *do* think about abortion, and so are not as well prepared to represent clients as they ought to be.

I was heartened by one law student who reminded his fellow students—in *WE*—about my record on freedom of speech. Also, he wrote, perhaps more telling for his audience, "in addition to his writings on the law, Mr. Hentoff is . . . the author of the liner notes to my favorite Bob Dylan album, *The Freewheelin' Bob Dylan.* I believe he would be a wonderful graduation speaker."

I've long believed that my liner notes on recordings would probably last longer than most of my other writings because listeners don't throw away music they especially like. But I never thought a liner note would help me get a gig as a commencement speaker.

I answered some of my critics in *WE*, but my champion, Leslie Dickson, who is strongly pro-choice, did a better job of it. Banning me because of my views on abortion, she wrote in *WE*, "would be censoring speech based on *his* exercise of free speech. Recently, Lani Guinier was taken under the wing of Northeastern's School of Law after being punished for *her* past exercise of speech [by President Clinton, who jettisoned her nomination as assistant attorney general for civil rights without even allowing her to defend her views before the Senate Judiciary Committee].

"I encourage the class to discover for themselves what Hentoff is all about," said Leslie. "He still has my vote!"

Several weeks before the commencement exercises, scheduled for May 25, 1995, I was again called by the school paper and asked what I planned to do about the demonstration that seemed very likely to take place during my speech. I said that since I didn't know what form the demonstration would take, I'd have to improvise—as I have a number of times in the past before hostile audiences.

Meanwhile, Leslie Dickson wrote in the law school student journal, "HE DOES NOT BELIEVE THE STATE SHOULD CRIMINALIZE ABORTION." (The capital letters are hers.)

Her attempt to bring facts into the controversy didn't seem to work. Leslie and I kept in touch while she worked a three-month co-op period at the Texas Civil Liberties Union. "Expect something at the graduation," she told me, "but I don't know what." And she said to the *Northeastern News*, "I'm absolutely sure something will happen." She added that there had been some talk that the students protesting would wear coat hangers as symbols of what women had to endure when abortion was illegal.

When I arrived in Boston on May 25, a law professor at Northeastern told me, "They've been playing it cool, but something's going to happen. Be prepared for anything."

One thing I was not prepared for was the reception David Hall, dean of the law school, received from the graduating class at commencement. They shouted, applauded, whistled, stomped. During my years at Northeastern, no administrator was so vividly appreciated, certainly not President Carl S. Ell.

Hall, one of the few black law school deans in the nation, apparently lives what he says: "Distrust in the legal system will only change when lawyers . . . rediscover their souls. . . . If we fail to ask or answer the question whether urban problems are for law schools to help solve, then not only will we lose our souls but . . . 'No justice, no peace' will be more than a protest slogan. It will become the inscription written on the tombstone of this justice system. And within the coffins will be our collective dreams of a just, fair, and productive society."

The dean introduced me, noting that in college he had learned a fair amount about jazz from reading my books and liner notes. I was not surprised that he, too, a soul seeker, has roots in jazz.

I came to the lectern, and from the 178 graduates there was a surprise. The applause was warm and rather prolonged, and nobody threw anything. I was relieved, but also kind of disappointed. I had been curious about how I would handle whatever kind of demonstration the protestors would mount.

I began by making what I said was an obvious point. Yet, obvious as it was, I had not heard it made by most of the multitude of law school professors and lawyers commenting on television and in print on the O.J. Simpson trial. If the defendant's name, I said, had been Frank Jones—whether he was black or white—the trial and the coverage would have been over a long time ago, and an execution date would probably have been set. While race is very often a determining factor in the routine denial of justice, so is class.

Of all the members of the Supreme Court, I added, the two justices most aware and angry about the class/race bias in the justice system were William O. Douglas and William Brennan. When I was interviewing Justice Brennan for a profile in *The New Yorker*—the former *New Yorker*—he told me how disappointed he was that so few law school graduates go into public-interest law. Most worry about how much money they're going to make.

Brennan, I said, would have been much encouraged had he known about the law school at Northeastern.

During my speech, preaching to the choir, I told the graduates about one of my heroes in the law—Steve Bright, director of the Southern Center for Human Rights, where the salary for everyone, from the director to the secretary, is $23,000 a year. Bright and his colleagues are often lawyers of last resort for people who are on death row because of prosecutors who savaged their constitutional rights and court-appointed defense lawyers who were often spectacularly incompetent. Northeastern law students, I noted, have worked in the Southern Center for Human Rights.

Another hero of mine—and, like Steve Bright, a friend—Anthony Griffin of Galveston, was probably not as familiar to the graduates. Griffin, who is black, has a brilliant record in voting rights, AIDS, race, and other discrimination cases. He was also a pro-bono general counsel for the Texas NAACP.

The state's ACLU affiliate had asked Griffin to be a voluntary unpaid lawyer defending the Grand Dragon of the Texas Knights of the Klan. He was being hauled into court by Texas officials demanding the Klan's membership list.

There had been persistent racist intimidation of blacks in certain public housing developments in Texas, and the state thought the Klan was deeply and nastily involved. If Texas officials could connect the addresses of certain members of the Klan with the places where this viciousness was taking place, they might be able to get indictments.

Anthony Griffin, who despised the Grand Dragon and his smoldering colleagues, was very much aware of the 1958 Supreme Court case *NAACP v. Alabama,* in which, on First Amendment grounds, the Court refused to permit the State of Alabama to get at the NAACP's membership lists because "Compelled disclosure of affiliation with groups engaged in advocacy may . . . expose these members to economic reprisal, loss of employment, and threat of physical coercion."

And in the late 1970s, an attempt by Texas itself to get the membership list of that state's NAACP was beaten down because of the precedent of *NAACP v. Alabama.* When Texas later went after the Klan's membership lists, it was again the First Amendment right of association that was being attacked by the state. And Anthony Griffin defends the First Amendment across the board—for anyone.

Because he believed the Klan was as protected by the First Amendment as the NAACP, Griffin was fired as general counsel of the Texas NAACP by the national office (Ben Chavis was then in charge). Griffin went on to receive the first annual William J. Brennan Award, which "recognizes a person or group for extraordinary commitment to the cause of free speech in America." Justice Brennan was there to tell Griffin how pleased he was that the Houston lawyer had started off the award.

At the Northeastern Law School commencement, I talked more about Brennan, including a recent comment he had made concerning the fight against the death penalty, which he, along with Thurgood Marshall, had led on the Court for many years:

"But even if it is not for me, as it was not for Justice Marshall, to finish the work, neither were we free to desist. The final labor, it seems, will be left to the brave and able hands and minds of those we leave behind."

I pointed to the graduates, who would keep on keeping on, and closed by saying, "I'd especially like to thank one of the graduates, Leslie Dickson—a brave young woman, a brave young lawyer."

As I left the stage, there was applause, no boos or hisses, no demonstration. What the hell was going on—or not going on?

The dean started handing the diplomas to the graduates, who, in single file, walked across the stage toward him. When he announced the name of Leslie Dickson, she broke out of the line to shake my hand and then went on to get her degree. As I said, a woman of courage.

As the granting of the degrees went on, I became aware that the protest had begun. It wasn't vocal. But a considerable number of women, and some men, had placed patches on their black robes. A red patch said, "Defend Abortion Rights." A purple-and-white patch declared the wearer as being "For the Freedom of Choice."

There was another emblem, sort of, in the ranks of graduates—a live emblem. Here and there on the line, four of the male graduates carried infants in their arms—or, rather, on one arm, so they could get their diploma with the other.

I would like to think that was a counter-message—for life. But I was told that at previous graduations, infants had also accompanied new lawyers as they received their degrees. It was not a counterdemonstration, I was told.

Anyway, I enjoyed seeing the babies. And I enjoyed seeing the free-expression, pro-choice patches. I really did. Between the two, however, it seemed to me that the infants were more compelling witnesses for choice.

YOU CAN GO HOME

AGAIN, SORT OF

When I came back to Boston to speak to the law school graduates, I didn't go all the way back to where I had grown up, in Roxbury. I had made that trip a few years before when I was in the city to promote my first book of memoirs, *Boston Boy*. On that occasion a reporter and a photographer from the *Boston Globe* were assigned to track me through my old neighborhood.

That would have been coming home with a flourish, if anyone on those streets had recognized me. But they were all black, and mostly young. From the predominantly Jewish boyhood of my neighborhood, Roxbury had become another kind of ghetto. A much more closed ghetto. At One Howland Street, where I had lived until I was nineteen, I saw huge locks on the doors, sometimes three of them on one door.

A woman who lived in what had been our apartment told me, "You never know what they're going to do. They'll rob you, they'll kill you. Life don't mean anything to them." Several of her neighbors nodded.

I remembered the only robbery—attempted robbery—I'd seen on Howland Street. It was during the Depression. The superintendent of our building caught a guy crawling through a window on the first floor—our window. He grabbed him and held him until the cops came. We cheered.

Our street, back then, wasn't all Jewish. At the upper end there were black families, and the cops never heard of any robberies there, either.

I was curious to see how my elementary school, the William Lloyd Garrison School, was holding up. Trailed by the reporter and the photographer, I walked up Elm Hill Avenue, a route I had taken every morning for six years, sent cheerily on my way by Fats Waller's "Your Feets Too Big," played on radio each morning, as a signature by a disc jockey, just before eight.

Turning the corner to the school, I expected it to be covered by graffiti. But the red-brick building was clean, cleaner than I remembered it. And although the houses on each side looked rundown, the school—and the freshly mown grass in front of it—could have been a Norman Rockwell painting.

Obviously, parents and other neighbors were making it clear that the school was a special place, not to be messed with.

We went down to Grove Hall, where I had spent a lot of time as a kid—the drugstore, with its supply of comic books; the bakery; and Siegel's Cafeteria, where intense men in black coats sipped scalding tea through sugar cubes as they compared notes about disappeared Jews in Europe and looked carefully through the lists of American casualties in the newspaper to see how many were Jewish. If there were only a few, they were disappointed. Jews had to be seen to be doing their share.

All those places were gone. The shells were boarded up. A few living stores still existed, but there were few customers. I had seen enough of the old neighborhood. Actually, I had seen nothing of *my* old neighborhood.

Almost ten years later I received a letter from Roxbury. The writer, Deahdra Butler-Henderson, was a black community organizer who was now devoting her considerable energy and persuasiveness to "Project in the Spirit / Mishkin Tefila." During my time there, Temple Mishkin Tefila was a synagogue at the top of Elm Hill Avenue, near the William Lloyd Garrison School. I was never inside, because it was a synagogue for prosperous Jews, while the *shul* I went to was primarily for Jews without much money, like my father. I didn't feel I belonged in Mishkin Tefila or its Hebrew school.

The Jews who had attended Mishkin Tefila, like the Jews I knew in my synagogue, were long gone. Mishkin Tefila's congregation had moved, as fast as they could, to the suburbs in the 1950s and 1960s. Most of the other Jews—there had been 100,000 in Roxbury and the adjoining districts of Dorchester and Mattapan—had moved wherever they could, so long as it was away from the blacks moving into their old neighborhoods.

"Why did we scare you?" one black woman asked of Jews years later.

The dynamics of the exodus have been outlined in the *Dorchester Community News* (November 3, 1995) by Sean Cahill:

"The transition of Roxbury, North Dorchester and Mattapan from mostly Jewish to mostly black was the result of a federal government housing program" that produced redlining and blockbusting, steering potential black homeowners exclusively into Jewish neighborhoods. Unscrupulous real estate brokers played upon people's fear and/or racism to get Jewish homeowners to sell their homes, then turned around and sold them to blacks at inflated prices."

The letter from Roxbury asked me if I would take part in what Deahdra Butler-Henderson described as a "healing process" between distrustful blacks and still-wary Jews with a resultant new institution, based in Mishkin Tefila, that would help revitalize the neighborhood.

The massive abandoned temple—as described by Sean Cahill—is "littered with broken glass, the inside almost completely gutted and the roof half gone." But Butler-Henderson had a grand plan that involved the resurrection of the temple and its transformation into a multicultural performing-arts center that would include classes for writers, as well as a permanent community museum that would celebrate, as she put it, these "ever-evolving neighborhoods."

What particularly intrigued me was her idea—as described by Patricia Smith in the *Boston Globe*—for a chronicle, on film and audiotape, of the life experiences of Jewish and African-American elders, with young residents of Roxbury, Dorchester, and Mattapan serving as interviewers. "The [black] interviewers will then tell the stories of their present-day neighborhood."

By March 1996, Deahdra Butler-Henderson had interested a growing number of Jews and blacks in her Project in the Spirit / Mishkin Tefila. It was time, she decided, to have an Easter-Passover dinner and a more or less formal inauguration of her plan to restore Mishkin Tefila to its former grandeur, but this time as a place of renewal for both Jews and blacks.

She asked me to be one of the speakers—part of the bridge, if it could be built, between the Jewish Roxbury of yore and the black Roxbury of now.

Because Mishkin Tefila was so dilapidated, the Easter-Passover dinner took place at the Morgan Memorial Goodwill Industries, an institutional building with informal employees.

There was a large assembly, Jewish and black, some whites who weren't Jewish, and many children. A woman rabbi gave the invocation. And that was a big cultural change. When I was a kid in Roxbury, there were no women rabbis. Indeed, there were no Reform or Conservative synagogues. God presided only over Orthodox *shuls*.

I began my talk by telling of growing up in Howland Street

in Roxbury. Jews lived, together, on two-thirds of the street, and blacks on the rest. I do not remember even a hello ever passing between blacks and whites. They were abstractions to each other. I was speaking directly to the kids in the room. We did not know each other's names. But I knew one of them, Ben Johnson. We had met through jazz in a place beyond Howland Street. We made, for a time, our own community.

Then I told the listeners of getting a job, when I was nineteen, on radio station WMEX in Boston, and, through a jazz program I had, of coming to know Duke Ellington, Dizzy Gillespie, Red Allen, Charles Mingus, and other powerfully singular players. They could not have been less abstract. So too, later, with others I got to know—Malcolm X, among others. Black and all insistently different.

But most whites do not know individual blacks, and vice versa. Moreover, when whites or blacks become racists, they act out of invincible ignorance because they literally do not *know* those whom they hate. Some of the youngsters celebrating the Mishkin Tefila renewal began to nod agreement.

And there *are* black racists, I told them. There is a mantra among many blacks that blacks can't be racists because they have no power. Only whites have the power to be racists.

It isn't so, I said. Among blacks I knew in Boston and later in New York, I saw internal racism—light-colored blacks demeaning darker blacks as inferior. And in a subsequent dimension of prejudice—when "black pride" began to be on the ascendant—dark blacks showed disdain for blacks who were "not black enough."

But the primary barriers, I said, to making it possible for the vast distance between blacks and whites to be at least somewhat narrowed are the abstractions, the stereotypes.

I also told them about the visit Kwame Turé, a black anti-Semite, paid to the University of Maryland in February 1990.

He used to be known as Stokely Carmichael, I said, the inventor of the "Black Power" term in the civil rights movement in the 1960s. Since then, he—like Louis Farrakhan—has attacked Jews as the main obstacle to the liberation of blacks. And he is fairly widely known for his equation "The only good Zionist is a dead Zionist."

At the University of Maryland he told the students, "Zionist pigs have been harassing us everywhere. . . . And when this anger rises, [we] will snap our fingers and finish them off."

In the wake of his speech at the University of Maryland, Turé left bitter Jewish students. But black students were angry at the Jews who had protested the invitation to Turé. ("No one can tell us whom to invite," the blacks said.)

But a professor let it be known that her classroom would be open after hours to anyone who wanted to come to talk about the growing tension on campus. Students did come, more each time.

There were no dramatic agreements, and there was a lot of caustic conversation. Eventually, however, one black student said to a Jewish student, "Now I know you as you. I never really *talked* to a Jew before. I don't necessarily like you or agree with you, but now I know *you*."

And there were Jewish students who said they too were getting to see the blacks in the room as individuals.

Getting past the stereotypes, though, is only a beginning, I said. The next stage is working together on something of real meaning to both of you. In Washington, a black student was co-editor of her high-school newspaper. The other editor was white, and the black student pointed out, "I don't go looking for white friends, but when I'm working with whites on something we both care about—like this newspaper—then we become friends."

"What Deahdra is building on the ruins of Temple Mishkin

Tefila," I said, ending my talk, "will be a place where everyone involved is known one by one, not as a member of a group. There aren't many places like that in this country—not yet."

And there was music that evening. A stately black woman sang soul music, based, in feeling and cadences, on spirituals. And my boyhood came strutting back when a klezmer band—the Kleznicks—appeared. In the Old Country, *klezmorim* were wandering improvisers, their roots in Yiddish music nourished by the distinctive sounds of the cultures they traveled through.

In this country, the klezmer bands were essential to weddings because their music was so jubilant, infectiously right for dancing. As a very small boy, on Howland Street in Roxbury, I would hear the singing trumpet and the dancing clarinet from a block away, and rush out of the house to get to the catering hall and look through the window at these astonishing musicians, who, without any music sheets in front of them, kept creating music that gave such pleasure that I desperately wished it would never stop.

Hearing this music again at the launching of Project in the Spirit / Mishkin Tefila made me realize that I had not so much come home again as found a new place where I felt at home.

The climax of the evening was the appearance of ten-year-old Amber Perry, a student at a public school in my old neighborhood. It would not be accurate to say she recited Maya Angelou's "Still Rise." She *became* the poem, bringing it to fiery life:

> . . . *You may shoot me with your words.*
> *You may cut me with your eyes.*
> *You may kill me with your hatefulness,*
> *But still, like air, I'll rise.* . . .
> *I'm a black ocean, leaping and wide,*
> *Welling and swelling I bear to the tide.*

Leaving behind nights of terror and fear. . . .
Into a daybreak that's wondrously clear
I rise
Bringing the gifts that my ancestors gave,
I am the dream and the hope of the slave.
I rise.
I rise.
I rise.

With the last "I rise!" Amber seemed to have become taller, not a child any longer.

The applause was long and loud, and as Amber basked in it she became a child again.

As I was leaving, I heard somebody mention that Deahdra, this black community organizer who created this coming together, is also part of a group involved in trying to bring nonviolence to Ireland. She is a member of Peacewatch there, and goes to Ireland from time to time. And in Boston, her Irish identification includes her presence on the advisory board of the Irish Immigration Center.

She reminded me of those Jewish women, fifty and more years ago, who seemed to be everywhere in the neighborhood—organizing, fund-raising, arranging marriages, and all the while taking care of their own families. She is in the tradition of the women you have to see to get things done.

BLACKS AND JEWS AND ME

When he was going to Boston Latin School, Leonard Bernstein lived around the corner from Mishkin Tefila and near my first alma mater, the William Lloyd Garrison School. Among other renowned musicians who started in Roxbury were Johnny Hodges and Harry Carney of the Duke Ellington orchestra, drummer Roy Haynes, and Ruby Braff (a Jewish trumpet player of whom Louis Armstrong was fond).

If these products of Roxbury brought pleasure, another has specialized in bringing fear—to Jews. Louis Farrakhan. I didn't know him when we both were there. He lived in the black part of Roxbury. But I was strongly influenced by a black man while I was still in Roxbury.

He was my first editor, William Harrison—a stern, wiry "race man," in the parlance of the time. He had an encyclopedic knowledge of black history and inequality. He had no patience with bigotry of any kind, including anti-Semitism. It drained energy, he told his black staff, that had to go into the politics of redistributing income and power.

Harrison was also a student of literature, and not only of black literature. He had lived in England for a time and, he once told me, had worked for T. S. Eliot on the *Criterion*. In race matters, as in literature, Harrison had an extraordinary range of knowledge and analytic skills.

When I knew him, William Harrison was the editor of *The Boston Chronicle*, a weekly addressed to the black communities of Boston, including Roxbury. I was nineteen when he asked me to write book reviews for the paper—a wide range of books. I had been recommended by my friend Ben Johnson, from the black part of Howland Street.

Harrison had only two rules: accuracy and clarity. Knowing how much he knew and how little I knew, I wrote those reviews very, very carefully. There was no pay—except for the privilege of being edited by William Harrison. Any stereotypes of blacks I'd had before knowing him had been swept away.

I didn't know any whites who read *The Boston Chronicle*, but what blacks did, and read, were largely unknown to the whites of the city. Years later, interviewing Larry O'Brien—who managed many of John F. Kennedy's campaigns—I asked why Kennedy had come so late to an awareness of racism, at home and across the land.

I remembered covering the March on Washington in 1963, when its leaders turned down Kennedy's request to address that historic civil rights assemblage because he had been tepid and contradictory on issues of black inequality. Later in the day, the pantheon of civil rights leaders allowed themselves to go to the White House for tea.

Answering my question, Larry O'Brien said, "Well, Jack didn't realize there were that many blacks in Boston. I mean, they just weren't seen in any numbers."

It depended, of course, on where you looked.

During my time in Boston, and for my first years in New York as an editor of *Down Beat*, many of the people I knew professionally and socially were black because we were in the same business—jazz.

From them, I heard and sensed no anti-Semitism. For the

most part, whatever resentment and anger they felt against whites was not compartmentalized but generic. For instance, I remember seeing Dizzy Gillespie on Broadway late one afternoon in the mid-1950s. He had just come from the office of his Jewish booking agent. Dizzy was exultant. "I told him," Dizzy said, "I finally told him. I don't work for *you*. You work for *me*." Not "You work for *me*, you Jewish bloodsucker."

Most jazz musicians reacted swiftly to any form of racism, from whomever it came. (Exceptions, in those and earlier years, were trips through the South, when physical survival was the priority.)

I saw Charles Mingus knock a white man out with one punch. The man hadn't said anything explicitly racist, but the attitude was there, and Charles decided on a preemptive punctuation to end the discussion.

Yet Mingus, who spoke out more plainly and fiercely about the exploitation of black musicians—by club owners and booking agents—than anyone else, never made it a Jewish issue.

In the 1950s there was a marked private and public change of attitude by black jazz musicians—particularly on the East Coast—toward whites, not specifically Jews. They were very conscious of the rising momentum of what A. Philip Randolph—the compelling labor and civil rights leader—called "The Unfinished Revolution."

In print, on the radio, on television, in conversations, there was the inescapable presence of the Freedom Riders and the sit-ins in the South, Dr. Martin Luther King, Malcolm X, the demonstrations up North, and the brutality of "Bull" Connor, among many other officially armed segregationists. And there was the spirit of what Thurgood Marshall later said: "I never have any trouble knowing I'm black. I just look at my hand."

Because of the rising black consciousness, there was pressure on black leaders to hire only black musicians. One black leader who would have no part of segregation in jazz was Miles Davis. Since Miles was famous for his contemptuous attitude toward Jim Crow in all its forms, he could hardly be called an Uncle Tom or an Oreo.

Still, there were mutterings about his hiring white pianist Bill Evans. "Hell," said Miles, "I'd hire someone who had green skin with purple polka dots—if he could play."

There was still, so far as I could see or hear, no discernible anti-Semitism among black players. Jews were just part of the white race, which, for some musicians, the world could have done without.

Outside of jazz, however, black anti-Semitism was growing. A predatory Jewish storekeeper or landlord—when there were still some Jews in black neighborhoods—meant that all Jews were predatory and bottomlessly greedy. Most blacks, to be sure, still took Jews one at a time, but black anti-Semites were obsessed—as white racists are obsessed.

In New York City, the long, traumatic citywide school strike of 1968, with a million kids on the streets, deepened the hatred of Jews among those blacks who were previously so disposed. The strike also gained new recruits to anti-Semitism, because the United Federation of Teachers—seen as a largely Jewish union—exercised the raw power of the strike to destroy an experimental black-run school district in Ocean Hill–Brownsville. The strike was led by the UFT's dread Al Shanker. (A Woody Allen movie at the time opened on a devastated planet Earth. Asked the cause, a survivor said, "Somebody gave an atom bomb to a guy named Al Shanker.")

The fact that there were also Jews who were continually critical of the UFT didn't change many black attitudes. Nor did the fact that the most comprehensive, carefully researched indictment of the teachers' union in this battle, a report titled "The Burden of Blame," was put together by the

New York Civil Liberties Union—headed by Ira Glasser, with a good many other Jews on the board, including me.

In the Ocean Hill–Brownsville schools, before the UFT recaptured the district, there were some new, young, very resourceful white teachers brought in by the black school administrators. Many of them were Jews. But the name that stayed in many black minds—all over the United States—was that of the late Al Shanker, who wouldn't give black-run schools a chance.

I did something during the strike that I never would have thought possible. In Boston, I was fifteen when I organized a union in the candy shop where I worked. Four years later I helped bring a union into the radio station I was working at then. Whenever I was working for someone else, it always seemed logical to get some protection against the boss, who was capable of turning me out into the street without warning.

Not surprisingly, I had never crossed a union picket line in my life. But I crossed a United Federation of Teachers picket line in 1968, and I also helped some parents in Greenwich Village open a school, helping to break the padlock myself. But in terms of black-Jewish relations, that didn't count. Nor did the work of other Jews who helped keep the black-run district going.

Blacks in other cities were intensely interested in the fate of Ocean Hill–Brownsville, and when it was eventually controlled again by the UFT, there was much black anger in the nation. Memories of that defeat reverberated for a long time. Black anti-Semites used Ocean Hill–Brownsville as a recruiting tool—citing Jews as the destroyer of black children.

But it's clear to me, listening to black radio all these years—in New York, Chicago, and other cities—that black anti-Semitism is hardly limited to memories of Ocean Hill–Brownsville. For example, on black radio and in the streets are theories that Jews must have had something to do with the

AIDS plague. Indeed, Steve Cokely, a Chicago "activist," has "discovered" that Jewish doctors were injecting the AIDS virus into black babies. Cokely later lectured on the subject at the University of Michigan under the auspices of an organization of black students there.

And as black scholars—Henry Louis Gates, for example— condemn black anti-Semitism, they are often reviled as Toms by some black nationalists and by members of Louis Farrakhan's Nation of Islam.

Minister Farrakhan became part of my own life during the 1984 presidential tournament.

During that campaign, Milton Coleman, a black reporter for the *Washington Post*, had, along with some other black reporters, heard Jesse Jackson, in an informal discussion, describe New York as "Hymietown." There is no evidence that Jackson had declared that session off the record, although he may have assumed that since only black reporters were present, they would not do him harm.

A white reporter at the *Washington Post* was preparing a long wrap-up on the Jackson campaign to that point, and Coleman told him about the "Hymietown" remark. The reference appeared deep in the story. It was not played as a big deal by the *Post*. But other papers and television networks did make a big deal out of it, and so did many Jewish organizations—and individuals. Jackson's campaign was blighted.

There was a split among black journalists over whether Coleman should have told the "Hymietown" story to a white reporter. Gil Noble devoted one of his *Like It Is* programs on WABC-TV to the debate. The show is directed primarily to black audiences. Present were Les Payne of *Newsday* and two other black journalists. I was the only white reporter on the program.

Payne argued that a journalist has to report what he or she sees and hears—if it's news. But the other black journalists said that, in this instance, a black reporter had a responsibility not to damage the campaign of a man in whom so many black people had placed so much hope.

Payne emphasized that no good is ever done to any people by hiding the truth. (It should be noted that in all of American journalism, Les Payne is one of the most vigorous pursuers of multifarious white racism.)

I said on the program that, as a Jew, I had written many pieces about Israel's brutalization of the Palestinians in the Occupied Territories, and had been accused by some Jews of betraying my people by providing ammunition to enemies of the Jewish state. Yet what I wrote was accurate, and to omit parts of a story is to falsify it.

A few nights later, Minister Farrakhan appeared on Ted Koppel's *Nightline* with, among others, my friend Roger Wilkins—formerly of the Justice Department, the *Washington Post*, and the *New York Times*. Milton Coleman was the subject. Farrakhan had previously addressed Milton Coleman in public:

"One day soon we will punish you with death."

If carried out, that punishment might, of course, have been quite a deterrent to other black reporters who might decide—by the tenets of their profession—to print facts that could lead to charges of their being "disloyal" to their people.

On *Nightline*, Farrakhan told Ted Koppel that not only truly responsible black journalists recognize the need for this higher loyalty. "On a recent show in New York City called *Like It Is*," Farrakhan said, "a respected Jewish writer named Nat Hentoff said that when he writes an article on someone, he *always* asks their position on Israel." Farrakhan continued, "Hentoff decides how he will write the article on the basis of that [person's] position on Israel."

He paused for dramatic effect and then said approvingly, "So he [Hentoff] is a Jew first and a writer afterwards."

At this point, Koppel—who knew my writings—tried to be helpful. "And that," Koppel said, "is Mr. Hentoff's decision to make."

Sure, it is Hentoff's decision to make—to be a propagandist. Thanks a lot, Ted.

Farrakhan, no doubt pleased that Koppel had confirmed that I was indeed in Israel's pocket, chimed in sanctimoniously, "That's right. That is Mr. Hentoff's decision to make."

And Roger Wilkins had not said a mumbling word.

I had been "exposed" to millions of viewers as a reporter who tailored his stories to fit ideological designs. In this business, all you have going for you is your credibility. Minister Farrakhan had just taken an ax to mine.

I didn't see Minister Farrakhan's tribute to me. That night, I was on a train coming home. Margot, who did see the program, was enraged. So angry that, talking on the phone to a friend, she dropped it, and then tried to get through to *Nightline*. But she only reached an operator who mechanically took her message.

I had the home phone number of one of *Nightline*'s producers, and woke her at about six the next morning, to get her attention.

No, she said, nobody ever gets rebuttal time on *Nightline*. But she'd tell Ted I'd called. When he came in, Koppel was told of my grievance, and watched the tape. I was invited to rebut—briefly. And briefly, I told the audience, "I am a journalist, first, second, and third. I use no political, religious, or ethnic criteria when I write."

Fair is fair. Farrakhan was asked to comment on what I had to say. Maybe he would admit unintended error. Following me on camera was Ted Koppel: "We contacted Mr. Farrakhan about Hentoff's response and Farrakhan said, 'What I spoke was true. I have no further comment.' "

I did, but my time was up.

Six months later I was interviewing a Chicago lawyer on another subject. Suddenly he said, "You know, I never would have thought you were the kind of reporter who would hide anything bad about Israel or anything else. I was very, very disappointed to hear that about you on *Nightline*."

I will never know how many viewers of *Nightline* took what Minister Farrakhan said about me as gospel. I'll also never know how much money I could have made if I had sued truth-teller Farrakhan for defamation. I might have become the landlord of the Nation of Islam, thereby embodying their most cherished stereotype of the Jew.

The first time I heard Minister Farrakhan's voice—at that Nation of Islam luncheonette in Harlem—he was telling me, from the jukebox, that "A White Man's Heaven Is a Black Man's Hell."

It didn't get to me. I thought it was kind of funny. But the minister's blessing of me on *Nightline* did get to me. I much preferred his displeasure.

He certainly continued to earn mine—all the more so as I visited college campuses throughout the country—more than ninety, over the past fifteen years. The degree of anti-Semitism, largely fueled by Farrakhan, was both disturbing and ominous. These students, after all, would become decision-makers, one way or another, in the wider world.

To begin with, groupthink abounds among some black students. There are exceptions, but individual dissent often either is suppressed or leads to expulsion from the group. Strengthening groupthink is the fact that some black students segregate themselves in separate residences and theme buildings with the supine approval of administrators, including college presidents.

Indeed, the thrust toward separatism has been so strong that Garry Trudeau once drew a "Doonesbury" strip in which a beleaguered college president, approached by a member of his staff, asks wearily, "What do the black students want now?"

Diffidently, the staff member answers, "Separate drinking fountains."

I have seen crudely anti-Semitic books on display at black student book sales; and the anti-Semitism at some black student papers could have been snugly fitted into the anti-Semitic tracts of white American fascists that I used to read more than fifty years ago.

At one college, Michigan State University, a pride of black students tried to end my lecture by shouting me down, but—like putting a cross in front of Dracula—I invoked Malcolm X's contempt for anti-Semitism, and they sat down again, sullenly.

At Kean College in New Jersey, I asked the head of the black student organization why his group hated Jews so much. Articulate, soft-spoken, he looked at me and said calmly, "Minister Farrakhan tells us who our enemies are."

I was not surprised to hear about a young Jewish woman, a student at UCLA, who, on the steps of the library, said aloud to no one in particular, "Why do they hate us so?"

Meanwhile, Farrakhan—who tells black students who their enemies are—was no longer a marginal figure in American life. In 1996, *Time* magazine anointed him one of the twenty-five most influential Americans. And the National Newspaper Publishers Association—comprising more than two hundred black papers in thirty-eight states—selected, for the first time in its history, a "Newsmaker of the Year." The overwhelming choice for the person who "has led blacks to a higher plateau" was Minister Farrakhan. The voters were "numerous grassroots and establishment leaders."

According to William Reed, the association's executive director, "some believe the sixty-two-year-old Jesus-quoting

Muslim has eclipsed even the stature of Martin Luther King at his apex."

The growing stature of Farrakhan struck me as somewhat reminiscent of nightmares of my boyhood. At that time, Father Charles E. Coughlin, a devout and skillful anti-Semitic orator, could well have been named one of the twenty-five most influential Americans. But no one, except for some Jews, seemed to care that on the edge of the twenty-first century, another religious leader—a powerful orator and a world-class hater of Jews—was both honored in the white mainstream media and vaulting over Martin Luther King among black newspaper publishers.

Though Farrakhan believes he is shaping and promulgating an indigenous black Manichaean explanation of the nation and the universe—blacks are the Light, and whites, especially Jews, are the Darkness—he actually has based his ecstatic anti-Semitism on classic white models.

Once I figured it out, I realized that Farrakhan's world-view indeed reflected that of the priest of the Shrine of the Little Flower in Royal Oak, Michigan—Father Coughlin. My parents and I used to listen to Coughlin on the radio; now I watch Farrakhan on C-Span. The world doesn't turn that much.

Coughlin used to publish a weekly newspaper, *Social Justice,* in which *The Protocols of the Elders of Zion*—a nineteenth-century tract, invented by the Tsar's secret police, about a worldwide Jewish conspiracy to take over the world—were given great and persistent prominence. The same durable *Protocols* have been sold at Nation of Islam mosques, and I have seen them lauded in black college newspapers.

The populist Catholic priest, on his radio programs—which had huge audiences across the country—took great pleasure in telling of his discovery that the international Communists, including most members of the Politburo, and the international bankers had one devil's mark in common. They were all Jews.

All these decades later, with Coughlin gone to his rest some-where, Farrakhan keeps anti-Semitic hopes alive. In a *New Yorker* profile of him, Henry Louis Gates tells of Farrakhan's speeches "in which he has talked about a centuries-old con-spiracy of international bankers—with names like Rothschild and Warburg—who have captured control over the central banks in many countries and who incite wars to increase the indebtedness of others and maximize their own wealth. . . .

"Farrakhan really does believe that a cabal of Jews secretly controls the world." Gates adds that Farrakhan—who also said this at a meeting of *Washington Post* editors and re-porters—believes that "there is a small group of Jews who meet in a Park Avenue apartment in New York or in Holly-wood to plan the course of [this] nation." He believes they meet regularly.

I do not believe that Farrakhan's Fruit of Islam—the blank-faced, bow-tied military wing of the Nation—will lead true be-lievers to conduct pogroms where Jews live and work. But his presence, and he sure has presence, helps keep me in touch with my boyhood and with what it has always been, here and there, to be a Jew.

When I was growing up in Boston, the cradle of abolition-ism, as William Harrison used to remind us, it was foolhardy of me to go out alone after dark and risk becoming prey to rov-ing bands of wild-eyed Christian Irish youngsters, whose most satisfying sport was to break the faces of Jews. One boy on my street got an icepick in his head and was never the same after-ward. I received only a busted nose ("You Jewish, kid?") and a lot of blood on my shirt.

Watching Farrakhan on television calling me—gener-ically—a "bloodsucker," and saying, head held high, that we Jews were planning to crucify him and would thereby be destroyed—I lived again in Roxbury, where both of us grew up. We have, of course, different memories. One of mine is of invading hooligans, breaking windows and pushing Jews into them. Like the newsreels of the time from Berlin.

I wouldn't crucify Farrakhan. Contrary to his fantasies, it's not a Jewish thing. But I have made him aware of my presence, writing about his support of slave dealers. For years, various international human-rights organizations have reported on the existence of chattel slavery in the Sudan. The Islamic rules of the country have encouraged Arab raiders and members of the official armed forces to capture and enslave black Christians and animists in the south of the country.

The raids have also resulted in many killings and rapes, and in the disruption of families. Black children are forced to convert to Islam. Entire villages are devastated.

Farrakhan—who has visited and been honored by the military government of the Sudan—has denied that slavery exists there. The irrefutable news that it does exist in the Sudan was revealed in parts of the American press by a courageous black reporter, Sam Cotton. With his help, and that of Christian Solidarity International—which has made frequent covert trips to the Sudan—I wrote about Farrakhan and slavery in the Sudan for the *Washington Post* as well as in the 250 other papers that take the column from my syndicate.

The columns indicted Minister Farrakhan for his silence. (Sam Cotton speaks of the "political and financial support" Farrakhan gets from countries that support the government of the Sudan—specifically Iran and Libya.)

Other newspapers, notably the *Baltimore Sun*, went on to focus on both the slave trade and the fact that Farrakhan, the self-described moral and political leader of all blacks, continued to ignore blacks in actual slavery while he condemns only the slavery of centuries ago.

The *Baltimore Sun* had accepted a challenge by Farrakhan.

At the National Press Club in Washington in 1996, Farrakhan had said angrily, "Where is the proof? If slavery exists, why don't you go as a member of the press, and you look inside Sudan, and if you find it, then you come back and tell the American people what you found."

The *Sun* thereupon sent two reporters—one black, one white—on a covert mission to the Sudan where, to directly answer Farrakhan, they *bought* two black slaves, whom they returned to their family.

ROOTS

When I talk to kids in schools, from elementary grades up, the questions are sometimes surprising. During the war between the New York teachers' union and black parents over control of the Ocean Hill–Brownsville schools, I was describing, to a fourth-grade class in Ocean Hill, how books are written and published. Raising his hand, a round, earnest boy asked me what royalty rate I was getting on my books.

A more common question is about influences. After I tell of some of the people and forces that helped shape my work—I. F. Stone and Duke Ellington, for instance—I'll be asked what my basic influences, my roots, are.

The most basic influences have been the legacies of liberty—from the Bill of Rights to jazz. And being a Jew. When I was a child, I overheard an old man say that a Jew must always have a bag packed so that, if need be, he can leave instantly. In the old country, my parents understood that. In this country they didn't have a bag by the door, but they knew that in many places in America—including Boston, where they lived—they were not, to say the least, welcome. My father, a traveling salesman all through New England and in parts of the South, came to know some gentiles with whom he could be comfortable. But my mother, spending all of her childhood and married years in the Jewish ghetto of Boston, was suspicious of all gentiles, and when I left the house at nineteen, her parting words were: "Never trust a goy."

My own early awareness of being a Jew was that it could be a harsh, narrow path of faith. For instance, I found out that the family of a son or daughter who married outside Judaism would sit in mourning for their child—just as if he or she were dead. To their parents, they *were* dead.

Years later, my parents essentially disowned me because my first wife was a non-Jew, Miriam Sargent. They finally relented. I was not dead yet.

I left the religious part of Judaism when I was thirteen. In the *shul*, on Yom Kippur, the holiest and most somber day of the Jewish year, I told God that I did not believe he existed, and challenged him to strike me dead then and there.

If there is a God, he or she must have been too busy for such a small fry.

Actually, I had become an atheist. Kierkegaard said it plainly: Belief in God, whatever one's religion, requires a leap of faith. In all these years I have not been able to make that leap.

And in all these years I have never stopped defining myself as a Jew. While still in my teens, I used to tell anyone who would listen that I would remain a Jew so long as there was anti-Semitism. Hardly a profound rationale. But that still means I will have this basis for staying a Jew from here to eternity.

There are other reasons—what might be called cultural reasons—that are shared by my children: a collective history of splendid accomplishments and horrifying pogroms, including the one in which concentration-camp commanders played Beethoven in their rooms in the quiet evening of a long, busy day.

And, most durably, for me, there is the perspective, as a Jew, of being an outsider. I felt this from the time I was old enough to take the trolley alone to Boston Latin School. On the trolley and in school, I was different. Blacks obviously have a stronger sense of being on the outside, on the margins. But Jews, whatever their economic class, are seldom so fully accepted by the goyim that they become insiders. And not being an insider has been a distinctive advantage to me as a journalist, novelist, and troublemaker.

My own standing as a Jew was severely questioned by many other Jews when I wrote accusingly of Israel's occupation of Palestinian territories and people. Yet, when quite small and just about able to walk, I had been sent up the block by my parents to collect money for trees to be planted in Palestine, the future home of the Jews. I was armed with a *pushka*, a small blue-and-white tin box for the ready donations.

We were all Zionists in my family, and I never stopped being one. But a Jewish state that ruled over so many non-Jews who wanted their own state was making Israel repellent in the world, and to many of its own citizens. In Israel, and later in New York, I interviewed and wrote about the colonels—male and female—in the Israeli army who started the Peace Now movement.

It was difficult, though not impossible, for hard-line Jews in America to call those colonels—all of whom had fought in one or more of Israel's wars—traitorous, self-hating Jews. But American Jews who called for an independent Palestinian state were to be condemned for eternity, and beyond, as self-hating Jews who betray the Jewish people.

Having written often and judgmentally that a true Jewish state would not repeatedly imprison Palestinians without presenting any evidence and without trial—as Israel did under what it called administrative detention—I received urgent requests on the phone and in letters that I commit suicide without delay. On a late-night radio talk show in New York, many calls came in during the two hours I was on. Every one was from a Jew devoutly wishing he or she were in the studio so that they could strangle—or otherwise exterminate—me.

One evening at New York's Central Synagogue, I was debating the former U.S. ambassador to the United Nations, Jeane Kirkpatrick, about Israel and the Occupied Territories. The Central Synagogue is eminently respectable, noted for the dignity of its rabbis and members.

The debate itself was rather mild. I was surprised that Jeane Kirkpatrick, otherwise well versed in international affairs, had limited knowledge of Israel—particularly the divisions between its political parties—and hardly any background in the diverse politics and strategies of the Palestinians. But she made some astute if predictable points, and besides, I liked her personally.

So I was having a good time until, on the right side of the auditorium, boos, shouts, imprecations—all directed at me—began to escalate. The boisterous editorial comments came from a block of seats. The rabbi looked embarrassed, as did the rest of the audience, which had hardly been on my side, but clearly were dismayed at such rudeness from Jews in their temple.

After the debate was over, the rabbi made a point of telling me that none of those Jews were familiar to him. They were not members of the congregation. Another official of the synagogue told me that the unruly Jews had been bused in from Brooklyn solely for that night's debates.

"Who bused them in?" I asked.

Nobody knew. The shouters had disappeared into the evening before I could ask them.

I have never been invited to the Central Synagogue since.

After all, if it hadn't been for me, its officials would not have been embarrassed.

One Sunday, not long after, my wife and I were watching Menachem Begin on CBS's *Face the Nation*. He was asked about a sharply critical comment concerning the Israeli occupation that had been written by Anthony Lewis of the *New York Times*. Begin looked at the questioner, looked at the camera, and dismissed any reference to Anthony Lewis by saying, "Mr. Lewis is not a friend of the Jewish people."

Margot looked at me. "From his point of view, he could have said the same about you, if he knew you existed."

Somebody in the Begin government knew my name. After being involved in a debate on the pages of the *Jerusalem Post*, I was told, not for attribution, that I was on an Israeli government list of people who were not exactly friends of the Begin government.

Yet I was more of a friend to Begin, on fundamental matters of Jewish identity, than he realized, even if he didn't know I existed.

In October 1982 I wrote in the *Village Voice* about the massacres in the Palestine refugee camps of Sabra and Shatila, carried out by Lebanese forces but facilitated by some Israeli soldiers stationed nearby. The reaction around the world was the worst Israel had experienced to that point, and Begin was at the center of the abuse and hatred.

In print, I had harshly, indeed viciously, attacked Ariel Sharon, who had manipulated the Israeli cabinet and army into the invasion of Lebanon, and I had not spared Begin for permitting the so-called "limited incursion" in the first place. But then Begin said something that made me realize that whether he knew it or not, or cared or not, we were soul brothers.

I began my column in the *Voice* with a poem, a memory:

*. . . All the children, astonished, ran to
meet the fear of death without tears . . .*

—MEMORIAL POEM BY JACOB
GLATSTEIN, TRANSLATED FROM THE
YIDDISH BY RUTH WHITMAN

Beneath this epigraph, I wrote:

"For this Rosh Hashanah 5743," I said, "the President of
Israel, Yitzhak Navon, sent greetings to all the Jews in the Di-
aspora. 'All Jews,' said President Navon, 'are responsible for
each other.'

"Or, at least, especially now, all Jews should try to understand each other. Menachem Begin, for instance. Begin, who
after the massacre in Sabra and Shatila, spoke from the heart
when he said, 'Goyim kill goyim, and they immediately come
to hang the Jews.'

"How insensitive, said a good many American Jews, some
of them his supporters. Can't he even make a show of compassion and restrain himself from saying things like that? And
from saying, yet again: 'No one will preach to us ethics and respect for human life.'

"And then there were those ads—those full-page ads in the
New York Times and the *Washington Post*. A number of enlightened Jews told me how embarrassed they had been by
those pronouncements. And especially by that headline:

BLOOD LIBEL

"The blunt prose that followed was credited to the Government of Israel, but you can hear the cadences, the very tart
sound, of Menachem Begin. Indeed, it was Begin himself who
ordered the Israeli Embassy in Washington to lay out $54,000
for the message: '. . . any direct or implicit accusation that the
IDF [the Israel Defense Force] bears any blame whatsoever
for this human tragedy is entirely baseless and without foun-

dation. The Government of Israel rejects such accusations with the contempt they deserve.'

"But the blame is inescapable. No matter how much genuine defiance the Prime Minister shows to the world. To all the world. To all the goyim.

"*Davar*, the Labor daily in Israel, answered those ads, on September 21:

" 'The Prime Minister went to synagogue yesterday; he should have gone to see the President, to hand in his resignation and to rid Israel of this Government which has turned Israel's image into something monstrous. The Prime Minister can go to synagogue for the Ten Days of Repentance and still not expiate his sin.'

"True. On the other hand, I think of a woman in Boston who has been so appalled, so humiliated, by all of this—not the least of it being the BLOOD LIBEL ads—that she has been talking of resigning from being Jewish.

"She should think more carefully about Menachem Begin. How he came to be what he is. And who is responsible for that. This man, who sounds like vinegar, and is accused of execrably bad taste for talking about goyim killing goyim and then coming to hang the Jews.

"The Begin Government's share of the responsibility for the deaths being clear, nonetheless it is interesting that everyone did come to hang the Jews while world indignation was still fresh and ferocious after the massacre. But for a significant period of time, hardly any attention was paid to the actual killers, the Christians, the followers of the Prince of Peace among the Lebanese forces.

"But I'm sure this did not surprise Mr. Begin. Martin Peretz, owner of *The New Republic*, calls him a 'zealot' and a 'fanatic.' Is there no more than that to say about this tormented, proud Jew?

"His father had been a leader of the Jews in Brest Litovsk,

Poland. His father was taken by the Nazis, and sacks full of rocks were arranged around his person. His father was then thrown into a river, with predictable consequences.

"Menachem Begin's mother was also murdered by the Nazis, as was his brother, Herzl. One of his close friends told *Newsweek*: 'He still believes Jews are the victims of hatred and prejudice: Jewish blood, the sight of helpless Jews being killed by enemies and pogroms. The fear of elimination and liquidation. That's what goes through his mind all the time.'

"And an aide of Begin said: 'He feels a duty to see that the Jewish people are safe. Not just Israel.'

"So, when Tom Wicker (*New York Times*) wrote that Begin's 'stonewalling' to prevent a real commission of inquiry showed 'contempt' for world opinion, Wicker didn't have it quite right.

"It was not contempt. It was fear. Fear that a real inquiry would reveal something awful that could harm Israel, that could harm the Jewish people everywhere, because Begin truly believes that all Jews are one. (Except those Jews who happen to be aggravating him at any given moment.) But did he have to use those embarrassing words, BLOOD LIBEL?

"Do you know what it is, this blood libel? For centuries, Jews were murdered because they were believed to be drinkers of blood. The blood of Christian children. Blood that Jews needed for their rituals. This blood libel began in Norwich, England, in 1144, and was soon spread enthusiastically all over Europe by goyim who actually believed that Jews had been created in the image of Satan.

"In France, for example, in 1247, a two-year-old Christian girl disappeared, and the next day her body was found in a ditch. Naturally the goyim came to hang the Jews. Three Jews were tortured until they 'confessed' to killing the child for her blood. Then they were sent to meet their maker in Hell.

"And never underestimate—as Begin knows—the ingenuity of the goyim when they want to get the Jews. In *The Roots of Christian Anti-Semitism* (Freedom Library Press/ Anti-Defamation League), Malcolm Hay notes that 'certain Christian fathers, when their children died, used to hide the dead bodies on Jewish premises, and then proceeded to extort money from the Jews by threatening to accuse them of having murdered the children to obtain the blood for the Paschal rites.'

"You think these blood libels against the Jews stopped when the darkness lifted and the Middle Ages were no more? Jews were tortured and killed for drinking the blood of Christian children into this very century. There was the grand 1903 Easter pogrom in Kishinev, Russia. The local bishop could have stopped it, but when asked if he really believed Jews were vampires, he said he surely did. And 118 Jewish men, women, and children were slaughtered. In Christ's name.

"In 1928, according to Ernest Volkman's *A Legacy of Hate: Anti-Semitism in America* (Franklin Watts), 'the rabbi of the Jewish community in Massena, New York, was summoned by the State Police and questioned about the custom among Jews of "offering human sacrifice at Yom Kippur." The question was asked in all seriousness while the police were investigating the disappearance of a four-year-old girl.'

"A mob of good Christians was already gathering in that New York town to take vengeance on the blood-drinking Jews who lived there. But their fun was spoiled when the four-year-old walked out of a nearby woods, unharmed.

"And, of course, when all was dark, under the Nazis, *Der Stürmer* regularly published vivid drawings of Jews sucking the blood of Christian children.

"So Menachem Begin was not just throwing words together for a catchy head to the ad. He was afraid, desperately afraid, that once again, Jews would be charged with having the blood of babies on their hands. That's why BLOOD LIBEL leapt from the top of the page.

"I suspect that it never occurred to Menachem Begin that goyim—to whom those ads were primarily addressed—would not know what blood libel is. How could they not know? They invented it.

"None of this is intended to make more of Menachem Begin as the head of the Jewish state than his record would indicate. Begin has become a great danger to Israel. His expansionist approach to Israeli security will destroy the Jewish character of the state if the West Bank and the Gaza Strip are annexed.

"Since Begin cannot change his own nature, he cannot negotiate with the Palestinians for their independence, because he does not see them as people, let alone as a nation. When he calls them 'animals walking on two feet,' he *says* he's talking about the terrorists; but since he appears to regard all Palestinians as terrorists, they see him as not seeing them at all.

"So, after a lifetime of fighting for a place where Jews will be free from the goyim and their murderous craziness, including blood libels, Menachem Begin looks out the window of his home and sees Jewish pickets calling him a murderer in Lebanon. Some of them have backgrounds much like his, but they came out different. Fear of the treacherous goyim did not freeze them, as it has Begin.

"But they—and we—should see Menachem Begin, and remember him, as a prisoner of those eternal goyim. Because not for a moment has he been free of them in his head.

"And they finally brought him down."

When I was in Israel, reporting for the *Village Voice*, I did not meet Mr. Begin. If I had, I might have told him of my mother, who, when she was a child in Minsk, was suddenly popped into the oven (unlit) by her mother. The avengers of Christ were about to pay another visit to the ghetto.

My mother's immediate family survived, but members of her extended family were killed, from time to time, just for being Jews. One was executed in 1905 for being a revolutionary.

We assumed that the Germans had finished off a number of other relatives, on both sides of the family, because we never heard from them again.

What I most vividly remember about Jerusalem are dead Jews. At Yad Vashem, the memorial of the Holocaust, there are rooms of ghosts. Photographs, for instance, of children who will soon—as in an unexpurgated fairy tale—be shoved into an oven, but with no one to rescue them.

After the rooms of those murdered by the Germans—I find it hard to distinguish between the Nazis and the Germans of those years, except for the German resistance—there is another room at Yad Vashem.

The war is over. The survivors of the concentration camps have been liberated. And on the wall of that room, with photographs, there is the story of some Polish Jews who, having survived the camps, were now returning to their homes in Kielce.

Ah, but Polish Christians live in those Jewish homes now, and these Poles are enjoying the property the Jews had to instantly leave behind years ago. They do not want to give any of this back. They have possession of it, so it is theirs.

How is the problem to be solved? Easy. Spread the word that these Jews have murdered a Polish boy to use his blood in the baking of matzoh. So, for almost an entire day, there was a pogrom, with forty-two Jews killed. Elie Wiesel wrote, "What happened in this place showed that 'ordinary people' could be as cruel as the killers in any death camps."

In Jerusalem, there is another place that exists to keep alive the memory of the Holocaust. It doesn't look like a museum at all. It looks like an eccentrically furnished, cluttered apartment out of a Dickens novel.

Yad Vashem is clean, almost sterile, and austere. Visiting international dignitaries, especially politicians, dutifully walk slowly through the rooms of Yad Vashem. But at this other place, near the top of one of Jerusalem's hills, the dignitaries do not come.

Yet it was at this place—seeing the clothes, the books of the forever disappeared—that I felt closer to the dead. I stared at some bars of soap on a shelf, and I turned to the ancient attendant. He nodded. "Jews," he said. "They used to be Jews."

I learned later that there is a dispute—and not only among the so-called Holocaust revisionists—as to whether any Jews actually were made into soap. But the old Jew in the shabby museum believed it. So did I.

MY CHILDREN: LAWYERS,

A MUSICIAN, A CIRCUS

PERFORMER

For all my carrying on about being a Jew, two of my progeny—Jessica and Tom—have married non-Jews. As did I the first time around, without feeling less Jewish. Tom and Jessica, like the other two, identify themselves as being of Jewish culture, if not the faith. And each is concerned about justice—which for me goes back to my childhood.

My father, an inveterate newspaper reader, would stop at a story of raw, arbitrary authority visited on some hapless soul, and say, "Un-Jewish. Very un-Jewish."

I wish he had been alive when attorney Alan Dershowitz, a master of unfeigned indignation, and I reversed an injustice against the Jewish people, or a few score of them. It was on Fire Island in New York, a summer place with a number of disparate communities. One of them, Point O' Woods, was a haven for WASPs. No Jews were permitted anywhere in that pristine retreat, and there was a formidable fence to make sure that we heathen were indeed kept out.

Point O' Woods had its own United States post office. One day, Alan Dershowitz and I, on bicycles, led a posse of Jews and several blacks up to the fence. We showed a functionary there a number of letters that we wished to mail. No way. "You want to mail a letter, go to the mainland."

Instead, we decided to exercise our First Amendment right to "petition the government for a redress of grievances." We wrote to the head of the U.S. Postal Service and the two United States senators from New York. The official word came back that Point O' Woods had to let us through the gate whenever we had letters to mail—or they would lose their very own United States post office.

So deep was their fear of contamination from Jews that the homeowners in Point O' Woods chose to do without the post office, and instead travel to the mainland to mail their letters.

It was one of the most satisfying victories I have ever experienced.

And it was repeated at our Jewish dinner table, as victories over illegitimate power have been for centuries. Not that we always agreed at the dinner table. Our children grew up as members of a continuing debating society. No subject was forbidden. Those years of learning how to cope with clashing ideas may have been a factor in Nick's and Tom's becoming lawyers.

My elder son, Nicholas, is a criminal defense lawyer in Phoenix. At first he was intrigued by journalism. As an intern at the *Wall Street Journal*, he had several front-page stories; and he worked another beat covering the Navajo Reservation for the *White Mountain Independent* in St. Johns, Arizona.

Having explored the combat zones of journalism, Nick decided to look into the law. After having won his license at the University of Arizona Law School, he clerked for a federal district judge in Phoenix. Nick became a lawyer there—first as a public defender and then as a solo practitioner.

He had the right temperament for it, including a zest for combat with prosecutors, police, and county sheriffs. He carries a (licensed) gun, and one of his avocations is improving his marksmanship at shooting ranges. Very un-Jewish, my father would have said.

I tell other lawyers and reporters about his cases as if they were mine. One I expect I shall be telling, until I can tell no more, brings me back to a boyhood fantasy of becoming another Clarence Darrow.

Dale Zamarripa, the youngest of eight children of migrant farm workers, had been an assistant orthodontist in the office of a Phoenix dentist for seven years. One day a fourteen-year-old patient called him from the Mesa Police Department and—with police listening in—accused Zamarripa of having sexually molested her for two years.

Zamarripa failed a polygraph test. A detective, Alden "Butch" Oates, then took him into a small room and told him that if he confessed, things would go more smoothly for him, and the girl's father might not press charges. Zamarripa, believing he was doomed anyway—because the failed polygraph test would be used against him in court—confessed.

When he found out the results of the test could not be admitted at trial, he tried to recant his taped confession. He failed in that too. The detective later said, "I didn't have to tell him the polygraph is inadmissible in court."

In jail for two months because he couldn't raise bail, Zamarripa was told by his public defender to go for a plea bargain because it would be almost impossible to undo the effect on a jury of a confession. And, said the lawyer, if he was convicted, he could be sentenced to two hundred years. Arizona's laws in this area are harsh. Zamarripa began to think of the plea bargain that would put him in prison for fifteen years. ("Maybe being free at fifty-five was better than never being free.")

After a second public defender was even less optimistic, Zamarripa, as a last resort, tried to find a private lawyer. As June Shih reported in the *Phoenix Gazette*: "Most lawyers they consulted wanted thirty thousand dollars to take the case. Zamarripa could only raise eight thousand dollars from his friends.

Nicholas Hentoff, an aggressive attorney, agreed to be co-counsel with the second public defender for eight thousand dollars."

As he thought about the case, Nick figured the alleged molestation of the girl would have been impossible over two years in an office without any doors and with continual traffic by patients and dentists.

As for the polygraph test, Nick brought in an expert polygrapher who testified that the protocol used by the police polygrapher was outdated, and there were other irregularities. Furthermore, Nick told the jury, his client's confession had been coerced.

A forensic psychiatrist, called by Nick, told the jury that Zamarripa was "a very compliant guy, the kind who believes that authorities are indeed authorities and police are good guys." Moreover, "the interview process itself is so overwhelming"— especially for compliant personalities—"that the immediate discomfort" is such "that you just want to get it over with."

During cross-examination of the detective who had obtained the confession, Nick persuaded the jury that the confession had indeed been coerced; moreover, he showed that there was a three-minute gap in the tape. What was missing? And why? The detective was vague.

Nick also brought in witnesses who created reasonable doubt as to the girl's truthfulness in other situations. And he argued that the accusation might have been planted in her mind by the psychiatrist treating her for depression.

Having deliberated for less than three hours after a six-week trial, the jury acquitted Zamarripa of four counts of child molestation, eight counts of sexual abuse, and two counts of sexual conduct with a minor.

Nick told the *Phoenix Gazette*, "It could have been devastating for me personally had he been convicted."

I believed him.

. . .

My younger son, Tom, became a lawyer, although his preference was to be a novelist. While he was an undergraduate at Wesleyan, he wrote a satirical novel. My wife and I—who would not have circulated a bad novel by one of our progeny because we would look bad, as well as the author—did send Tom's novel around because it worked. It sharply illuminated what, years later, came to be called "political correctness" on campus.

The religion of "political correctness," however, was already rooted among some liberals. It was flourishing, for instance, at the *Village Voice*, where I continued to enjoy being a heretic. P.C. was also becoming evident among some editors at publishing houses. Before I unwisely sent Tom's book to a number of firms, my agent had tried to persuade a series of houses to publish my first detective novel, *Blues for Charlie Darwin.*

That book, based in part on months of hanging out with homicide detectives, was about police and their prey—and, as on the streets, it was sometimes hard to distinguish between them in my novel. The language was multiculturally offensive and, I think, funny.

My detective novel traveled a long time before finding a publisher. It had been rejected by a dozen firms, and the comments of some of the editors who turned it down presaged the fate of Tom's novel—and later, the full flower of political correctness to come: "Some of the characters are racist and anti-Semitic. Do they reflect Hentoff's own views?" "There is nobody I can identify with in this novel. I thought Hentoff was a liberal."

Eventually, *Blues for Charlie Darwin* found a home at William Morrow because of Hillel Black, then an editor there, and it was published successfully in Europe and South

America, where sensitivity to uncivil language is apparently not yet in full bloom. One of my ambitions, when I was living in France on a Fulbright in 1950, was to have Gallimard publish one of my books someday. And, Gallimard did adopt this prickly novel.

I should have advised Tom to wait until the Zeitgeist changed before sending out his novel, which has yet to be published. He tried college journalism, and became editor of *The Argus*, the student paper at Wesleyan. During his time at the top, he was almost defenestrated. The staff could hardly have been more sensitive to any language that might wound blacks, women, the handicapped, and Aleuts. They confronted Tom one day and demanded that from then on, the word *freshman* never be used in *The Argus*. That sexist term was to be replaced with *freshperson*.

Tom informed the staff that the change would be made only over his dead body. Fortunately a vote was not taken on this option. I understand that since he left, the Wesleyan campus abounds with freshpersons each fall, according to *The Argus*.

Tom went on to Columbia University Law School and spent summers at the NAACP Legal Defense Fund in Los Angeles and the ACLU's National Security Project in Washington. After graduation he became an associate at Williams and Connolly in Washington, the firm founded by the justly legendary Edward Bennett Williams. He is married to Sally Sloan of National Public Radio, and they have a child, Hugo. Tom specializes in First Amendment and intellectual-property law. He remains an unreconstructed skewerer of political correctness in all its forms, and he has become a crisply analytical, resourceful lawyer, the kind I used to dream of being.

. . .

My daughter Jessica was a reader from her very early years. I can't remember her without a paperback in the hip pocket of her jeans. I expected, as did she, that she would become a professor somewhere. At the State University of New York at Purchase, she majored in sociology, and her senior thesis was titled, "With It and For It: Circus People as a Deviant Subculture."

Her interest in circus life had already become passionate. SUNY-Purchase offered a month of alternative courses in between the regular semesters. Jessica took one in circus arts, given by an actual circus performer. A Pied Piper, as it turned out. She had found her life's work.

First, Jessica learned and then mastered juggling. Always fond of fun, she had no trouble becoming a clown as well. She was now equipped for a summer on the road with Circus Kingdom, a Christian show that performed at prisons, orphanages, and homes for the mentally disturbed, as well as for other audiences.

During a subsequent summer, she made a living, sort of, doing street shows—in New York and Montreal. In addition to juggling, she engaged in fire-eating. I thunderously disapproved of her ingesting fire, and she finally agreed to stop, taking to the trapeze instead. I did not think I had won a significant victory.

As part of her apprenticeship, Jessica was in a long-term—physically and emotionally painful, often excruciatingly difficult—course of study with two former members of the Moscow Circus, Nina Krasavani and Gregory Fedin.

With them, Jessica learned, again and again, the art of staying alive on a trapeze. For a long time I boycotted her performances—out of protest and fear. Not long after she took to the air, she had called early on a Sunday morning: "Hi, Dad. I'm in Kansas City. In the hospital. I fell twenty feet last night. Fortunately I landed on the softest part of my anatomy."

It had happened at a place called Worlds of Fun. Years later a reporter for *St. Louis* magazine noted that Jessica "suffered a fractured pelvis, a dislocated shoulder, and a worried father." Thereafter, Jessica and I argued bitterly and raucously during my long-distance attempts to get her to stay on the ground.

My internist, Dr. Paul Esserman, a kindly man, watched Jessica in a trapeze performance at the Brooklyn Academy of Music. "I saw her up there," he told me, "and I couldn't help myself. I stood up and spread out my arms, I was so afraid she'd fall."

Jessica and her partner did not use a net. It was, she told me, a violation of the European tradition. I bought her a net, and it was never used.

While refusing to see her perform, I marveled at the clippings she sent. When Circus Flora played Denver, the *Rocky Mountain News* took special note of "two laughing girls in white tights and iridescent gauze who hang their heels from a silver ring." Jessica also rode bareback on a huge horse.

When the circus performed at the Spoleto Festival in Charleston, South Carolina, Jennifer Dunning of the *New York Times* wrote: "The honors for the most imaginative act must go to the Hentoff and Hoyer Duo, two young women who hang from each other's hands, knees, and heels in exotic configurations high above the audience."

And in his book, *The New American Circus* (University Press of Florida), Professor Ernest Albrecht cited Jessica as one of "the significant forces in the modern circus."

My laughing, exotic, influential daughter called one night to say that after a performance, several of the seasoned European circus artists on the show applauded her and her partner. It was like a young tenor saxophonist being told by Ben Webster, "You've got it!"

I gave up. I ended my boycott. I finally recognized that since I have obsessions, why shouldn't she?

When Circus Flora stopped at Saratoga Springs, in upstate New York, I traveled there, expecting to avert my eyes from those two young women so far up, and without a net.

My fear grew as, ever smiling, they climbed the rope to the trapeze. (Jessie later admitted that in her difficult learning days with the insistent Russians, she would think, as she climbed up a rope, "I could have been a teacher, I could have been a lawyer.")

Once the act began, however, I became so involved in the gracefully intricate choreography that I forgot to be afraid.

In my mail, from the road, there was a photograph of Jessica, on the ground, stroking a young lion at her feet while a zebra looked into the middle distance. "How many Jewish girls," she wrote me, "get to listen to lions roaring at night; look out their window and see elephants (have you watched an elephant go swimming?); play with chimpanzees; and wake up to baby bears nibbling their fingers?"

Around that time, backstage at a circus, an elderly European circus performer asked Jessica, "You Jewish?" Yes, said Jessica. "And you're in the circus? I thought Jews were smart."

In one of the troupes with which my daughter has performed, the closing number had the whole cast singing "May All Your Days Be Circus Days!" She remembers that "the ringmaster would sound out the lyrics, we'd all be standing around the ring, and I'd wave at the people, incredibly happy that all my days *are* circus days."

When she was married in a circus tent to Michael Killian in St. Louis, where she now lives, Dr. David Harris, the Methodist minister who gave Jessica her first circus job, officiated at the wedding. Jessica, in white, rode down the aisle into the center of the ring on a large dashing black horse. As the father of the bride, I was under instructions to take her off the horse. I didn't do it gracefully, but I didn't drop her.

Jessica now has her own circus—the Everyday Circus—that performs for kids' parties, civic celebrations, and other festive occasions. And for years she has worked with a creation of hers, the St. Louis Arches, a young black gymnastic team that specializes in daring, precise, rapid-fire acrobatic acts.

Now a circus impresario and teacher, Jessica remembers that when she was a teenager, she didn't think she would ever be able to climb a tree. Her very young children, Elleana, Keaton, and Kellin, are now part of her Everyday Circus. They have never known anything but circus days.

Miranda, the circus performer's younger sister, is a musician. She had—it seems to me—always been a musician. When Mandy was ten, she played guitar and sang with a decent respect for music. But soon her obsession was to become a pianist. From a temporary brother-in-law who was passing through the family, I bought a white upright piano with—it was later discovered—a near-fatal crack in its soundboard. Nonetheless, for years Mandy extracted intriguing sounds from that terminal instrument for six hours nearly every day.

When she was sixteen I bought her a Baldwin piano, and she played until, it seemed, she became the piano. When it was silent, she listened to recordings by Sarah Vaughan, Billie Holiday, Duke Ellington, and especially Bill Evans, the self-doomed, deeply introspective jazz pianist. One of her other favorites was Annie Ross, a singer of quick, swinging wit.

Mandy began working gigs around New York. Her choice of vocation gave me much vicarious pleasure. I had been mesmerized by music since I was a child running to hear a Jewish klezmer band at a wedding hall down the street. And in the *shul*, the deep song of the improvising cantors, the hazzans, penetrated my very soul, if an atheist has a soul.

For years, wanting to get somewhere, anywhere, into the making of music, I played clarinet. Classical music. I didn't have a clue about how to improvise, although Mandy tells me that if she had been around then, she could have taught me how to improvise in half an hour.

My fantasy—through childhood and for some years thereafter—was to be hired by Duke Ellington and, bowing to the audience, take a seat alongside Johnny Hodges, Ben Webster, and Harry Carney in the reed section. That fantasy died of invincible reality. Then I had another—one of my children would be so striking a musician that she'd be recruited by Ellington or Count Basie.

And here was a daughter who, if not eventually selected to be in the jazz pantheon, might at least go on the road with a trio and be asked back for return gigs. In New York she played dates with small combos of her own, gradually veering away from straight jazz and from songs by other composers. She had studied composition at the Manhattan School of Music, where she got a master's as well as a bachelor's degree so that she could pay the rent—by teaching—until stardom came.

Her formal studies in composition didn't get in the way of her natural storytelling skills. Her songs were wry distillations of love-as-Russian-roulette, and were very funny in a self-deprecating way. Her sound—dark and resonant—was immediately identifiable.

She was becoming what used to be called a cabaret singer. I still hoped she would play into my fantasies by returning at least partially to jazz. She was still talking like a jazz musician. Reading some of my reviews of various players, she'd shake her head and say, "How can you criticize someone's performance when you can't play any jazz yourself?" That reminded me of Horace Silver, the most amiable of jazz pianists off the stand, saying to me years ago, before Mandy was born, "You wrote in *Down Beat* that I play 'angular' piano. What does that mean? Can you show me how and where on the keyboard I played this 'angular' passage?"

After a while there was another change in Mandy's playing, singing, and writing. She plunged into rock. I could no longer hear her lyrics; they were overwhelmed by the electronics.

That inability to listen beyond the past wasn't my fault, Mandy told me. "It is the way people of your generation," she said, "hear music." She and people of *her* generation, she went on, listen in a fundamentally different way so far as textures, rhythms, the inner meanings of words, and especially feelings, are concerned.

I was too old, in sum, to know when a synthesizer was singing to me. I tried Duke Ellington's apothegm: "There are only two kinds of music—good and bad."

She looked at me. "To whom?" she said.

Mandy changed again. I heard her in a Greenwich Village club with a largely jazz combo—the Miranda Hentoff Band. I liked seeing that in print. I'd always wanted to have a band, but I had wound up being only a one-man band.

After the clanging, raucous rock, I could now hear her lyrics again, her voice soaring over the band's crisp, often exhilarating drive. ("I used to think that time is all you need," she sang. "Finally I see how many ways you leave.")

During all those years, Mandy was teaching composition, theory, and piano at the Harlem School of the Arts; at various public magnet schools and non-magnet schools; at the Victoria Arts Center Institute in Melbourne, Australia; and at Lincoln Center in New York. She also has had a large number of private pupils—from the children of Itzhak Perlman to those of Sting.

I was one of her students once. As a parent who has spent much of his life writing about music while unable to be a credible musician—or, for that matter, any kind of real musician—I had a singular experience one afternoon at Lincoln Center.

Mandy was lecturing—with musicians on stage for illustration. She was explaining the structure, from the inside out, of Bartok's "Sonata for Two Pianos and Percussion." The audience consisted of music teachers, professional musicians, students, and officials of Lincoln Center.

Mandy cast steady, penetrating light on Bartok's intentions and conclusions in the work. With wit and contagious enthusiasm, she personified music as adventure, as continual self-discovery. I had been listening to that work from my early twenties, but she brought me far beneath the surface.

I looked at the stage and remembered the child somehow extracting music from a cheap white piano with a cracked soundboard. You never know what a child of yours will become, but I never could have imagined the evolution of these four kids—with surprises still to come.

FURTHER ADVENTURES

IN THE SKIN TRADE

Through the years I have usually not told my children of various death threats I've received—and other confrontations with unhappy readers. But I do tell of some that have taken a particularly dramatic—or somewhat humorous—turn.

Some years ago, for instance, during the time when "We Shall Overcome" was the mantra of the black-and-white civil rights movement, I was walking, at twilight, down a side street in Greenwich Village. Suddenly a dozen or so young black men—actually, more boys in appearance than men—materialized.

They surrounded me, and their leader, apparently in the mood for conversation before engaging in the business at hand, asked with menacing amiability, "Who are you? What do you do?"

"I'm a writer," I said.

"What do you write about?"

Combining guile with accuracy, I said, "Civil rights, discrimination against blacks."

He smiled, as did his companions. "You write about us, right?"

I skipped adding that I didn't write only about delinquents among blacks.

"Yeah."

A few weeks before, I had spent much of the night with a gang of predatory white youths in the Chelsea area. It was an assignment for *The Reporter* magazine. At one point, as we were going through a very dark underground passage, I heard one of the warriors behind me say, "We could off the reporter right here." He was overruled.

"Where do you write about us?" the young black leader, still smiling, asked me in the gathering darkness.

"In *The Reporter*, *Village Voice*, other places."

"Well, then you owe us, right? You get money writing about us, we got to get our share, right? Without us, you'd have nothing to write about."

It seemed a reasonable point, a sort of free-marketplace-of-ideas mugging. Besides, what choice did I have?

I gave him whatever I had, a ten and a five, as I remember. He pocketed the money and waved his troops to follow him down the street. He turned briefly and smiled.

Less beguiling was hearing on the radio one day that I was on a select list of whites whose critical writings on some blacks had qualified them to be sent into eternity. I was listening to WLIB, a black New York radio station. The host at the time was Clayton Riley, an articulate, chronically angry teacher and sometimes writer for the *New York Times*, the *Village Voice*, and other publications.

During one of Riley's broadcasts, he declared, "There are doctrinaire white supremacists trying to destroy us. . . . This has to do with the race war that is going on in this country. People can sleep and shrug their shoulders if they want to, but we are at war. . . . Every black public figure is under attack. . . . The racial divide is growing wider and wider.

"We talk about what Colin Powell said: 'You find the

enemy, you isolate it, you kill it.' [And among those] we want to put on that list is Nat Hentoff.

"Remember my telling you the story about Miles Davis. A broadcaster asked him, 'Miles, what would you do if you found out you had an hour left to live?' Miles said, 'I'd like to spend it strangling a white boy.'

"Well, we have added to the list of white boys Miles would like to have strangled—and let us say *would like to*. Miles Davis didn't go out and strangle nobody. . . .

"I must tell you, folks, you can believe this if you want to or believe it or not, if you choose to do that. I don't know a black man who would not say to another black man, 'I dream *constantly*, dream about, fantasize about, strangling a white boy.'

"Now a lot of folks will say to me, 'Hey, you shouldn't say that. People will misunderstand.' I don't *care* if people misunderstand. It's symbolic, you know. We're talking about metaphors, talking about irony, that's what the blues is made of.

"We're going to add John Taylor [a reporter then for *New York* magazine] to the list of white boys Miles Davis would like to have strangled. You know, 'If I had an hour to live, I'd like to spend it strangling a white boy!' . . . Everybody who has put our lives on the line, whether it is Jim Sleeper [then of the New York *Daily News*] or Nat Hentoff. They are the enemy, and you have to remember that Colin Powell said, 'You find the enemy, you isolate it, you kill it!' That is what you do with Nat Hentoff [and the others] who are attempting to murder us."

Miles Davis got a bum rap from Riley. Miles was not the author of that deep yearning to spend one's last breath by ending the breathing of a white boy. It was said by a young, mercurial black nationalist in the Village.

Miles Davis disliked a lot of people, regardless of race,

creed, or any other category. But he despised all forms of racism, and fought it in and out of the music business.

Listening to Clayton Riley's broadcast, I was torn between being a First Amendment protector and a target. Had Clayton Riley engaged in incitement to kill? He had said, by way of avoiding that indictment, "We're talking about metaphors, talking about irony." And earlier, during the same broadcast, he noted, "This is all satire. We're speaking metaphorically here."

Let us suppose it was all metaphor and irony. David Duke, after all, used to say his critics took some of what he said too literally. A certain amount of hyperbole and sardonic playfulness is endemic to public discourse, especially on talk radio.

Yet, when I heard the "strangling" part of the tape, I remembered some of the death threats I've gotten through the years. Some were couched in what I guess could be called metaphorical language, but how could I be sure of what was coming now—especially from those of Clayton Riley's listeners unacquainted with metaphor or irony?

A death threat, however phrased, can be very scary. It's supposed to be. It is certainly not an invitation to further dialogue.

As for the law, however, was Riley vulnerable for a charge of incitement to terminal violence? Not according to a Supreme Court precedent. He was protected by the 1969 Supreme Court decision in *Brandenburg v. Ohio*. There the leader of a Ku Klux Klan klavern had been convicted in the lower courts of advocating violence to effect political change. Angry that the president, Congress, and the Supreme Court were, he claimed, giving preference to blacks, he *said* he and his boys in the hood would eventually go to Washington to take care of those depriving him and other whites of their rights.

The Supreme Court reversed the conviction, ruling that

violence can lawfully be advocated *unless* the speaker is engaged in "inciting or producing *imminent* lawless action"—that is, if the speaker urges that violence be committed right then and there. Also, the advocacy must be likely to incite or produce actual violence. That is, the speaker must be addressing people who are ready and willing to commit the violence right then and there. Incitement alone isn't enough.

Clayton Riley was not advocating that the stranglings begin immediately, nor was he addressing a specific group of people who were prepared to grab white throats then and there—so far as I knew.

So Riley was free and clear of any legal sanctions for broadcasting his hit list.

But there were some acutely frustrated blacks in New York. One or two listeners, hearing Riley that day, could have been inspired to strike a resounding blow in that race war in America that Riley described. I wasn't hard to find.

It didn't happen. Still, imperfect pacifist that I am, I thought, for a while, of carrying a knife.

Clayton Riley was outspoken again on the air. Bob Grant, a very popular white talk-show host then on WABC, was attacked by callers and hosts on WLIB for what they described as chronic racism. Jesse Jackson, among others, picketed the WABC studios and called for a boycott of Grant's sponsors as a way to take him off the air.

Riley, however, vigorously disagreed with this strategy on free-speech grounds. "I stand with anyone on WABC," Riley said, "on their right—as it is my right—to speak. There is no halfway point on this, if you believe in free speech. I want to *know* what's out there.

"Without the First Amendment, we would not be able to do our programs at WLIB. It's because we have the First Amendment now that we're able to have black newspapers and the range of opinions across the spectrum." If the First

Amendment were weakened, "WLIB would be the first radio station to go. I am opposed to boycotting WABC."

This white boy applauded Riley in my column in the *Voice*. Soon after, Riley was fired. Too brusque to the callers, management said. Too soft on Bob Grant, I thought. I was glad I hadn't called the cops on Mr. Riley.

SWINGING THE BILL

OF RIGHTS

I tell the story of Clayton Riley in secondary schools and colleges when I'm asked to speak on the First Amendment and the rest of the Bill of Rights. It's a way of making freedom of speech real—not just an abstraction in a civics lesson.

One day, on the way to talk to kids in rural Pennsylvania about their legacy of liberty, I visited Justice Brennan in his chambers at the Supreme Court. I told him where I was going, and Brennan said, "Tell them stories! You've got to get the words of the Bill of Rights off the page and into their lives."

During part of that trip, I was accompanied by an official of a school district, and one afternoon she warned me that the school we were about to visit was in a very poor area. Apart from what they got in school, the kids had no cultural advantages. Their parents didn't take them to museums or symphony concerts in the cities not too far away. So, she said, "The kids are, well, not likely to fully understand what you'll be saying."

At first they didn't seem to be all that quick, but that was my fault because I was slow in getting to the stories. I started by asking if they knew what the Fourth Amendment is. There was a dense silence until a brave student asked, "The right to bear arms?" That didn't work, and no one else tried. I went on, forgetting Justice Brennan's advice, and talked abstractly about privacy and the guarantee in the Constitution that no arm of the state can invade an American's home or business without a search warrant—and that warrant cannot be issued by a judge unless there is probable cause to believe that a crime is going on, or has taken place. And the warrant is illegal unless it particularly describes the place, persons, or things to be searched or seized.

The students nodded dimly—until I told them a story:

When the British ruled here, I began, their troops could, at will, break into anyone's home or business with a "writ of assistance"—a general search warrant. With these "blank check" writs, the soldiers would brutally turn everything, including the colonists, upside down.

The class was showing interest. I went on to tell them about the Boston lawyer James Otis, a passionate advocate for individual freedoms, as he argued, in 1761, for four hours before the Massachusetts Supreme Court against those humiliating general search warrants.

James Otis lost that day in court, but his arguments reverberated through the colonies. A young lawyer, watching in the courtroom that day, wrote an entry in his diary that night. Describing Otis as "a flame of fire," he said, "The Child, Independence was then and there born." The young lawyer, I told the class, was John Adams, who was to become our second president.

And because of the anger of the colonists at the general search warrants, I went on, we now have the Fourth Amendment in the Bill of Rights to prevent *our* government from coming into our homes and businesses to search and seize at will. Justice Brennan believes, I added, that those British searches that so enraged the colonists were the most immediate precipitating cause of the American Revolution.

Some of the kids were leaning forward at their desks. It

as—from their—as if they were discovering America. And so they were.

Not all my days in the public schools ring the liberty bell. There are times when their faces are blank, and I'm afraid that many of the students will grow up to be as ignorant of our liberties as presidents, members of Congress, and high-school principals.

But, like Johnny Appleseed, I keep on keeping on. Some of my most vivid memories are of what happened in some of those classrooms, and after. For example, one morning in a public high school in Colorado, I was talking—with actual stories—of the First Amendment right to petition the government for a redress of grievances. A week before, the principal had ruled that the students had no right to circulate, at a coming football game, some complaints about the governance of the school. The game took place the day after we explored the First Amendment, and sheets of protest spread throughout the stands.

When the furious principal threatened reprisals, the students reminded him that he was the "government" of that school, and so the First Amendment applied to him. The students enjoyed instructing a principal about the basics of Americanism.

In a sense, the former chairman of the House Internal Security Committee may have been right in characterizing me as an itinerant subversive.

AT THE JAZZ BAND BALL

For many years, I spent much of my time with those embodiments of free expression—jazz musicians—and was a familiar presence at the clubs where the music was played. That largely stopped as I began to write and lecture on the law and the courts; on attacks on free speech from the left and the right; on health-care rationing; on the Peace Now forces in Israel; on capital punishment; and on euthanasia.

Nights, instead of checking out rhythm sections, I read legal briefs or medical journals. I miss the company of jazz players, although we occasionally meet on the street.

Many of the musicians I knew well are gone. The only photographs I have on my desk, aside from those of my family, are of jazz musicians, most of them dead. They recall good times when we were together at one jazz band ball or another.

Dizzy Gillespie, for one. Louis Armstrong once said of Fats Waller that "when he entered a room, you could see a gladness in all the people there."

So it was with Dizzy. He wasn't always sunny, by any means. He reacted swiftly and stingingly to any hint of Jim

Crow. But the warmth of the man, his constant curiosity and delight in learning new possibilities—in music and in the rest of his life—was infectious. And the quick precision of his wit was an extension of his trumpet playing, or maybe the other way around.

There is a description of Dizzy by the musician-historian Gene Lees that distills his spirit. Lees and a photographer had arranged to meet Dizzy at a small park in Minneapolis. As they approached, they saw Dizzy, who did not see them: "Lost in some musical thought, Dizzy was softly dancing, all alone there in the sunlight."

In the 1980s there was to be a concert in Dizzy's honor at Lincoln Center. He would be leading a big band. I hadn't seen Dizzy, except as part of an audience, for a few years, and I decided to come to the rehearsal. In the hallway, Dizzy was talking with someone, saw me, ran over, and grabbed me in a bear hug. To the man he was talking to, Dizzy, grinning, explained, "It's like seeing an old broad you used to go with."

This old broad has seldom been so honored.

Along with Dizzy, I have a photograph of Sidney Bechet, the moon-faced, invincibly stubborn soprano saxophonist from New Orleans who could overpower anyone who shared the stand with him. Even Wild Bill Davison, whose trumpet didn't need a microphone even in a football stadium, could not compete, in terms of presence, with Bechet.

In Paris, I heard him sit in with a band of white New Orleans revivalists, Frenchmen who had memorized the ancient recordings, including—as it sounded—the record scratches. Bechet lifted them all up with his long, straight horn and propelled them into making real jazz, their own jazz.

"There's this mood about the music," Bechet said of jazz, "a kind of need to be moving. You can't just set it down and hold it. Those Dixieland musicianers, they tried to do that;

they tried to write the music down and kind of freeze it. Even when they didn't arrange it to death, they didn't have any place to send it; that's why they lost it. You just can't keep the music unless you move with it."

For me, the memory that most deeply illuminates the meaning of this music that keeps moving goes back to a bitterly cold winter night in Boston when I was eighteen. It had been snowing for days, and all public transportation had been shut down. At Symphony Hall, across town from where I lived in Roxbury, a Duke Ellington concert was scheduled for that night.

I decided to walk there, even though the snow in some places was quite deep. My parents thought I was crazy, not for the first time, but like Sidney Bechet, I was not to be deterred. At least, I figured, hardly anyone else would be there, so that the music would be directed almost entirely to me.

It was a long, hard walk, ice tricking me into falling and the cold cutting through my earmuffs. When I got to Symphony Hall, I was stunned to see it was packed. We congratulated ourselves and each other for knowing what was important in life, contrary natural forces notwithstanding.

The main event at the concert was the first performance—in Boston, anyway—of Ellington's "Black, Brown and Beige," a history of blacks in America. The sounds and shapes were of more than survival. Much more. At the core of the suite was a deep, clear blues, but there was also much celebrating.

Through the music, I saw pictures, moving pictures, of field workers, jubilant dancers at the news of liberation, and church congregations speaking directly to the ultimate presence.

I was familiar with classical music; and in the same hall I had recently heard an ecstatic performance of Beethoven's Ninth Symphony, directed by Serge Koussevitzky. But the interweaving colors, rhythms, and voicings of Ellington's por-

trait of a people—his history of centuries of agony and triumph—resounded so in my mind that I was hardly aware of
walking home through the treacherous snow and ice.

As for what his music did for Ellington, one of his sidemen
told me once, "He's found the way to stay young. Watch him
some night in the wings. Those bags under his eyes are huge,
and he looks beat and kind of lonely. But when we begin to
play, he strides out on the stand, the audience turn their faces
to him, and the cat is a new man."

So, still, am I when I listen to Ellington and Dizzy and
Lester Young and Billie Holiday and much else in jazz. Musicians used to tell me that playing jazz kept them young. So
does listening.

Another jazzman—the most subtly original of them all—
practically lived to play. And, involuntarily, he was a Pied
Piper to many musicians who wanted to be unique, as he was.
Not in the least maliciously, they kept stealing from him.

Wearing his customary porkpie hat and long black coat,
Lester Young, or Prez—as tenor saxophonists called him because he had influenced so many of them—was standing at the
back of Birdland one night in the mid-1950s. On the stand was
Paul Quinichette, a tenor saxophonist whose Prez-like sound
and phrasing made Young say softly about his clone, "They
don't leave anything anymore for Prez himself to play."

The lament was more ironic than true because Young,
a lonely, very shy man—who once said his horn was his life—
tried, through the years, "to play different because this is later,
and that was then." But Prez was well aware of having shaped
the playing and thereby the careers of scores of jazzmen—
among them Stan Getz, Zoot Sims, Paul Desmond, Gerry
Mulligan, John Coltrane, and Charlie Parker.

During his formative years, Parker said, "I was crazy about
Lester. He played so clean and beautiful." Unlike another

reigning influence on the tenor, Coleman Hawkins—whose style could be as aggressive as a thunderstorm with torrential chordal improvisations—Lester was light, graceful, witty, unerringly swinging, and full of subtle surprises. As Prez put it, "I'm always loose in space, lying out there somewhere."

However, before he became widely known with Count Basie in the mid-1930s, Young was regarded as tonally defective by many of his contemporaries. Billie Holiday, his friend and supporter—the respect was mutual—recalled, "When he first started, everyone thought his tone was too *thin*. And I told Lester, 'It doesn't *matter* because you have a *beautiful* tone, and you *watch*, after a while, everybody's going to be copying *you*.' "

Billie, smiling, told me that story after her prophecy had come true.

In his playing, Prez always, as drummer Jo Jones said, "told a story." He was not in the least interested in technical displays. And to get inside each song, he once said to me, "a musician should know the lyrics of the songs he plays. A lot of musicians nowadays don't. That way they're just playing the chord changes. Most of the time I spend in listening to records is listening to singers and picking up the words right from there." His favorite vocalist, by far, was Frank Sinatra.

He surprised me one afternoon when he told me that a key early influence on his playing had been Frank Trumbauer, the limpid white alto saxophonist most often heard with Bix Beiderbecke. "He always told a little story," Lester explained.

For Prez, it was never the same story. He could not abide being predictable.

Lester could be genial and funny, but most often he was alone, even when he was with someone. His own feelings were easily bruised, and so he was careful of the sensibilities of others. The result was that sometimes he figured it was safer to keep quiet.

Off the stand as well as on, Prez's credo was, "It's got to be sweetness, man. Sweetness can be funky, filthy, or anything. But not loud."

Prez generally did not read jazz critics. They got his playing wrong, he said to jazz historian Bob Perlongo, so why should he depend on their accuracy in describing other musicians? "They keep saying I'm a cool jazz tenor or bebopper or something. But I play *swing* tenor."

Although he did selectively incorporate in his playing what he liked in modern jazz, Prez was the embodiment of the way of swinging that delighted in melodic improvisation.

In his later years—Prez was forty-nine when he died in 1959—his dependence on gin got worse, and he had great difficulty eating. Still, there were some nights when he told gently compelling stories on his horn that were far more intimate, I expect, than he had put into words for many years.

The last time I saw Prez—two years before he died—was in the CBS television studio on West 57th Street where "The Sound of Jazz" was soon to be aired "live." There was a starkly furnished room off the studio, with white walls and black and white tile on the floor. It could have been a setting for Vermeer, except that the Dutch painter might not have known what to make of the man, alone, in a porkpie hat and a long black coat seated on a chair, very close to the leather case holding his horn.

Prez was sick and weak and didn't have the energy—or the desire—to join the musicians next door swapping stories of past gigs.

Young just sat there, waiting for his cue. Later, on the show, he blew the cleanest, most beautiful, and deepest blues I had ever heard. I looked for him after we had gone off the air, but he had disappeared.

Prez was beyond category, like many of his itinerant colleagues. He improvised his life, as well as his music, but he couldn't resolve all the dissonant chords in his head.

I have a photograph of him on my desk—gesturing at a friend, outside a store window. Prez is smiling. Like his music, that picture makes me feel I'm in the sunlight. Prez never knew it, but he was an essential part of my life.

THE UNEASY LEGEND:

BOB DYLAN

One non-jazz musician I came to know evolved into a fabled superstar.

In 1961, Margot and I were living in Greenwich Village, around the corner from Gerde's Folk City, an informal gathering place for folk singers—both beginners and the more or less professional. A regular performer was a youngster who always wore a leather cap, blue jeans, and well-worn desert boots. Born Robert Zimmerman in the bleak mining town of Hibbing, Minnesota, he was known in Greenwich Village as Bob Dylan.

Margot thought he looked like her, but was unimpressed with his music. Most of his songs then, for instance, could not have existed had it not been for Woody Guthrie, his idol.

I was not an enthusiast either. Dylan played rudimentary guitar, and as for his voice, I agreed with a Missouri folk singer who said Dylan's sound was like that of "a dog with his leg caught in barbed wire."

Later that year, a *New York Times* critic, Robert Shelton, wrote a review of a Dylan performance at Gerde's Folk City: "Although only twenty years old, Bob Dylan is one of the most distinctive stylists to appear in a Manhattan cabaret in months. . . . A searing intensity pervades his songs. . . . His music-making has the mark of originality and inspiration, all the more noteworthy for his youth. Mr. Dylan is vague about his antecedents and birthplace, but it matters less where he has been than where he is going, and that would seem to be straight up."

Shelton's review led to a recording contract with Columbia on the insistent advice of John Hammond—who had been instrumental in the beginning careers of Count Basie and Billie Holiday, among many others. Hammond produced the first Dylan recording, and when it was released, he called me one afternoon. I was reviewing music for a number of places at the time.

"I know you get a lot of records," Hammond said, "and I expect the Bob Dylan is lost in some pile, but I wish you'd dig it out. He's a real talent."

Because I respected Hammond's judgment, I dug the record out, and Dylan was somewhat more arresting on it than he had been at Gerde's.

Rapidly, Dylan became a solid seller on records and filled clubs and concert halls. I wrote the liner notes for his second album, and as we got to know each other somewhat, I wrote a profile of him in *The New Yorker*.

Despite the justly vaunted checking staff at *The New Yorker*, Dylan cozened them and me with a tale of having, as a young loner, run away from home to go on the road with Big Joe Williams, a blues singer of the old, rural, wandering tradition.

It turned out that although Dylan later recorded with Big Joe Williams, he had not, as a youngster, run away from home for ambulatory instruction from Big Joe.

I wrote about Dylan in other publications, and I'd occasionally see him on the street in the Village. Invariably he'd ask about something I was writing about him, "When's it coming out? When's it coming out?" At the same time, he would say to others that he wasn't in the least interested in what was written about him.

By 1965, Dylan had become an international celebrity with huge record sales and sold-out concert appearances. His songs, particularly "The Times They Are A-Changin' " and "Blowin' in the Wind," had become anthems of the exuberantly rebellious young.

Dylan could no longer be found on the streets of the Village. He had become remote, avoiding interviewers. There was a growing aura of mystery about him, as if he were a cult figure, and in a way he was.

Playboy asked me to do one of the magazine's long, presumably probing interviews with him, and he accepted. We talked for two hours. It was a straight-ahead session, with Dylan speaking plainly and seriously about the misinterpretations of some of his songs and some parts of his life.

I edited the interview for clarity, not at all for content, and showed it to Dylan. *Playboy*'s question-and-answer interviews then had to get the approval of the subject, while profiles of a person—which included interviews with others, pro and con, and were driven by the writer's viewpoint—were not seen by the subject in advance.

One Saturday morning I was in my office when the phone rang. It was Dylan. He was furious. *Playboy* had sent him *its* edited version of the interview, and, said Dylan, it was all fucked up. Not only had parts of it been removed, but new quotes from Dylan—none of which he had said—had been inserted.

"Listen," I said to the raging Dylan, "they still need your approval of the final piece. Tell them go to hell. Tell them they can't print it."

There was a long pause. "No," Dylan said. "We're going to do a new interview. Right now."

"Right now" took about five hours. I had no tape recorder

in the office, and so my writing hand did not fully recover for a couple of days.

As soon as we started, I knew where Dylan was going. This was going to be a huge send-up of an interview—surrealistic, mocking, careeningly irresponsible, a carnival-like kaleidoscope of life-changing hidden meanings.

I played the straight man. Or rather, the fool.

For years ever since, Dylan exegetes, writing about the now notorious interview, have noted what a square I was for asking those dumb questions that so totally missed Dylan's brilliantly elliptical wisdom. One exception was Anthony Scaduto's book, *Bob Dylan: An Intimate Biography* (Signet), which, in all other respects as well, is the most accurate chronicle of Dylan's odyssey.

Here's an excerpt from the interview featuring the nonstop improvising Bob Dylan:

PLAYBOY [me]: What made you decide to go the rock-and-roll route?

DYLAN: Carelessness. I lost my one true love. I started drinking. I wind up in Phoenix. I get a job as a Chinaman. I start working in a dimestore, and move in with a thirteen-year-old girl. Then this big Mexican from Philadelphia comes in and burns the house down. I go down to Dallas. I get a job as a "before" in a Charles Atlas "before and after" ad. I move in with a delivery boy who can cook fantastic chili and hot dogs. Then this thirteen-year-old girl from Phoenix comes and burns the house down.

The next thing I know I'm in Omaha. It's so cold there, by this time I'm robbing my own bicycles and frying my own fish. I move in with a high school teacher who also does a little plumbing on the side, who ain't much to look at, but who's built a refrigerator that can turn newspapers into lettuce. Everything's going good until that delivery boy shows up and tries to knife me. Needless to say, he burned the house down, and I hit the road. The first guy that picked me up asked me if I wanted to be a star. What could I say?"

PLAYBOY [me]: And that's how you became a rock-and-roll singer?

DYLAN: No, that's how I got tuberculosis.

Ten years later, I encountered a hostile Bob Dylan. In 1975 he went on the road with the Rolling Thunder Revue—Joan Baez, Allen Ginsberg, T-Bone Burnett, Bob Neuwirth, Ronee Blakley, and Jack Elliott.

Jann Wenner, proprietor of *Rolling Stone*, asked me to write about the tour. I went to see the star and was told Dylan wouldn't see me. Period. He was angry at my wife and me.

In an article in the Sunday *New York Times*, I had quoted Margot as saying that Dylan was still "The Kid," but an older, sour kid.

"Tell your master," I said to Dylan's emissary, "that I'm going to do the story anyway."

It was easy. Joan Baez was an old friend. I knew Allen Ginsberg, and I soon established a camaraderie with some of the musicians and other cast members.

When I was ready to write, a message came from the master of the revels. Dylan would see me now. I sent back word that I didn't need him. I had my story—or, rather, stories.

As related in my *Rolling Stone* piece, one of the stories is from a musician in the band:

"Joan and Bob are doing a duet. She's really moving, I mean dancing. She starts doing the Charleston and the audience is digging it and we're digging it. Dylan though, he's plunking his guitar, moving his eyes around quick like he does, looking at Joanie, looking at us, looking at the audience. Like, 'What the hell is she doing that's going over so big?'

"It's over, and Joan walks offstage, grinning, sees a friend in the wings and says to him, 'You won't be hearing *that* number from this little old duo on this tour.' She's right. Bob's never called for that tune since. He couldn't stand the competition. Big as he is, in some ways he's still a kid scrambling for his turf."

And there is a story of the Rolling Thunder Revue in Toronto:

Seated at the back of the stage is Dylan's mother, Betty Zimmerman. She is pulled up and onto stage center and begins to dance and wave to the audience, none of whom, she is sure, knows who she is.

It is getting near the start of the second chorus and Joan Baez, chronically gracious, pulls Mrs. Zimmerman toward the lead mike, the principals' mike. "All of a sudden," Joan told me, "Dylan kicks me in the ass. Gently. It was his way of saying, 'I think I'd rather sing this chorus than have my mother do it.' So I had to gracefully Charleston Mrs. Zimmerman back a few steps and then leap to the mike and sing with Bob."

And there, back a few steps, was Mrs. Zimmerman, arms flailing, dancing to Woody Guthrie's "This Land Is Your Land" and the music of her own child. The first time she's ever been on stage with that child.

And put in her rightful place.

Still, after all these years, I remain connected, in a way, with Dylan. I was interviewing, while writing this book, an ABC television investigative reporter, Bob Zelnick, about affirmative action. I gave my name, and the first thing he said was, "Are you the Nat Hentoff who wrote the notes for Bob Dylan's second album, *Freewheelin' Bob Dylan*?"

I get the same question from some of my children's friends, lawyers of a certain age, and other passersby. Reflected glory, if that's the word.

"HE HAS COME TO THE DEFENSE
OF SOME OF THE MOST LOATHSOME
HUMAN BEINGS IN OUR SOCIETY"

I once told one of Duke Ellington's sidemen that I was un-accustomed to getting awards, but would like to become accustomed. He laughed and said the time would come. And it did.

Soon after I was told by *The New Yorker* that—to my sur-prise—I had retired from that magazine, I was also surprised by the National Press Foundation in Washington. Its director told me that I was about to receive—in February 1995—an award for lifetime distinguished contributions to journalism. Previous winners had included Eugene Roberts, Robert May-nard, David Broder, and Fred Friendly—the last named being a man I knew and much admired, and had worked with on a number of his televised seminars on constitutional law.

When I got to Washington for the presentation of the award, I met one of the jurors. The head of the foundation had told me the selection committee's decision was unanimous. She laughed upon hearing this. "Well," she said, "we had a lively session before the voting."

It turned out—not at all to my pro-choice wife's surprise—that some members of the selection committee had reserva-tions about honoring anyone who was pro-life. But somehow, despite my heresy, I was not turned away.

What made the evening especially memorable for me was Meg Greenfield's introduction. The editor of the *Washington Post's* editorial page had, ten years before, asked me to write a regular column for her, and that had led to the column's being seen regularly in over two hundred newspapers. It was a boyhood dream astonishingly fulfilled. When I was a kid, and my father would bring home five of Boston's eight daily papers, I'd read the columnists first and clip out some of the pieces to put in a scrapbook alongside my unsyndicated comments.

I had known Meg slightly when we both worked for Max Ascoli's *The Reporter* long ago. Actually, she was one of the more renowned reporters, and I was a freelancer in the back of the magazine.

In the years I have been writing the column—"Sweet Land of Liberty"—for the *Washington Post*, I doubt if I talked to her more than three times. I had no idea what she thought of the column, but she did keep it.

Hearing her on the night of the award, I was surprised at what she said about me. I quote from her introduction because I don't care whether it's self-serving. It's an award in itself:

"Nat Hentoff has been in our business for around forty years now. In that time, the tribe has truly multiplied. Where there once would be tens or maybe hundreds of reporters and headscratchers covering government activities, there now will routinely be thousands. But journalism has not just become more populous. It has also suffered a terrible fate. It has become—I don't even like to say it—chic. . . .

"Nat Hentoff is not chic. Never has been, as those of us who have known him over the centuries can attest. Never will be. Count on it.

"On the contrary, he has other, often opposite attributes. He is independent, not tribal, in his views. And he is stubborn—not to put too fine a point on it, he is terminally stubborn."

My wife nodded vigorously.

"This description, of course, is what all journalists these days affect to be. . . . But there is a difference. Hentoff is what others only say they are; and he does what others only imagine they do.

"In an age when so many among us claim courage for taking on individuals and institutions that they couldn't be more safe in attacking—targets that will automatically win them praise, not censure, among the people whose opinions they care most about—Hentoff takes real risks, challenges icons and ideas that are treasured in the community he lives in. He puts on his skunk suit and heads off to the garden party, week after week, again and again.

"He defends the First Amendment against the predations of the liberals—of which he is one—as well as the conservatives. He asserts the civil liberties claims of the citizen, irrespective of politics or position, not just of those with whom he may sympathize on the issue. To tell the truth, he has come to the defense of some of the most loathsome human beings in our society when he knew that their fundamental rights—and by extension the rights of all—were being endangered. . . . Journalism doesn't get any better than Nat Hentoff. . . ."

Meg did not—as *The New Yorker* had—announce my retirement. So, with my skunk suit at hand, I continue to greatly enjoy writing the column, "Sweet Land of Liberty," for the *Washington Post*.

I ended my acceptance speech that night by conjuring up Izzy Stone, who, in 1945, was in Czechoslovakia, and couldn't get an exit visa. But he showed up in Paris. "I rode out," he explained to a puzzled colleague, "on top of a train."

I wish, I told the audience of reporters and editors, there

were an aerial photograph of the short, curly-haired, dimpled reporter, with his thick glasses—embodying the free press as a high-riding, solitary, stubborn pilgrim. Just like he was at home.

I went on to recall that someone had once asked Izzy what he wanted out of life—or, as Duke Ellington said in one of his songs, "What Am I Here For?"

Izzy's answer was, "To be free to follow no master other than my own compulsions. To live up to my idealized image of what a true journalist should be—and still be able to make a living for my family."

"What more," Izzy said, "could anyone ask?"

Toward the end of the evening, a very well-known reporter and analyst came up to me. I had admired her work for a long time, but we'd never met. "I want to thank you," she said, "for your pro-life writings. They're a great help. Some of us can't say openly that we believe as you do. But when a pro-life comment comes from you—with your civil liberties credentials—it means a lot."

Hearing that was my third award that night.

Not, however, according to my unyieldingly pro-choice wife.

As Izzy Stone said, "It's a good life."

A NOTE ON THE TYPE

The text of this book was set in Plantin, a typeface first cut in 1913 by the Monotype Corporation of London. Though the face bears the name of the great Christopher Plantin (ca. 1520–1589), who in the latter part of the sixteenth century owned, in Antwerp, the largest printing and publishing firm in Europe, it is a rather free adaptation of designs by Claude Garamond made for that firm. With its strong, simple lines, Plantin is a no-nonsense face of exceptional legibility.

Composed by Creative Graphics,
Allentown, Pennsylvania
Printed and bound by Quebecor Printing,
Martinsburg, West Virginia
Designed by Anthea Lingeman